THE KNITTING ALL AROUND
STITCH DICTIONARY

150 new stitch patterns to knit top down,
bottom up, back and forth & in the round

WENDY BERNARD

photographs by THAYER ALLYSON GOWDY
prop & wardrobe styling by KAREN SCHAUPETER

STC CRAFT / NEW YORK

CONTENTS

INTRODUCTION

IN KNITTING, THERE ARE ONLY TWO stitches: knit and purl. From those two stitches come a seemingly infinite number of combinations for creating fabrics that look and feel different. Most of us start out by learning to make a knit stitch, which produces Garter stitch when worked every row. Next, we learn to add purls to the mix to create Stockinette stitch. Last, we combine the two to make ribbing. And whether we're knitting flat (back and forth) or in the round, these basic stitches can serve us well for a long, long time. But at some point, most of us hunger for a little more variety—what would happen if we played around with our knits and purls? Enter stitch dictionaries. These are books—like this one—filled to the brim with stitch patterns. I don't know a knitter who doesn't have at least one beloved and well-used volume.

As a knitwear designer, I am known for creating garment designs that are knit from the top down, often in the round (for example, a sweater knit from the neckline to the bottom hem in one piece). But during my early years while I was still honing my skills, I discovered that most stitch dictionaries only included instructions for knitting stitch patterns back and forth from the bottom up (for example, as you would knit a sweater in pieces—front, back, and sleeves—starting at the bottom hem). At first, I took it upon myself to translate every stitch pattern I used for my designs in silence, just my needles and me. And then it occurred to me that I could share the fruits of my labor: my instructions for knitting in different directions. And so I wrote the *Up, Down, All-Around Stitch Dictionary*, which was published in 2014. My instincts were right. There are, indeed, *many* other knitters who desire stitch patterns written for knitting in different directions. And they no longer have to go it alone. The response to my first stitch dictionary was so positive that right away I wanted to write another one (and, fortunately, my publisher was all for it).

For this second volume I carefully selected over 150 additional stitch patterns that I love. You can use this volume on its own or in combination with the first. There are only four stitch patterns that are repeated in both volumes, and that is because they are so universal that I think they need to be included in every stitch dictionary: Stockinette stitch, Garter stitch, 1x1 Rib, and 2x2 Rib.

As with the first volume, I present the instructions for each stitch pattern in both flat and in-the-round versions. They are all written out line by line for those who prefer written stitch patterns, and most are also charted for those who like following charts.

In many cases, the stitch patterns will look the same whether knit from the bottom to the top or from the top down. There are times, especially in the case of lace patterns, when they won't look exactly the same, so I have created a top-down version that isn't identical but will give you similar results (as is the case with Fern Grotto on page 168).

All of these stitch patterns are perfect for using in top-down or bottom-up garments and accessories. I've provided a project in each of the chapters to get you started thinking about how to incorporate them. You can follow the instructions exactly as written, but you can also swap in another stitch pattern for the one I used if you want. And if you're in a design-it-on-my-own mood, you'll find six

formulas at the back of the book starting on page 262: Socks in Two Directions, Hats in Two Directions, and Triangular Shawls in Two Directions. In the *Up, Down, All-Around Stitch Dictionary*, I included "from scratch" formulas for a lace stole, mittens, and a top-down cable hat. If you have both books, mix and match to your heart's content.

It makes me so happy to see knitters' eyes light up when they realize that all the work of converting these stitch patterns has been done for them and they can get down to the enjoyment of knitting rather than having to pull out graph paper and a pencil and figure it out for themselves. And when I think of how many thousands of other stitch patterns exist, I hunger to tackle those as well! Whatever the future holds (volume 3 perhaps?!), my greatest hope is that you'll use these new tools to elevate your skills and to create one-of-a-kind items for yourself and for the people you care about. xx

STITCH DICTIONARIES are like cookbooks—you can't have just one! Not only are they great sources of inspiration, they also offer endless ideas for customizing existing knitting patterns or even designing from scratch. First things first, though: After you've chosen a stitch pattern or two, you need to swatch. This will help you decide if you like how the stitch pattern works with the yarn you've selected.

Why Swatch?

Swatching gives you a chance to spend some time working with your yarn—taking it for a test drive and getting to know it before you get down to the nitty gritty of casting on for the actual project. It will help you to control both the size of the finished project and the feel of your knitted fabric. And it will give you invaluable information about how the knitted fabric will look and wear.

At one time or another, most knitters have happily knitted a garment, then tried it on and discovered, to their dismay, that it didn't fit! Knitting a swatch and then checking your gauge will help you to avoid this mishap, and if you check and recheck your gauge and overall measurements as you progress, you'll be even more likely to finish with a project that is the exact size you planned for it to be.

Another reason to swatch is to find out how your needles and yarn work together. Every yarn, be it wool, synthetic, or cotton, acts differently with different needles. Metal needles with sharp tips may not play well with fuzzy mohair, for example. Nubby cotton, on the other hand, may not behave with bamboo needles. Looking at your swatch, ask yourself: Does the yarn show off the pattern? Or does the colorway get in the way? Does it pill? Does the yarn bloom (expand) after washing? What about colorfastness? Does the color run out of the yarn when you wash it?

Part of the fun of knitting is finding a pattern you love and marrying it with yarn in your stash or from your favorite yarn store, so there's no reason to shy away from this process. Remember, swatching is your friend. Just grab some needles and yarn and see where it takes you. If the drape or gauge is off and there's nothing you can do to make it work, think of it this way: You'll be saving that yarn for a different project. If everything seems to jive, then go for it! And don't forget to ask the salespeople at the yarn store—they are a treasure trove of good advice.

How to Swatch

In most knitting patterns, a gauge, or tension, is given for a 4″ (10 cm) square. Your swatch should be at least this size or even bigger, not counting the nonrolling edge, in order to give you the most accurate reading.

Using the yarn and needles suggested in the pattern or the yarn of your choice, cast on the number of stitches—or more—required to achieve a square of at least 4″ (10 cm). If you're not sure of the number of stitches you might need, refer to the ball band on your yarn. Also, allow at least two stitches on each side of the swatch to work in a nonrolling edge like Garter stitch.

Most knitting patterns will give you a gauge and tell you which stitch pattern to use to measure the gauge. For example, the gauge might be listed as 20 stitches over 4″ (10 cm), or 5 stitches per inch (2.5 cm), in Stockinette stitch. If no stitch pattern is given, Stockinette stitch is generally assumed. If you're designing on the fly, choose a stitch pattern and experiment away! Just be sure to keep track of your needle size (more about this later).

Once you've knitted your swatch, bind off or place the live stitches on a closeable holder or waste yarn (if you bind off too tightly, your reading might be off—that is why I suggest placing live stitches on a holder that won't squish the stitches while keeping them from unraveling). Then launder and dry the swatch as you intend for the project you're planning. The key is to treat your swatch exactly as you plan on treating your project after it is complete. That way, your swatch will give you the most accurate representation of your finished project.

HOW SELECTION OF YARN AFFECTS YOUR PROJECT

After choosing your project, the first step is to decide what yarn to use. While many knitters prefer to use the yarn that is indicated in the pattern, many others like to substitute yarn from their local yarn store or from their stash. The fiber content of your yarn is probably the most important factor to consider. For example, if you have a hat pattern that calls for merino wool and you swap it out for cotton, not only will your hat become floppy, it will also probably grow. And unless you have prior experience with the same cotton yarn, you will most definitely end up with a hat that is different than the hat in your pattern even if you obtain the correct gauge. This is because cotton has very little stretch or memory, unlike wool, which will stretch but will also snap back. The solution: Swatch!

If you're making a lace swatch, you'll also want to block it after you wash it. To block, soak the swatch in water, squeeze out the excess, and then pin it to a dry towel or soft, absorbent surface to dry. Some swatches, like ribs, should be stretched only very slightly to get an accurate stitch count. Freshly knitted ribs can pull in quite a lot, but ribbed fabric is meant to pull in and provide a snug fit, so you shouldn't stretch them too much. Trust your gut—imagine how you want your ribs to behave in your garment and go for it.

Once your swatch is dry, measure your gauge between the Garter or nonrolling selvage stitches using a tape measure or stitch gauge. If your stitch count is less than the called-for

stitch count in your knitting pattern, you'll need to go down a needle size. The converse will be true if you have too many stitches to the inch. For example, if your pattern advises you to use size US 8 (5 mm) needles with a worsted-weight yarn to obtain a gauge of 18 stitches over a 4″ (10 cm) square and you find that you have 20 stitches, you'll have to re-swatch using a larger needle.

But what about row gauge? Some people will tell you that the row gauge isn't all that important, but it actually is. When you shape portions of a sweater, like sleeves for example, if you work the decreases (in the case of a top-down sweater) and the instructions tell you to decrease every sixth round and your row gauge

doesn't match the row/round gauge in the pattern, your sleeves may come out either too short or too long. In the worst case scenario, you may reach the cuff without having completed all your decreases. Or let's say you're following a charted knitted pattern rather than written-out instructions that tell you to knit to a particular length. If you knit each row in the chart and your row gauge is off, again you might end up with an item that is too short or too long. If you find that your row gauge is off by more than a row, consider swatching with a different size needle or even a different type of needle. It does sound strange, but some knitters find that switching from bamboo to metal or vice versa affects their row gauge, so give it a go! If you can't get row gauge no matter what, don't worry. Just be sure to measure, measure, measure as you go.

swatching in the round

If you are planning to knit in the round—especially when making a garment—you might consider making a gauge swatch in the round. Many knitters who knit in the round understand that their knitting tends to be tighter when knitting that way and can account for it, but if you're not sure, go ahead and try your hand at knitting a swatch in the round and checking it against a swatch you've made flat. If you're wondering why some people knit tighter while knitting in the round it is because they purl more loosely than they knit. And since you aren't purling when knitting in the round (at least with Stockinette stitch), there is a tendency for in-the-round knitting to have a slightly tighter gauge than flat knitting.

There are two basic ways to go about making an in-the-round swatch. My preferred method is to use double-pointed needles, join in the round, and make a tube, but you can also cast on stitches to one double-pointed needle and instead of turning after your first row and working a wrong-side row, slide the stitches to the right-hand end of the needle and continue working right-side rows only, which will give you a flat, "in-the-round" swatch. As you work in this manner, drape the working

yarn loosely across the wrong side after each row is complete. You might also work more than just two nonrolling edge stitches on either side of the main stitch pattern, since swatching in this way will produce a slightly looser edge. Once the swatch is done, bind off your stitches, and cut the strands of yarn so the swatch lies flat. Or, if the swatch seems reasonably tidy, just leave the loose strands alone. Either way, you will end up with a swatch that you can read. Although I know how to work both types of swatches, I find the "flat" version to be fiddly and a little cumbersome, so I prefer the tube—but that is just my personal preference. Try out both methods and see which one you like best!

keeping track of needle size

I've learned the hard way that keeping track of my needle size when swatching is paramount! I can't tell you how many times I've finished and blocked a swatch and then promptly forgotten the needle size I used.

To combat this, I've come up with two tried-and-true ways to keep track without having to attach a tag to my swatch. Of course, if you like to attach tags, you can. But even though I understand the importance of swatching and heartily embrace the concept, I get so excited to start my project that I often forget or don't want to take the time to properly label my work. If you suffer from a similar affliction, the first way to "label" your swatch is to simply purl the same number of stitches as the number-size of the needle on the right side of the swatch. Then, you can go back and read the number of purl stitches and know what size needle you used for that section of the swatch.

Sometimes I will use multiple needle sizes in the span of a swatch, which means, of course, that it will be a much longer rectangle instead

DO SWATCHES LIE?

Well, in a word: sometimes. There, I said it. Swatches lie . . . sometimes. The thing is, unless you're making a swatch-sized item, chances are your gauge will change once the resulting project is actually finished and worn. In other words, the swatch won't lie about itself, being swatch-sized and all, but once that swatch turns into a full-sized garment or blanket with a bit of heft, the gauge will most likely loosen.

The good news is that a gauge swatch will give you a hint—a very good hint—about the final size of your garment. Your swatch will tell you other great things too—for example, whether or not the yarn looks nice in your chosen stitch pattern or if the drape of the fabric is what you're looking for.

In the end, the best way to approach and embrace swatching is to just do it. Swatch! And then wash and block the swatch to see how it behaves (see page 10). If you're making a big, big sweater with heavy yarn, consider hanging the swatch over the edge of a counter to dry. If you suspect the garment will be extra heavy, then fasten a binder clip to the end of the swatch to weigh it down. This will tell you if the row gauge will easily stretch out or relax once the garment is worn. If you decide to use a binder clip, examine your yarn's weight and the size of the project. If it will be a super-large and heavy project, then choose the binder clip size accordingly: If you select one that is either too heavy or too light, you won't be able to accurately assess the stretch factor.

of a 4″ (10 cm) square and that I will have to "relabel" my swatch with purl stitches each time I change needles. Another solution is to tie knots in the tail of the yarn, as in the photo on page 12. So, if I used a size US 7 needle, I'll tie seven knots in the tail. For a size US 10½ needle, I'll tie ten knots, then leave a long space, then tie an eleventh for the ½; if I'm working with the purl stitch marking method, I'll purl 10 stitches, knit 1, then purl an eleventh. The space between knots or purl stitches is the reminder that I used a 10½, as opposed to an 11. If you're used to referring to needle size by metric units and want to use this method, here's a conversion table:

METRIC SIZE	US SIZE
2	0
2.25	1
2.75	2
3.25	3
3.5	4
3.75	5
4	6
4.5	7
5	8
5.5	9
6	10
6.5	10½
8	11
9	13
10	15

Following the Charts in This Book

Before you dive in, it's a great idea to read through this section to ensure that knitting from the charts in this book is fun and easy for you. The charts vary based on the direction in which you are knitting: top-down, bottom-up, back-and-forth, or in the round. In some cases, you'll see that there is one chart for all directions, and in others, there are two or even more. They are all labeled for you, so just keep them in mind as you work.

WHAT TO DO WITH ALL OF THOSE SWATCHES

If you knit swatches as often as I do, you'll find a way to put them to good use. Some very organized people put their swatches in a notebook along with the corresponding label to keep for future reference. Others save them and sew them together to make a crazy quilt of sorts. I've seen them used as pockets, too. You can also use them to practice techniques like I-cord edgings, picking up and knitting, or duplicate stitch. Another idea is to use them as coasters—that's what I do!

Each chart shows you what the stitch pattern looks like when you're looking at it from the right side of the work. I try to use symbols that look like the actual stitches, so that when you look at the chart, you are able to see where you are in the pattern as you go. These charts are numbered on the edges to help you keep track of what row (or round) you are on.

When you're working back and forth as you would in a flat pattern with a right side and a wrong side, the numbers on the right-hand edge of the chart indicate right-side rows, and the numbers on the left indicate wrong-side rows. Row 1 indicates the first row of the chart that you will work. When Row 1 is on the left side of the chart, that means you start with a wrong-side row. For right-side rows, you will always work the chart from right to left. For wrong-side rows, you work from left to right. For a chart that shows a stitch pattern that is worked in the round, there will only be numbers on the right side, since you only work right-side rounds. If a chart displays both the flat and in-the-round stitch pattern (see the charts for Wheat Cable on page 141), you will only have numbers on the right side; the rows that aren't numbered will be wrong-side rows when working flat.

When you're looking at a wrong-side row, you have to work the symbol so that it will appear correctly on the right side. For example, a blank white square indicates a knit stitch. Obviously, you'll knit that stitch on the right side, but what would you do on the wrong side to create a stitch that will be a knit stitch on the right side? The answer is "purl," of course! If you ever have questions, there is a key that will tell you how the stitch should be worked; if it is to be handled differently depending on which side of the work you're on, that will be indicated. As an example, to produce a decrease that looks just like a k2tog on the right side, you work a p2tog on the wrong side. So, the key will say "K2tog on RS, p2tog on WS."

A trick of mine is to place a sticky note above the row (or round) that I'm working so I can see how my new stitches are matching up with the previously worked stitches. This helps me catch mistakes quickly.

Every stitch repeat is indicated below each chart, and the row/round repeats are shown to the right. In many cases, the repeat takes up the entire chart (see Diagonal Broken Rib, page 69). Sometimes, when working flat, there will be one or more extra stitches on either side (or both sides) of the main pattern repeat (see Banded Basket Stitch Flat, page 34, and Honeycomb Smocking Flat, page 90). This is so that the end of the stitch pattern mirrors the beginning. In this case, you will work x stitches before the repeat (if there are any), y stitches in the repeat the appropriate number of times for your pattern, then end with the last z stitches to mirror the pattern.

There is no need to mirror the stitch pattern when the piece is worked in the round, so you will rarely see extra stitches on an in-the-round chart. Occasionally there are one or more set-up rows or rounds at the beginning of a chart that are worked before the main pattern begins (see Interlocking Rings in the Round, page 123). You will usually work these rows/rounds once only, then repeat the designated pattern rows/rounds. If the repeat (stitch or row/round) doesn't take up the entire chart, there will be a heavy vertical or horizontal line before and/or after the repeat to help you keep track of the repeat.

Occasionally, in some patterns, a pattern repeat will shift a few stitches to the right or left to accommodate stitches within the pattern, like a decrease worked at the end of a repeat, or a cable or other multi-stitch motif that overlaps into the following repeat. For example, in the Star Stitch pattern on the following page and on page 85, the repeat shifts 2 stitches to the left on Row 4 to accommodate the "make star" motif. A similar shift is required on Round 3 of the In the Round chart.

With some stitch patterns that are worked in the round, the pattern might be worked across the beginning-of-the-round marker, beginning or ending one or more stitch(es) before or after the marker (see English Lace in the Round, page 167). The symbols and the chart key will tell you how to work these extra stitches. Many times you will need to shift the marker to keep the pattern flowing properly.

You might also see a gray-shaded square in a chart; this is a "no-stitch" square. When you see this, all you do is skip over that stitch and don't work it at all. No-stitch squares are

The pattern repeat for Star Stitch is shifted to accommodate the star motif, which overlaps the next repeat.

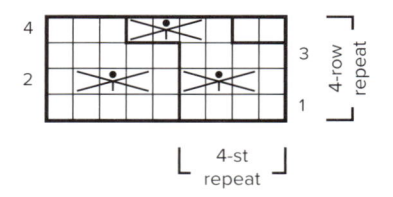

STAR STITCH FLAT

4 · 3 · 4-row repeat · 2 · 1 · 4-st repeat

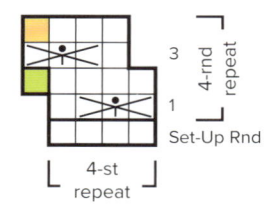

STAR STITCH IN THE ROUND

3 · 4-rnd repeat · 1 · Set-Up Rnd · 4-st repeat

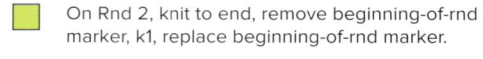

Make star

☐ (green) On Rnd 2, knit to end, remove beginning-of-rnd marker, k1, replace beginning-of-rnd marker.

☐ (yellow) At end of Rnd 4 only, knit to end, reposition beginning-of-rnd marker to before last st; slip last st back to left-hand needle, to be worked in make star at beginning of Rnd 1.

inserted into the chart in two situations: One is to tell you that a stitch is no longer available because a decrease has been worked without an increase to replace the stitch. You can find examples of this on page 150 in the chart for the Sausage Cables.

The second, less common, situation is where the no-stitch square serves as a placeholder on the first row or rows of a chart for an increase that will happen later in the chart (see Lucina Shell Lace, page 177). The no-stitch squares on Rows 1–4 provide space for the yarnovers that will be worked on Rows 3 and 5. This enables us to create a chart that is clear and easy to read.

when the written pattern and charts don't match

If you are working from both the written-out instructions and the chart, there will be times when they don't appear to match each other. Never fear! The end result will always match, but they may differ in how the repeats are set up on some of the rows. Why? With written-out instructions, you can shift where the pattern repeat is on each row for the most efficient and easy-to-memorize way of working it. For example, in Diagonals on page 27, the pattern repeat for Row 1 is p3, k5, which is super-easy to memorize. When you get to Row 3, the pattern repeat shifts 2 stitches to the right, so that the row now starts with p1, k5 before it gets back to p3, k5. Rather than make the pattern repeat for Row 3 be p1, k5, p2, we just give you some extra stitches at the beginning of the row and start the repeat

FRONT

BACK

WHEN IS REVERSIBLE TRULY REVERSIBLE?

In this book, you'll find a number of stitch patterns that are labeled "reversible." When a stitch pattern is truly reversible, the composition of knits and purls make the right side and the wrong side exactly the same. There are other situations where the stitch pattern looks *nearly* the same on both sides. Finally, there are instances where it looks nice on both sides, but the pattern is different on each side. In the first case, the stitch patterns will be labeled as "fully reversible." In the latter two, they will be labeled as two-sided, indicating

that the right and wrong sides will not be exactly the same. Examples of patterns that look nearly the same on both sides are Slip Stitch Mesh on page 101 (and above) and Indian Cross Stitch on page 86. Garter stitch on page 22 and most simple ribs are truly reversible, and it is impossible to tell the right side from the wrong side. All reversible stitch patterns in this book make great choices for items that show both sides, like scarves, stoles, caps with turned-up brims, and sweaters with collars that show both sides.

later, enabling you to continue working the familiar p3, k5 repeat.

If we created the chart to match the written instructions exactly, the vertical stitch repeat line(s) would zigzag, making the chart less easy to follow.

Just know that the charts in this book are visual representations of the patterns, and are presented in the clearest manner possible. In the end, the finished pattern will be exactly the same whether you work it from the text or from the chart—follow whichever works best for you.

Working with Mosaic Stitch Patterns

The most common forms of knitted colorwork are Fair Isle, or stranded knitting, and intarsia, and both of them require that you manage more than one color of yarn at a time. Mosaic knitting, a term coined by Barbara G. Walker in the late 1960s, is a less common form of colorwork, but a fun one that only requires that you manage one color at a time.

Basically, mosaics are two-color slip-stitch designs. One color is worked across a right-side row, and then the same color is worked back along the wrong-side row while the second color waits at the opposite edge.

You can work mosaic patterns flat or in the round, and in Stockinette stitch or Garter stitch. The choice is entirely up to you! You can see examples of the mosaics in Chapter 6 starting on page 213. Other than choosing your texture, there are only two things that you need to consider when working mosaic stitch patterns. First, every slipped stitch is slipped with the yarn to the wrong side (whether working flat or in the round) and second, the rows/rounds are always worked in pairs. This means that you will work a row or round in the indicated color, then the next row or round will be worked with the same color. On the second row/round in the pair, you will work (knit or purl) the same stitches that you worked on the previous row/round, and slip the same stitches that you slipped. When working a flat piece, to work in Stockinette stitch, purl the worked (non-slipped) stitches on wrong-side rows; to work in Garter stitch, knit the worked stitches on wrong-side rows. When working in the round, to work in Stockinette stitch, knit all worked stitches on all rounds; to work in Garter stitch, knit the worked stitches on the first round of each pair and purl them on the following round.

When looking at a flat mosaic chart, notice that each horizontal row of squares represents two rows of knitting, one right-side row that runs from right to left and one wrong-side row that runs from left to right. The rows are numbered on both sides, with odd numbers for right-side rows on the right and even numbers for wrong-side rows on the left. When looking at in-the-round mosaic charts, you'll note that the chart rounds are numbered only on the right side of the chart, and that all the numbers are odd; you will work each even-numbered round exactly the same as the preceding odd-numbered round.

In this book, you'll notice that the two colors are labeled as "Dark" (D) or "Light" (L), corresponding to the dark or light boxes. In the flat charts, the first stitch in each row indicates which color you use to work that row. In the in-the-round charts, there is a column to the right of the chart that indicates which color you use to work that round. Note that you will always alternate one pair of dark rows/rounds with a pair of light rows/rounds. So, on every right-side row that begins with a dark square, you knit all the dark stitches and slip all the light stitches purlwise, always with the yarn to the

Hanging Fruit, page 230

wrong side. Alternatively, on every row that begins with a light square, you knit all the light stitches and slip all the dark stitches.

When working a mosaic stitch pattern from the chart, just work from the bottom of the chart to the top, paying attention to the vertical line(s) indicating the pattern repeat. These repeats act the same as the asterisk you find in written patterns. The stitches that appear outside the repeat lines are just edge stitches, and you work them at the beginning and at the end of your pattern while repeating the stitches within the lines until you reach the last edge stitches. When working in the round, all you do is work the stitches within the repeat. It's that simple! xx

ABOUT THE SWATCHES IN THIS BOOK

All the swatches in this book started out with enough stitches to create at least a 4" (10 cm) square. In some cases, due to the nature of the stitch pattern and the pattern multiples, the swatch is rectangular. When I knitted them, I started with two rows of Garter stitch and two edge stitches on each side in Garter stitch. I ended all of the swatches with two more rows of Garter stitch and then bound off. Because they are made with alternating light and dark colors, the mosaic swatches have a striped effect along the Garter edges. Disregard these stripes as they are not a part of the actual mosaic stitch pattern. When in doubt, look at the chart.

CHAPTER 1

KNITS & PURLS

KNITTERS OF ALL LEVELS can form super-attractive, and even intricate, designs by using the most basic knits and purls. No fancy maneuvers or acrobatics—like knitting below or slipping stitches, twists or yarnovers—needed. In most cases, these stitch patterns are easily memorized and show off to great effect, especially when worked in solid colors. An extra bonus of using only knit and purl stitches in stitch patterns is that the finished product often looks good on both sides, or is even totally reversible. Two examples of reversible patterns are Lozenges on page 47 and Crenellated Pattern on page 48. Either would be perfect for a scarf or a stole where both sides will show. xx

STITCHES

STOCKINETTE STITCH
GARTER STITCH
STOCKINETTE STITCH
  TRIANGLES
BOX STITCH
DIAGONAL CHECKS
STRING OF BEADS
DIAGONALS
MOSS CIRCLES
MOSS STITCH ZIGZAG
BROKEN DIAGONAL
  CHECK
PURL TEXTURE
THERMAL STITCH
BANDED BASKET STITCH
HARRIS TWEED
PENNANTS

RIPPLE PATTERN
KNIT AND PURL
  DIAMONDS
PURL ZIGZAG
FLUTED TRIANGLES
IMITATION LATTICE
LITTLE CHECKS 1
LITTLE CHECKS 2
SWEDISH BLOCK
LOZENGES
CRENELLATED PATTERN
DOUBLE DIAMOND
  BROCADE
SEERSUCKER STITCH
SQUARES

PROJECT

SEERSUCKER PULLI

Stockinette Stitch

FLAT

(any number of sts; 2-row repeat)

ROW 1 (RS): Knit.

ROW 2: Purl.

Repeat Rows 1 and 2 for Stockinette Stitch Flat.

IN THE ROUND

(any number of sts; 1-rnd repeat)

ALL RNDS: Knit.

Garter Stitch (FULLY REVERSIBLE)

FLAT

(any number of sts; 1-row repeat)

ROW 1: Knit.

Repeat Row 1 for Garter Stitch Flat.

IN THE ROUND

(any number of sts; 2-rnd repeat)

RND 1: Knit.

RND 2: Purl.

Repeat Rnds 1 and 2 for Garter Stitch in the Round.

Stockinette Stitch Triangles (FULLY REVERSIBLE)

BOTTOM-UP FLAT

(multiple of 5 sts; 6-row repeat)

ROW 1 (RS): Knit.

ROW 2: *K1, p4; repeat from * to end.

ROWS 3 AND 4: *K3, p2; repeat from * to end.

ROW 5: *K1, p4; repeat from * to end.

ROW 6: Knit.

Repeat Rows 1–6 for Stockinette Stitch Triangles Bottom-Up Flat.

BOTTOM-UP IN THE ROUND

(multiple of 5 sts; 6-rnd repeat)

RND 1 (RS): Knit.

RND 2: *K4, p1; repeat from * to end.

RND 3: *K3, p2; repeat from * to end.

RND 4: *K2, p3; repeat from * to end.

RND 5: *K1, p4; repeat from * to end.

RND 6: Purl.

Repeat Rnds 1–6 for Stockinette Stitch Triangles Bottom-Up in the Round.

BOTTOM-UP FLAT & IN THE ROUND

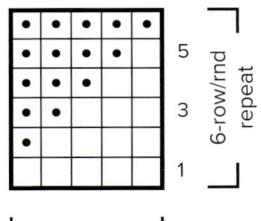

5-st repeat

TOP-DOWN FLAT & IN THE ROUND

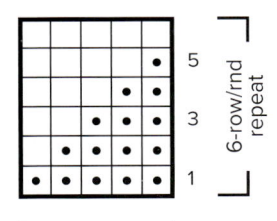

5-st repeat

TOP-DOWN FLAT

(multiple of 5 sts; 6-row repeat)

ROW 1 (RS): Purl.

ROW 2: *P1, k4; repeat from * to end.

ROWS 3 AND 4: *P3, k2; repeat from * to end.

ROW 5: *P1, k4; repeat from * to end.

ROW 6: Purl.

Repeat Rows 1–6 for Stockinette Stitch Triangles Top-Down Flat.

TOP-DOWN IN THE ROUND

(multiple of 5 sts; 6-rnd repeat)

RND 1 (RS): Purl.

RND 2: *P4, k1; repeat from * to end.

RND 3: *P3, k2; repeat from * to end.

RND 4: *P2, k3; repeat from * to end.

RND 5: *P1, k4; repeat from * to end.

RND 6: Knit.

Repeat Rnds 1–6 for Stockinette Stitch Triangles Top-Down in the Round.

Box Stitch (FULLY REVERSIBLE)

FLAT

(multiple of 4 sts + 2; 4-row repeat)

ROW 1 (RS): *K2, p2; repeat from * to last 2 sts, k2.

ROWS 2 AND 3: P2, *k2, p2; repeat from * to end.

ROW 4: Repeat Row 1.

Repeat Rows 1–4 for Box Stitch Flat.

IN THE ROUND

(multiple of 4 sts; 4-rnd repeat)

RNDS 1 AND 2: *K2, p2; repeat from * to end.

RNDS 3 AND 4: *P2, k2; repeat from * to end.

Repeat Rnds 1–4 for Box Stitch in the Round.

FLAT

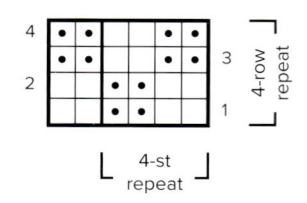

IN THE ROUND

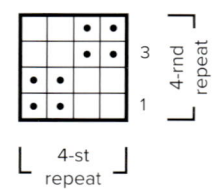

Diagonal Checks (FULLY REVERSIBLE)

FLAT

(multiple of 5 sts; 8-row repeat)

ROW 1 (RS): *P1, k4; repeat from * to end.

ROW 2: *K3, p2; repeat from * to end.

ROW 3: *P3, k2; repeat from * to end.

ROW 4: *P1, k4; repeat from * to end.

ROW 5: *K1, p4: repeat from * to end.

ROWS 6 AND 7: *K3, p2; repeat from * to end.

ROW 8: *K1, p4; repeat from * to end.

Repeat Rows 1–8 for Diagonal Checks Flat.

IN THE ROUND

(multiple of 5 sts; 8-rnd repeat)

RND 1: *P1, k4; repeat from * to end.

RND 2: *K2, p3; repeat from * to end.

RND 3: *P3, k2; repeat from * to end.

RND 4: *P4, k1; repeat from * to end.

RND 5: *K1, p4; repeat from * to end.

RND 6: *K2, p3; repeat from * to end.

RND 7: *K3, p2; repeat from * to end.

RND 8: *K4, p1; repeat from * to end.

Repeat Rnds 1–8 for Diagonal Checks in the Round.

FLAT & IN THE ROUND

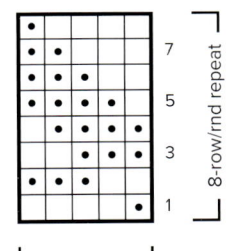

5-st repeat

8-row/rnd repeat

String of Beads

FLAT

(multiple of 8 sts + 1; 8-row repeat)

ROW 1 (RS): *K1, p2, k3, p2; repeat from * to last st, k1.

ROWS 2-4: Knit the knit sts and purl the purl sts as they face you.

ROW 5: K2, *p2, k1, p2, k3; repeat from * to last 7 sts, p2, k1, p2, k2.

ROWS 6-8: Repeat Row 2.

Repeat Rows 1–8 for String of Beads Flat.

FLAT

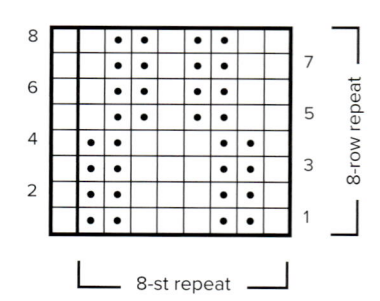

IN THE ROUND

(multiple of 8 sts; 8-rnd repeat)

RNDS 1-4: *K1, p2, k3, p2; repeat from * to end.

RNDS 5-8: K2, *p2, k1, p2, k3; repeat from * to last 6 sts, [p2, k1] twice.

Repeat Rnds 1–8 for String of Beads in the Round.

IN THE ROUND

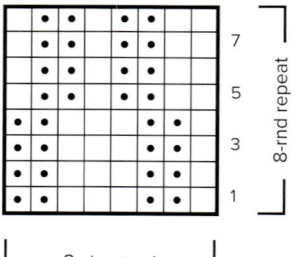

Diagonals (TWO-SIDED)

FLAT

(multiple of 8 sts + 6; 8-row repeat)

ROW 1 (RS): *P3, k5; repeat from * to last 6 sts, p3, k3.
ROW 2: P4, *k3, p5; repeat from * to last 2 sts, k2.
ROW 3: P1, k5, *p3, k5; repeat from * to end.
ROW 4: K1, p5, *k3, p5; repeat from * to end.
ROW 5: K4, *p3, k5; repeat from * to last 2 sts, p2.
ROW 6: K3, *p5, k3; repeat from * to last 3 sts, p3.
ROW 7: K2, p3, *k5, p3; repeat from * to last st, k1.
ROW 8: P2, k3, *p5, k3; repeat from * to last st, p1.
Repeat Rows 1–8 for Diagonals Flat.

FLAT

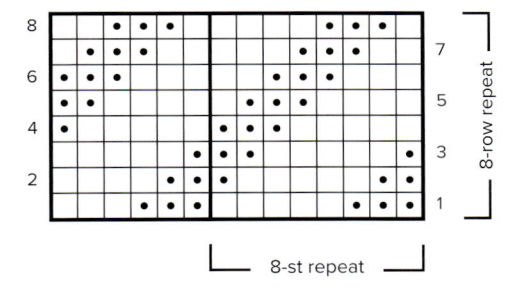

8-row repeat
8-st repeat

IN THE ROUND

(multiple of 8 sts; 8-rnd repeat)

RND 1: *P3, k5; repeat from * to end.
RND 2: P2, *k5, p3; repeat from * to last 6 sts, k5, p1.
RND 3: P1, *k5, p3; repeat from * to last 7 sts, k5, p2.
RND 4: *K5, p3; repeat from * to end.
RND 5: K4, *p3, k5; repeat from * to last 4 sts, p3, k1.
RND 6: K3, *p3, k5; repeat from * to last 5 sts, p3, k2.
RND 7: K2, *p3, k5; repeat from * to last 6 sts, p3, k3.
RND 8: K1, *p3, k5; repeat from * to last 7 sts, p3, k4.
Repeat Rnds 1–8 for Diagonals in the Round.

IN THE ROUND

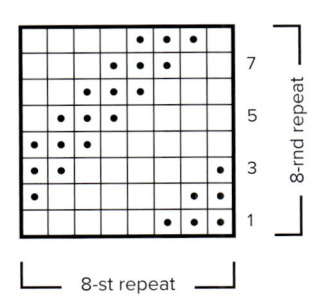

8-rnd repeat
8-st repeat

Moss Circles

FLAT

(multiple of 12 sts + 1; 16-row repeat)

ROW 1 (RS): K3, *[p1, k1] 3 times, p1, k5; repeat from * to last 10 sts, [p1, k1] 3 times, p1, k3.

ROW 2: P4, *[k1, p1] twice, k1, p7; repeat from * to last 9 sts, [k1, p1] twice, k1, p4.

ROWS 3 AND 4: Repeat Rows 1 and 2.

ROW 5: K1, p1, *k3, p1, k1, p1; repeat from * to last 5 sts, k3, p1, k1.

ROW 6: K1, *p1, k1, p7, k1, p1, k1; repeat from * to end.

ROW 7: [K1, p1] twice, *k5, [p1, k1] 3 times, p1; repeat from * to last 9 sts, k5, [p1, k1] twice.

ROWS 8–11: Repeat Rows 6 and 7.

ROW 12: Repeat Row 6.

ROW 13: Repeat Row 5.

ROW 14: Repeat Row 2.

ROWS 15 AND 16: Repeat Rows 1 and 2.

Repeat Rows 1–16 for Moss Circles Flat.

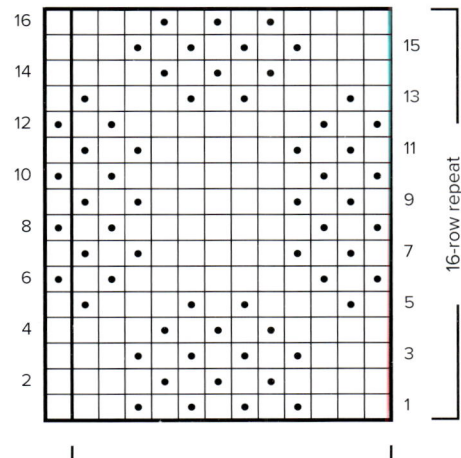

IN THE ROUND

(multiple of 12 sts; 16-rnd repeat)

RND 1: K3, *[p1, k1] 3 times, p1, k5; repeat from * to last 9 sts, [p1, k1] 3 times, p1, k2.

RND 2: K4, *[p1, k1] 3 times, p1, k7; repeat from * to last 8 sts, [p1, k1] twice, p1, k3.

RNDS 3 AND 4: Repeat Rnds 1 and 2.

RND 5: K1, p1, *k3, p1, k1, p1; repeat from * to last 4 sts, k3, p1.

RND 6: P1, k1, p1, *k7, [p1, k1] twice, p1; repeat from * to last 9 sts, k7, p1, k1.

RND 7: [K1, p1] twice, *k5, [p1, k1] 3 times, p1; repeat from * to last 8 sts, k5, p1, k1, p1.

RNDS 8–11: Repeat Rnds 6 and 7.

RND 12: Repeat Rnd 6.

RND 13: Repeat Rnd 5.

RND 14: Repeat Rnd 2.

RNDS 15 AND 16: Repeat Rnds 1 and 2.

Repeat Rnds 1–16 for Moss Circles in the Round.

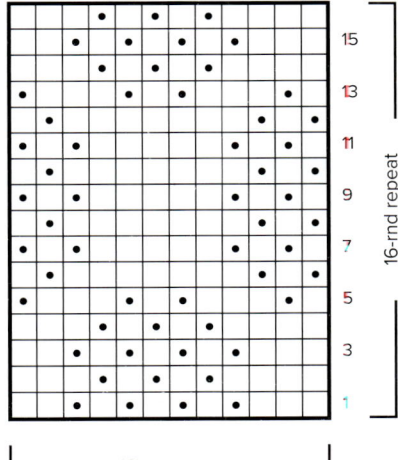

Moss Stitch Zigzag (TWO-SIDED)

FLAT

(multiple of 9 sts; 10-row repeat)
ROW 1 (RS): [K1, p1] twice, *k4, [p1, k1] twice, p1; repeat from * to last 5 sts, k4, p1.
ROW 2: *P4, [k1, p1] twice, k1; repeat from * to end.
ROW 3: [K1, p1] 3 times, *k4, [p1, k1] twice, p1; repeat from * to last 3 sts, k3.
ROW 4: P2, *[k1, p1] twice, k1, p4; repeat from * to last 7 sts, [k1, p1] twice, k1, p2.
ROW 5: K3, *[p1, k1] twice, p1, k4; repeat from * to last 6 sts, [p1, k1] 3 times.
ROW 6: *[K1, p1] twice, k1, p4; repeat from * to end.
ROW 7: Repeat Row 5.
ROW 8: Repeat Row 4.
ROW 9: Repeat Row 3.
ROW 10: Repeat Row 2.
Repeat Rows 1–10 for Moss Stitch Zigzag Flat.

IN THE ROUND

(multiple of 9 sts; 10-rnd repeat)
RND 1: [K1, p1] twice, *k4, [p1, k1] twice, p1; repeat from * to last 5 sts, k4, p1.
RND 2: *[P1, k1] twice, p1, k4; repeat from * to end.
RND 3: [K1, p1] 3 times, *k4, [p1, k1] twice, p1; repeat from * to last 3 sts, k3.
RND 4: K2, *[p1, k1] twice, p1, k4; repeat from * to last 7 sts, [p1, k1] twice, p1, k2.
RND 5: K3, *[p1, k1] twice, p1, k4; repeat from * to last 6 sts, [p1, k1] 3 times.
RND 6: *K4, [p1, k1] twice, p1; repeat from * to end.
RND 7: Repeat Rnd 5.
RND 8: Repeat Rnd 4.
RND 9: Repeat Rnd 3.
RND 10: Repeat Rnd 2.
Repeat Rnds 1–10 for Moss Stitch Zigzag in the Round.

FLAT & IN THE ROUND

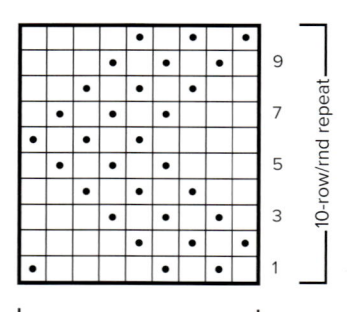

10-row/rnd repeat

9-st repeat

Broken Diagonal Check

FLAT

(multiple of 8 sts; 8-row repeat)

ROW 1 (RS): *K6, p2; repeat from * to end.
ROW 2: P1, *k2, p6; repeat from * to last 7 sts, k2, p5.
ROW 3: K4, *p2, k6; repeat from * to last 4 sts, p2, k2.
ROW 4: P3, *k2, p6; repeat from * to last 5 sts, k2, p3.
ROW 5: K2, *p2, k6; repeat from * to last 6 sts, p2, k4.
ROW 6: P5, *k2, p6; repeat from * to last 3 sts, k2, p1.
ROW 7: Purl.
ROW 8: Repeat Row 2.
Repeat Rows 1–8 for Broken Diagonal Check Flat.

IN THE ROUND

(multiple of 8 sts; 8-rnd repeat)

RND 1: *K6, p2; repeat from * to end.
RND 2: K5, *p2, k6; repeat from * to last 3 sts, p2, k1.
RND 3: K4, *p2, k6; repeat from * to last 4 sts, p2, k2.
RND 4: K3, *p2, k6; repeat from * to last 5 sts, p2, k3.
RND 5: K2, *p2, k6; repeat from * to last 6 sts, p2, k4.
RND 6: K1, *p2, k6; repeat from * to last 7 sts, p2, k5.
RND 7: Purl.
RND 8: Repeat Rnd 2.
Repeat Rnds 1–8 for Broken Diagonal Check in the Round.

FLAT & IN THE ROUND

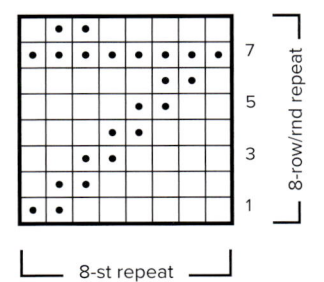

8-st repeat

8-row/rnd repeat

Purl Texture

FLAT

(multiple of 6 sts; 8-row repeat)

ROW 1 (RS): *K3, p3; repeat from * to end.

ROW 2: Purl.

ROW 3: Knit.

ROW 4: Purl.

ROW 5: *P3, k3; repeat from * to end.

ROWS 6–8: Repeat Rows 2–4.

Repeat Rows 1–8 for Purl Texture Flat.

IN THE ROUND

(multiple of 6 sts; 8-rnd repeat)

RND 1: *K3, p3; repeat from * to end.

RNDS 2–4: Knit.

RND 5: *P3, k3; repeat from * to end.

RNDS 6–8: Knit.

Repeat Rnds 1–8 for Purl Texture in the Round.

FLAT & IN THE ROUND

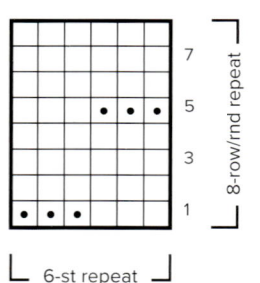

Thermal Stitch

FLAT

(multiple of 4 sts + 2; 4-row repeat)

ROW 1 (RS): *K2, p2; repeat from * to last 2 sts, k2.

ROW 2: P2, *k2, p2; repeat from * to end.

ROW 3: Knit.

ROW 4: Purl.

Repeat Rows 1–4 for Thermal Stitch Flat.

IN THE ROUND

(multiple of 4 sts; 4-rnd repeat)

RNDS 1 AND 2: *K2, p2; repeat from * to end.

RNDS 3 AND 4: Knit.

Repeat Rnds 1–4 for Thermal Stitch in the Round.

FLAT

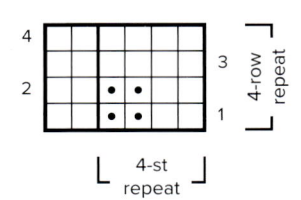

IN THE ROUND

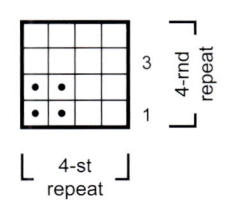

Banded Basket Stitch (TWO-SIDED)

FLAT

(multiple of 9 sts + 6; 10-row repeat)

ROW 1 (RS): *P6, k3; repeat from * to last 6 sts, p6.

ROWS 2–6: Knit the knit sts and purl the purl sts as they face you.

ROW 7: K6, *p3, k6; repeat from * to end.

ROWS 8–10: Repeat Row 2.

Repeat Rows 1–10 for Banded Basket Stitch Flat.

IN THE ROUND

(multiple of 9 sts; 10-rnd repeat)

RNDS 1–6: *P6, k3; repeat from * to end.

RNDS 7–10: *K6, p3; repeat from * to end.

Repeat Rnds 1–10 for Banded Basket Stitch in the Round.

FLAT

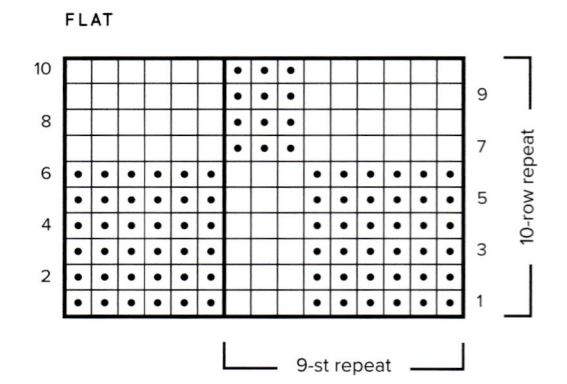

IN THE ROUND

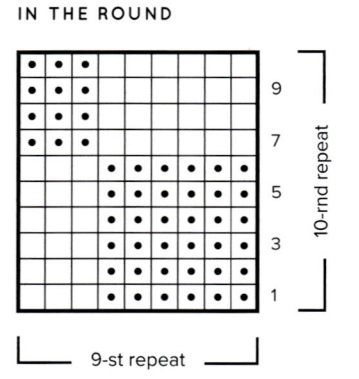

Harris Tweed (TWO-SIDED)

FLAT

(multiple of 6 sts + 3; 12-row repeat)

ROW 1 (RS): *K3, p3; repeat from * to last 3 sts, k3.

ROWS 2-3: Knit the knit sts and purl the purl sts as they face you.

ROW 4: Knit.

ROWS 5-6: Repeat Row 2.

ROWS 7: Repeat Row 1.

ROWS 8-9: Repeat Row 2.

ROW 10: Purl.

ROW 11: Knit.

ROW 12: Purl.

Repeat Rows 1–12 for Harris Tweed Flat.

FLAT

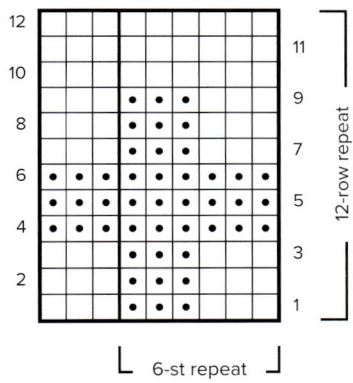

6-st repeat

IN THE ROUND

(multiple of 6 sts; 12-rnd repeat)

RNDS 1-3: *K3, p3; repeat from * to end.

RNDS 4-6: Purl.

RNDS 7-9: Repeat Rnds 1–3.

RNDS 10-12: Knit.

Repeat Rnds 1–12 for Harris Tweed in the Round.

IN THE ROUND

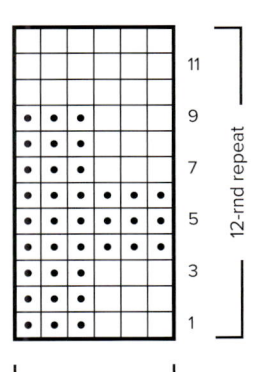

6-st repeat

Pennants (FULLY REVERSIBLE)

FLAT

(multiple of 9 sts; 16-row repeat)

ROW 1 (RS): *P1, k8; repeat from * to end.

ROW 2: *P7, k2; repeat from * to end.

ROW 3: *P3, k6; repeat from * to end.

ROWS 4 AND 5: *P5, k4; repeat from * to end.

ROW 6: Repeat Row 3.

ROW 7: Repeat Row 2.

ROW 8: Repeat Row 1.

ROW 9: *K8, p1; repeat from * to end.

ROW 10: *K2, p7; repeat from * to end.

ROW 11: *K6, p3; repeat from * to end.

ROWS 12 AND 13: *K4, p5; repeat from * to end.

ROW 14: Repeat Row 11.

ROW 15: Repeat Row 10.

ROW 16: Repeat Row 9.

Repeat Rows 1–16 for Pennants Flat.

FLAT & IN THE ROUND

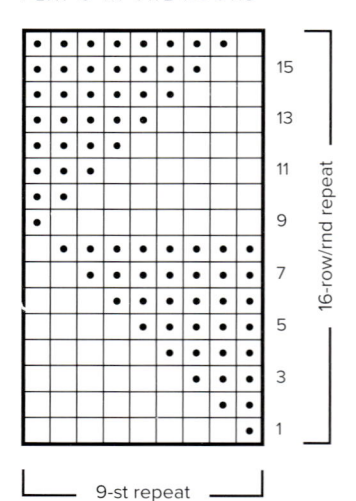

9-st repeat

IN THE ROUND

(multiple of 9 sts; 16-rnd repeat)

RND 1: *P1, k8; repeat from * to end.

RND 2: *P2, k7; repeat from * to end.

RND 3: *P3, k6; repeat from * to end.

RND 4: *P4, k5; repeat from * to end.

RND 5: *P5, k4; repeat from * to end.

RND 6: *P6, k3; repeat from * to end.

RND 7: *P7, k2; repeat from * to end.

RND 8: *P8, k1; repeat from * to end.

RND 9: *K8, p1; repeat from * to end.

RND 10: *K7, p2; repeat from * to end.

RND 11: *K6, p3; repeat from * to end.

RND 12: *K5, p4; repeat from * to end.

RND 13: *K4, p5; repeat from * to end.

RND 14: *K3, p6; repeat from * to end.

RND 15: *K2, p7; repeat from * to end.

RND 16: *K1, p8; repeat from * to end.

Repeat Rnds 1–16 for Pennants in the Round.

Ripple Pattern (TWO-SIDED)

FLAT

(multiple of 8 sts + 6; 10-row repeat)

ROW 1 (RS): *K6, p2; repeat from * to last 6 sts, k6.

ROW 2: K1, *p4, k4; repeat from * to last 5 sts, p4, k1.

ROW 3: *P2, k2; repeat from * to last 2 sts p2.

ROW 4: P1, *k4, p4; repeat from * to last 5 sts, k4, p1.

ROW 5: K2, *p2, k6; repeat from * to last 4 sts, p2, k2.

ROW 6: P6, *k2, p6; repeat from * to end.

ROW 7: Repeat Row 4.

ROW 8: *K2, p2; repeat from * to last 2 sts, k2.

ROW 9: Repeat Row 2.

ROW 10: P2, *k2, p6; repeat from * to last 4 sts, k2, p2.

Repeat Rows 1–10 for Ripple Pattern Flat.

FLAT

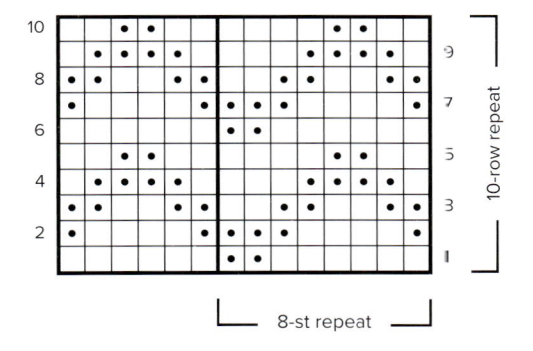

8-st repeat

10-row repeat

IN THE ROUND

(multiple of 8 sts; 5-rnd repeat)

RND 1: *K6, p2; repeat from * to end.

RND 2: P1, *k4, p4; repeat from * to last 7 sts, k4, p3.

RND 3: *P2, k2; repeat from * to end.

RND 4: K1, *p4, k4; repeat from * to last 7 sts, p4, k3.

RND 5: K2, *p2, k6; repeat from * to last 6 sts, p2, k4.

Repeat Rnds 1–5 for Ripple Pattern in the Round.

IN THE ROUND

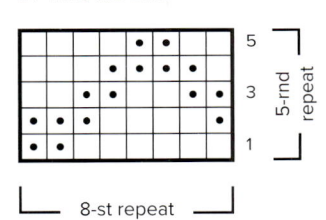

8-st repeat

5-rnd repeat

Knit and Purl Diamonds (FULLY REVERSIBLE)

FLAT

(multiple of 10 sts + 1; 16-row repeat)

ROW 1 (RS): K5, *p1, k9; repeat from * to last 6 sts, p1, k5.

ROW 2 AND ALL WS ROWS: Knit the knit sts and purl the purl sts as they face you.

ROW 3: K4, *p3, k7; repeat from * to last 7 sts, p3, k4.

ROW 5: K3, *p5, k5; repeat from * to last 8 sts, p5, k3.

ROW 7: K2, *p7, k3; repeat from * to last 9 sts, p7, k2.

ROW 9: *K1, p9; repeat from * to last st, k1.

ROW 11: Repeat Row 7.

ROW 13: Repeat Row 5.

ROW 15: Repeat Row 3.

ROW 16: Repeat Row 2.

Repeat Rows 1–16 for Knit and Purl Diamonds Flat.

IN THE ROUND

(multiple of 10 sts; 16-rnd repeat)

RNDS 1 AND 2: K5, *p1, k9; repeat from * to last 5 sts, p1, k4.

RNDS 3 AND 4: K4, *p3, k7; repeat from * to last 6 sts, p3, k3.

RNDS 5 AND 6: K3, *p5, k5; repeat from * to last 7 sts, p5, k2.

RNDS 7 AND 8: K2, *p7, k3; repeat from * to last 8 sts, p7, k1.

RNDS 9 AND 10: *K1, p9; repeat from * to end.

RNDS 11 AND 12: Repeat Rnds 7 and 8.

RNDS 13 AND 14: Repeat Rnds 5 and 6.

RNDS 15 AND 16: Repeat Rnds 3 and 4.

Repeat Rnds 1–16 for Knit and Purl Diamonds in the Round.

FLAT

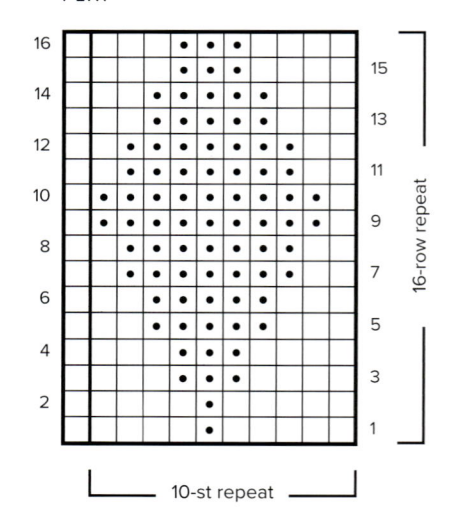

10-st repeat

16-row repeat

IN THE ROUND

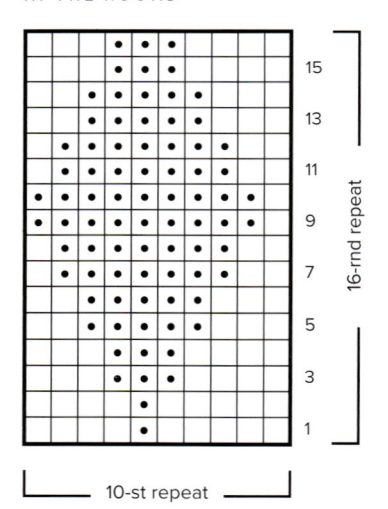

10-st repeat

16-rnd repeat

Purl Zigzag

FLAT

(multiple of 5 sts; 10-row repeat)

ROW 1 (RS): *P1, k4; repeat from * to end.

ROW 2: P3, *k1, p4; repeat from * to last 2 sts, k1, p1.

ROW 3: K2, *p1, k4; repeat from * to last 3 sts, p1, k2.

ROW 4: P1, *k1, p4; repeat from * to last 4 sts, k1, p3.

ROW 5: *K4, p1; repeat from * to end.

ROW 6: *P4, k1; repeat from * to end.

ROW 7: Repeat Row 5.

ROW 8: Repeat Row 4.

ROW 9: Repeat Row 3.

ROW 10: Repeat Row 2.

Repeat Rows 1–10 for Purl Zigzag Flat.

IN THE ROUND

(multiple of 5 sts; 10-rnd repeat)

RND 1: *P1, k4; repeat from * to end.

RND 2: K1, *p1, k4; repeat from * to last 4 sts, p1, k3.

RND 3: K2, *p1, k4; repeat from * to last 3 sts, p1, k2.

RND 4: K3, *p1, k4; repeat from * to last 2 sts, p1, k1.

RND 5: *K4, p1; repeat from * to end.

RND 6: *P1, k4; repeat from * to end.

RND 7: Repeat Rnd 5.

RND 8: Repeat Rnd 4.

RND 9: Repeat Rnd 3.

RND 10: Repeat Rnd 2.

Repeat Rnds 1–10 for Purl Zigzag in the Round.

FLAT & IN THE ROUND

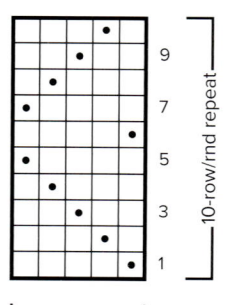

Fluted Triangles

FLAT

(multiple of 8 sts; 8-row repeat)

ROW 1 (RS): *K4, p4; repeat from * to end.

ROW 2: P1, *k3, p5; repeat from * to last 7 sts, k3, p4.

ROW 3: K4, *p2, k6; repeat from * to last 4 sts, p2, k2.

ROW 4: P3, *k1, p7; repeat from * to last 5 sts, k1, p4.

ROW 5: *P4, k4; repeat from * to end.

ROW 6: *P5, k3; repeat from * to end.

ROW 7: *P2, k6; repeat from * to end.

ROW 8: *P7, k1; repeat from * to end.

Repeat Rows 1–8 for Fluted Triangles Flat.

IN THE ROUND

(multiple of 8 sts; 8-rnd repeat)

RND 1: *K4, p4; repeat from * to end.

RND 2: K4, *p3, k5; repeat from * to last 4 sts, p3, k1.

RND 3: K4, *p2, k6; repeat from * to last 4 sts, p2, k2.

RND 4: K4, *p1, k7; repeat from * to last 4 sts, p1, k3.

RND 5: *P4, k4; repeat from * to end.

RND 6: *P3, k5; repeat from * to end.

RND 7: *P2, k6; repeat from * to end.

RND 8: *P1, k7; repeat from * to end.

Repeat Rnds 1–8 for Fluted Triangles in the Round.

FLAT & IN THE ROUND

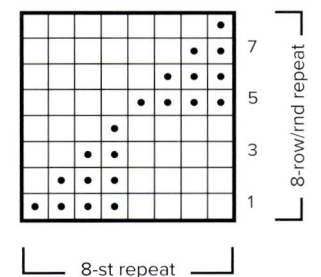

8-row/rnd repeat

8-st repeat

FRONT

BACK

Imitation Lattice (TWO-SIDED)

FLAT

(multiple of 12 sts + 1; 24-row repeat)

ROW 1 (RS): K4, *p5; k7; repeat from * to last 9 sts, p5, k4.

ROW 2 AND ALL WS ROWS: Knit the knit sts and purl the purl sts as they face you.

ROW 3: K3, *p3, k1, p3, k5; repeat from * to last 10 sts, p3, k1, p3, k3.

ROW 5: K2, *p3, k3; repeat from * to last 5 sts, p3, k2.

ROW 7: *K1, p3, k5, p3; repeat from * to last st, k1.

ROW 9: P3, *k7, p5; repeat from * to last 10 sts, k7, p3.

ROW 11: P2, *k9, p3; repeat from * to last 11 sts, k9, p2.

ROW 13: Repeat Row 9.

ROW 15: Repeat Row 7.

ROW 17: Repeat Row 5.

ROW 19: Repeat Row 3.

ROW 21: Repeat Row 1.

ROW 23: K5, *p3, k9; repeat from * to last 8 sts, p3, k5.

ROW 24: Repeat Row 2.

Repeat Rows 1–24 for Imitation Lattice Flat.

IN THE ROUND

(multiple of 12 sts; 24-rnd repeat)

RNDS 1 AND 2: K4, *p5; k7; repeat from * to last 8 sts, p5, k3.

RNDS 3 AND 4: K3, *p3, k1, p3, k5; rep from * to last 9 sts, p3, k1, p3, k2.

RNDS 5 AND 6: K2, *p3, k3; repeat from * to last 4 sts, p3, k1.

RNDS 7 AND 8: *K1, p3, k5, p3; repeat from * to end.

RNDS 9 AND 10: P3, *k7, p5; repeat from * to last 9 sts, k7, p2.

RNDS 11 AND 12: P2, *k9, p3; repeat from * to last 10 sts, k9, p1.

RNDS 13 AND 14: Repeat Rnds 9 and 10.

RNDS 15 AND 16: Repeat Rnds 7 and 8.

RNDS 17 AND 18: Repeat Rnds 5 and 6.

RNDS 19 AND 20: Repeat Rnds 3 and 4.

RNDS 21 AND 22: Repeat Rnds 1 and 2.

RNDS 23 AND 24: K5, *p3, k9; repeat from * to last 7 sts, p3, k4.

Repeat Rnds 1–24 for Imitation Lattice in the Round.

FLAT

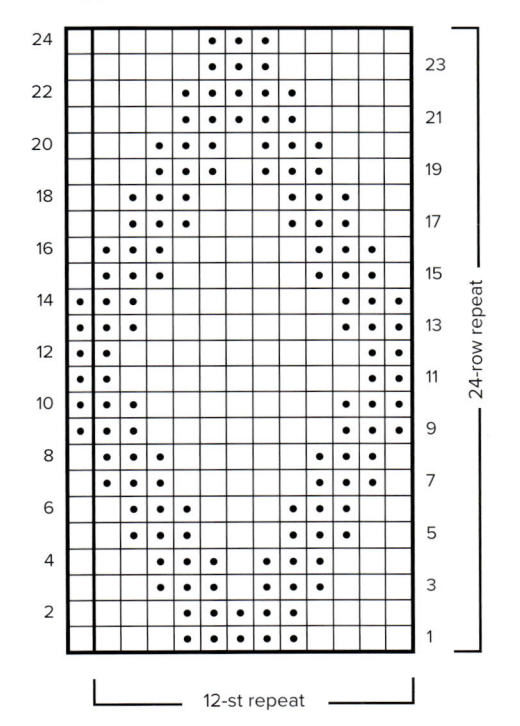

24-row repeat

12-st repeat

IN THE ROUND

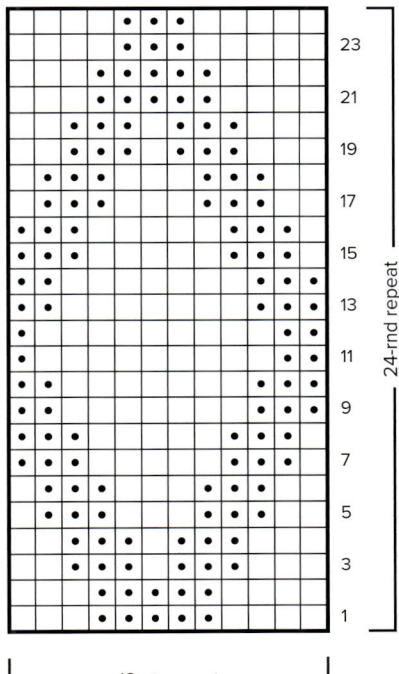

24-rnd repeat

12-st repeat

Little Checks 1

FLAT

(multiple of 10 sts + 1; 10-row repeat)

ROW 1 (RS): Purl.

ROW 2: K4, *p3, k7; repeat from * to last 7 sts, p3, k4.

ROWS 3 AND 4: Knit the knit sts and purl the purl sts as they face you.

ROW 5: Purl.

ROW 6: Knit.

ROW 7: K2, *p7, k3; repeat from * to last 9 sts, p7, k2.

ROWS 8 AND 9: Knit the knit sts and purl the purl sts as they face you.

ROW 10: Knit.

Repeat Rows 1–10 for Little Checks 1 Flat.

IN THE ROUND

(multiple of 10 sts; 10-rnd repeat)

RND 1: Purl.

RNDS 2–4: P4, *k3; p7; repeat from * to last 6 sts, k3, p3.

RNDS 5 AND 6: Purl.

RNDS 7–9: K2, *p7, k3; repeat from * to last 8 sts, p7, k1.

RND 10: Purl.

Repeat Rnds 1–10 for Little Checks 1 in the Round.

IN THE ROUND

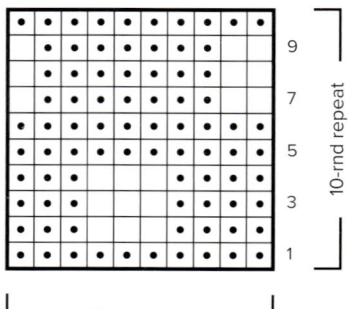

FLAT

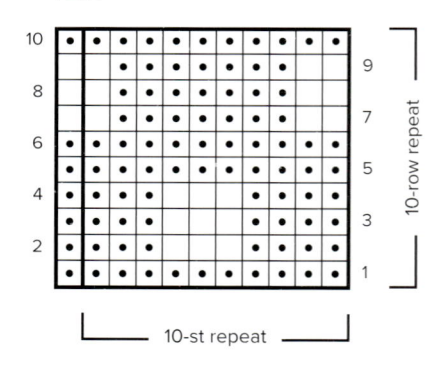

Little Checks 2

FLAT

(multiple of 6 sts + 3; 16-row repeat)

ROW 1 AND ALL RS ROWS (RS): Knit.

ROW 2: Knit.

ROWS 4 AND 6: P3, *k3, p3; repeat from * to end.

ROWS 8 AND 10: Knit.

ROWS 12 AND 14: K3, *p3, k3; repeat from * to end.

ROW 16: Knit.

Repeat Rows 1–16 for Little Checks 2 Flat.

IN THE ROUND

(multiple of 6 sts; 16-rnd repeat)

RND 1 AND ALL ODD-NUMBERED RNDS: Knit.

RND 2: Purl.

RNDS 4 AND 6: *K3, p3; repeat from * to end.

RNDS 8 AND 10: Purl.

RNDS 12 AND 14: *P3, k3; repeat from * to end.

RND 16: Purl.

Repeat Rnds 1–16 for Little Checks 2 in the Round.

FLAT

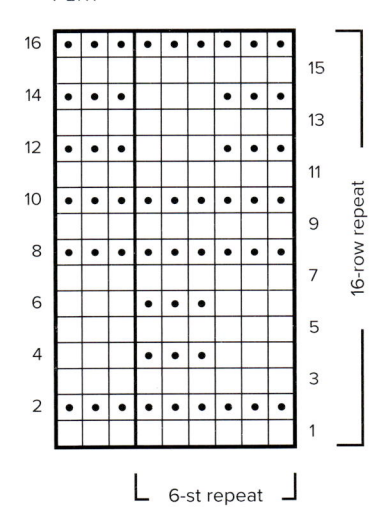

16-row repeat

6-st repeat

IN THE ROUND

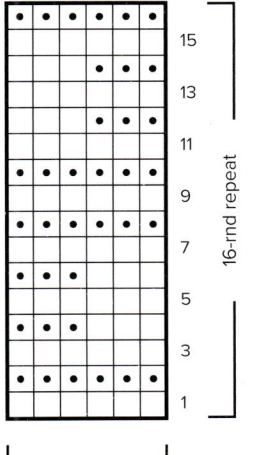

16-rnd repeat

6-st repeat

Swedish Block (TWO-SIDED)

FLAT

(multiple of 6 sts + 2; 8-row repeat)

ROW 1 (RS): *K2, p4; repeat from * to last 2 sts, k2.

ROWS 2 AND 3: P2, *k4, p2; repeat from * to end.

ROWS 4–8: Knit the knit sts and purl the purl sts as they face you.

Repeat Rows 1–8 for Swedish Block Flat.

IN THE ROUND

(multiple of 6 sts; 8-rnd repeat)

RNDS 1 AND 2: *K2, p4; repeat from * to end.

RNDS 3–8: *P2, k4: repeat from * to end.

Repeat Rnds 1–8 for Swedish Block in the Round.

FLAT

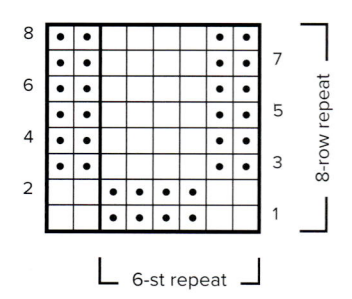

IN THE ROUND

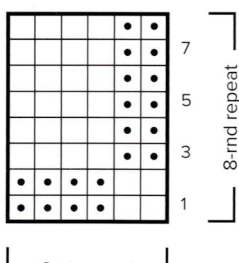

Lozenges (FULLY REVERSIBLE)

FLAT

(multiple of 5 sts; 8-row repeat)

ROW 1 (RS): *P1, k4; repeat from * to end.

ROWS 2 AND 3: *P3, k2; repeat from * to end.

ROW 4: Repeat Row 1.

ROW 5: *K4, p1; repeat from * to end.

ROWS 6 AND 7: *K2, p3; repeat from * to end.

ROW 8: Repeat Row 5.

Repeat Rows 1–8 for Lozenges Flat.

IN THE ROUND

(multiple of 5 sts; 8-rnd repeat)

RND 1: *P1, k4; repeat from * to end.

RND 2: *P2, k3; repeat from * to end.

RND 3: *P3, k2; repeat from * to end.

RND 4: *P4, k1; repeat from * to end.

RND 5: *K4, p1; repeat from * to end.

RND 6: *K3, p2; repeat from * to end.

RND 7: *K2, p3; repeat from * to end.

RND 8: *K1, p4; repeat from * to end.

Repeat Rnds 1–8 for Lozenges in the Round.

FLAT & IN THE ROUND

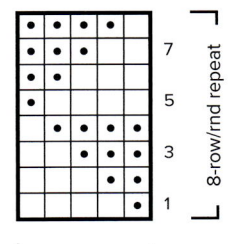

Crenellated Pattern (TWO-SIDED)

FLAT

(multiple of 24 sts; 24-row repeat)

ROW 1 (RS): *K2, p2, k8, p2, k2, p8; repeat from * to end.

ROW 2 AND ALL RS ROWS: Knit the knit sts and purl the purl sts as they face you.

ROW 3: *K2, p8, k2, p2, k8, p2; repeat from * to end.

ROW 5: *K8, p2, k2, p8, k2, p2; repeat from * to end.

ROW 7: *P6, k2, p2, k8, p2, k2, p2; repeat from * to end.

ROW 9: *K4, p2, k2, p8, k2, p2, k4; repeat from * to end.

ROW 11: *P2, k2, p2, k8, p2, k2, p6; repeat from * to end.

ROW 13: *P2, k2, p8, k2, p2, k8; repeat from * to end.

ROW 15: Repeat Row 11.

ROW 17: Repeat Row 9.

ROW 19: Repeat Row 7.

ROW 21: Repeat Row 5.

ROW 23: Repeat Row 3.

ROW 24: Repeat Row 2.

Repeat Rows 1–24 for Crenellated Pattern Flat.

IN THE ROUND

(multiple of 24 sts; 24-rnd repeat)

RNDS 1 AND 2: *K2, p2, k8, p2, k2, p8; repeat from * to end.

RNDS 3 AND 4: *K2, p8, k2, p2, k8, p2; repeat from * to end.

RNDS 5 AND 6: *K8, p2, k2, p8, k2, p2; repeat from * to end.

RNDS 7 AND 8: *P6, k2, p2, k8, p2, k2, p2; repeat from * to end.

RNDS 9 AND 10: *K4, p2, k2, p8, k2, p2, k4; repeat from * to end.

RNDS 11 AND 12: *P2, k2, p2, k8, p2, k2, p6; repeat from * to end.

RNDS 13 AND 14: *P2, k2, p8, k2, p2, k8; repeat from * to end.

RNDS 15 AND 16: Repeat Rows 11 and 12.

RNDS 17 AND 18: Repeat Rows 9 and 10.

RNDS 19 AND 20: Repeat Rows 7 and 8.

RNDS 21 AND 22: Repeat Rows 5 and 6.

RNDS 23 AND 24: Repeat Rows 3 and 4.

Repeat Rnds 1–24 for Crenellated Pattern in the Round.

FLAT & IN THE ROUND

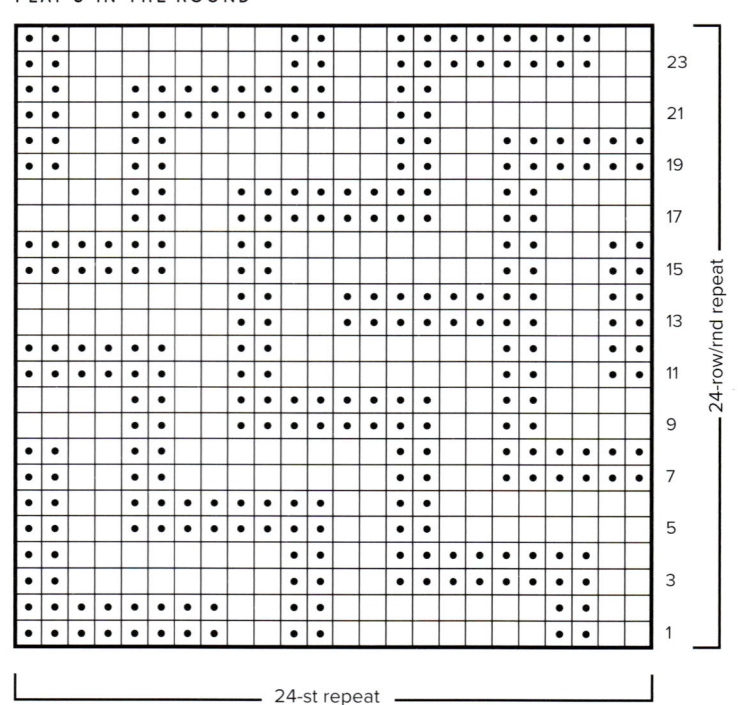

24-row/rnd repeat

24-st repeat

FRONT

BACK

Double Diamond Brocade

FLAT

(multiple of 12 sts; 12-row repeat)

ROW 1 (RS): *K5, *p2, k10; repeat from * to last 7 sts, p2, k5.

ROW 2 AND ALL WS ROWS: Knit the knit sts and purl the purl sts as they face you.

ROW 3: K3, *p2, k2, p2, k6; repeat from * to last 9 sts, p2, k2, p2, k3.

ROW 5: K1, *p2, k6, p2, k2; repeat from * to last 11 sts, p2, k6, p2, k1.

ROW 7: P1, *k10, p2; repeat from * to last 11 sts, k10, p1.

ROW 9: Repeat Row 5.

ROW 11: Repeat Row 3.

ROW 12: Repeat Row 2.

Repeat Rows 1–12 for Double Diamond Brocade Flat.

IN THE ROUND

(multiple of 12 sts; 12-rnd repeat)

RNDS 1 AND 2: *K5, *p2, k10; repeat from * to last 7 sts, p2, k5.

RNDS 3 AND 4: K3, *p2, k2, p2, k6; repeat from * to last 9 sts, p2, k2, p2, k3.

RNDS 5 AND 6: K1, *p2, k6, p2, k2; repeat from * to last 11 sts, p2, k6, p2, k1.

RNDS 7 AND 8: P1, *k10, p2; repeat from * to last 11 sts, k10, p1.

RNDS 9 AND 10: Repeat Rnds 5 and 6.

RNDS 11 AND 12: Repeat Rnds 3 and 4.

Repeat Rnds 1–12 for Double Diamond Brocade in the Round.

FLAT & IN THE ROUND

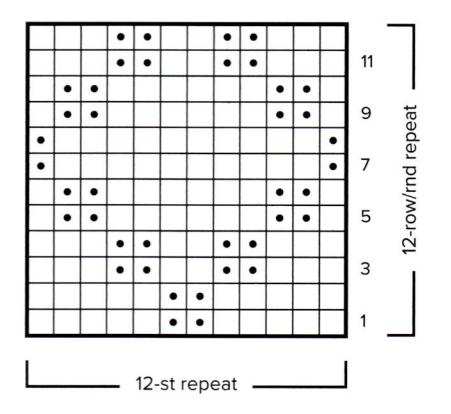

Seersucker Stitch

FLAT

(multiple of 4 sts + 1; 8-row repeat)

ROW 1 (RS): *K1, p1; repeat from * to last st, k1.

ROW 2 AND ALL WS ROWS: Knit the knit sts and purl the purl sts as they face you.

ROW 3: *P1, k3; repeat from * to last st, p1.

ROW 5: Repeat Row 1.

ROW 7: K2, *p1, k3; repeat from * to last 3 sts, p1, k2.

ROW 8: Repeat Row 2.

Repeat Rows 1–8 for Seersucker Stitch Flat.

FLAT

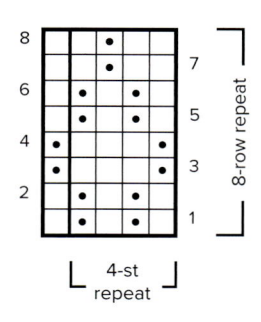

4-st repeat

IN THE ROUND

(multiple of 4 sts; 8-rnd repeat)

RNDS 1 AND 2: *K1, p1; repeat from * to end.

RNDS 3 AND 4: *P1, k3; repeat from * to end.

RNDS 5 AND 6: Repeat Rnd 1.

RNDS 7 AND 8: K2, *p1, k3; repeat from * to last 2 sts, p1, k1.

Repeat Rnds 1–8 for Seersucker Stitch in the Round.

IN THE ROUND

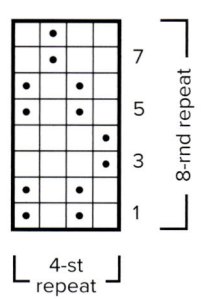

4-st repeat

Squares (TWO-SIDED)

FLAT

(multiple of 10 sts + 2; 12-row repeat)

ROW 1 (RS): Knit.

ROW 2: Purl.

ROW 3: *K2, p8; repeat from * to last 2 sts, k2.

ROW 4: Knit the knit sts and purl the purl sts as they face you.

ROW 5: *K2, p2, k4, p2; repeat from * to last 2 sts, k2.

ROWS 6–10: Repeat Row 4.

ROWS 11 AND 12: Repeat Rows 3 and 4.

Repeat Rows 1–12 for Squares Flat.

IN THE ROUND

(multiple of 10 sts; 12-rnd repeat)

RNDS 1 AND 2: Knit.

RNDS 3 AND 4: *K1, p8, k1; repeat from * to end.

RNDS 5–10: *K1, p2, k4, p2, k1; repeat from * to end.

RNDS 11 AND 12: Repeat Rnds 3 and 4.

Repeat Rnds 1–12 for Squares in the Round.

FLAT

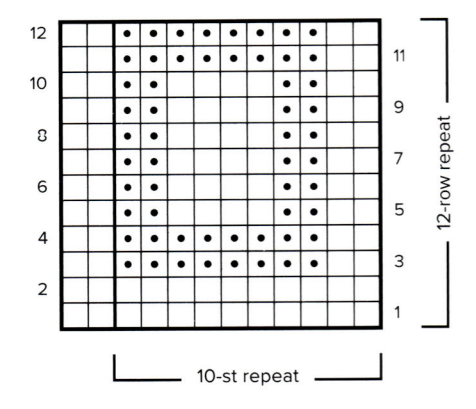

10-st repeat

IN THE ROUND

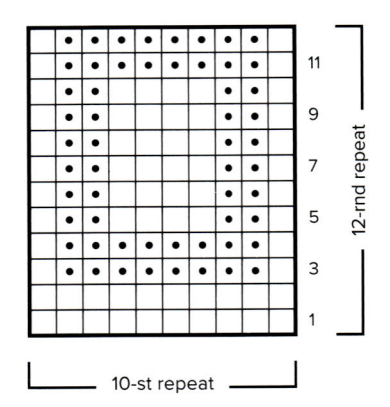

10-st repeat

Seersucker Pulli

This is a top-down pullover with a textured cowl neck and cuffs. The Seersucker Stitch pattern has an in-the-round stitch multiple of 4, so if another stitch catches your eye and you want to try your hand at swapping out stitch patterns, go ahead! Just take a look at the Stitch Multiple Index on page 282 to find a substitute with the same stitch multiple. If you prefer another with a different stitch multiple, feel free to adjust the cast-on number, do a stealth decrease or increase right before you separate the neck from the Sleeves, and knit on. Just remember to do the same maneuver once you get to the sleeve cuffs.

SIZES

X-Small (Small, Medium, Large, 1X-Large, 2X-Large, 3X-Large)

FINISHED MEASUREMENTS

30¼ (33, 37¼, 41, 45¼, 49¾, 51½)" [77 (84, 94.5, 104, 115, 126.5, 131) cm] chest

YARN

Blue Sky Alpacas Extra (55% baby alpaca, 45% fine merino; 218 yards / 150 grams): 5 (5, 6, 6, 6, 7, 7) hanks #3516 Still Water

NEEDLES

Sizes X-Small and Small only: one 24" (61 cm) long circular needle size US 8 (5 mm)

One 29" (74 cm) long circular needle size US 8 (5 mm)

One or two 24" (61 cm) long or longer circular needles or one set of five double-pointed needles (dpn) size US 8 (5 mm), as preferred for Sleeves

Change needle size if necessary to obtain correct gauge.

NOTIONS

Stitch markers in 2 colors; waste yarn

GAUGE

18 sts and 22 rows = 4" (10 cm) in Stockinette stitch (St st)

STITCH PATTERN

Seersucker Stitch

(multiple of 4 sts; 8-rnd repeat)

RNDS 1 AND 2: *K1, p1; repeat from * to end.

RNDS 3 AND 4: *P1, k3; repeat from * to end.

RNDS 5 AND 6: Repeat Rnd 1.

RNDS 7 AND 8: K2, *p1, k3; repeat from * to last 2 sts, p1, k1.

Repeat Rnds 1–8 for Seersucker Stitch.

SEERSUCKER STITCH

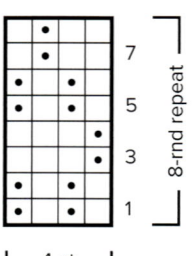

8-rnd repeat

4-st repeat

COLLAR

With long circular needle (use 24"/61 cm for X-Small and Small and 29"/74 cm for all other sizes), CO 116 (120, 124, 128, 132, 136, 140) sts. Join for working in the rnd, being careful not to twist sts; pm color A for beginning of rnd. Begin Seersucker Stitch; work even until 4 vertical repeats of pattern have been completed. Purl 1 rnd (Turning Rnd). Work 4 more vertical repeats.

YOKE

SET-UP RND: K24 for Right Sleeve, pm color B, k34 (36, 38, 40, 42, 44, 46) for Front, pm color B, k24 for Left Sleeve, pm color B, knit across Back to end.

SHAPE RAGLAN

NOTE: Change to longer circular needle if necessary for number of sts on needle.

INCREASE RND: Continuing in St st (knit every rnd), increase 8 sts this rnd, then every other rnd 16 (17, 18, 20, 21, 22, 24) times, as follows: K1, M1-r, [knit to 1 st before next color B marker, M1-l, k1, sm, k1, M1-r] 3 times, knit to last st, M1-l, k1—252 (264, 276, 296, 308, 320, 340) sts [58 (60, 62, 66, 68, 70, 74) sts each Sleeve; 68 (72, 76, 82, 86, 90, 96) sts each for Front and Back].

BODY

JOIN BACK AND FRONT: Transfer next 58 (60, 62, 66, 68, 70, 74) sts to waste yarn for Right Sleeve, removing markers, CO 0 (1, 4, 5, 8, 11, 10) st(s) for underarm, reposition color A marker for new beginning of rnd, CO 0 (1, 4, 5, 8, 11, 10) st(s) for underarm, knit to next marker, transfer next 58 (60, 62, 66, 68, 70, 74) sts to waste yarn for Left Sleeve, removing markers, CO 0 (2, 8, 10, 16, 22, 20) sts for underarm, knit to end—136 (148, 168, 184, 204, 224, 232) sts remain. Continuing in St st, work even until piece measures 9 (9, 9, 8¾, 9½, 9¾, 10)" [23 (23, 23, 22, 24, 25, 25.5) cm] from underarm.

NEXT RND: Change to Seersucker St; work even until 3 vertical repeats of pattern have been completed. BO all sts loosely knitwise.

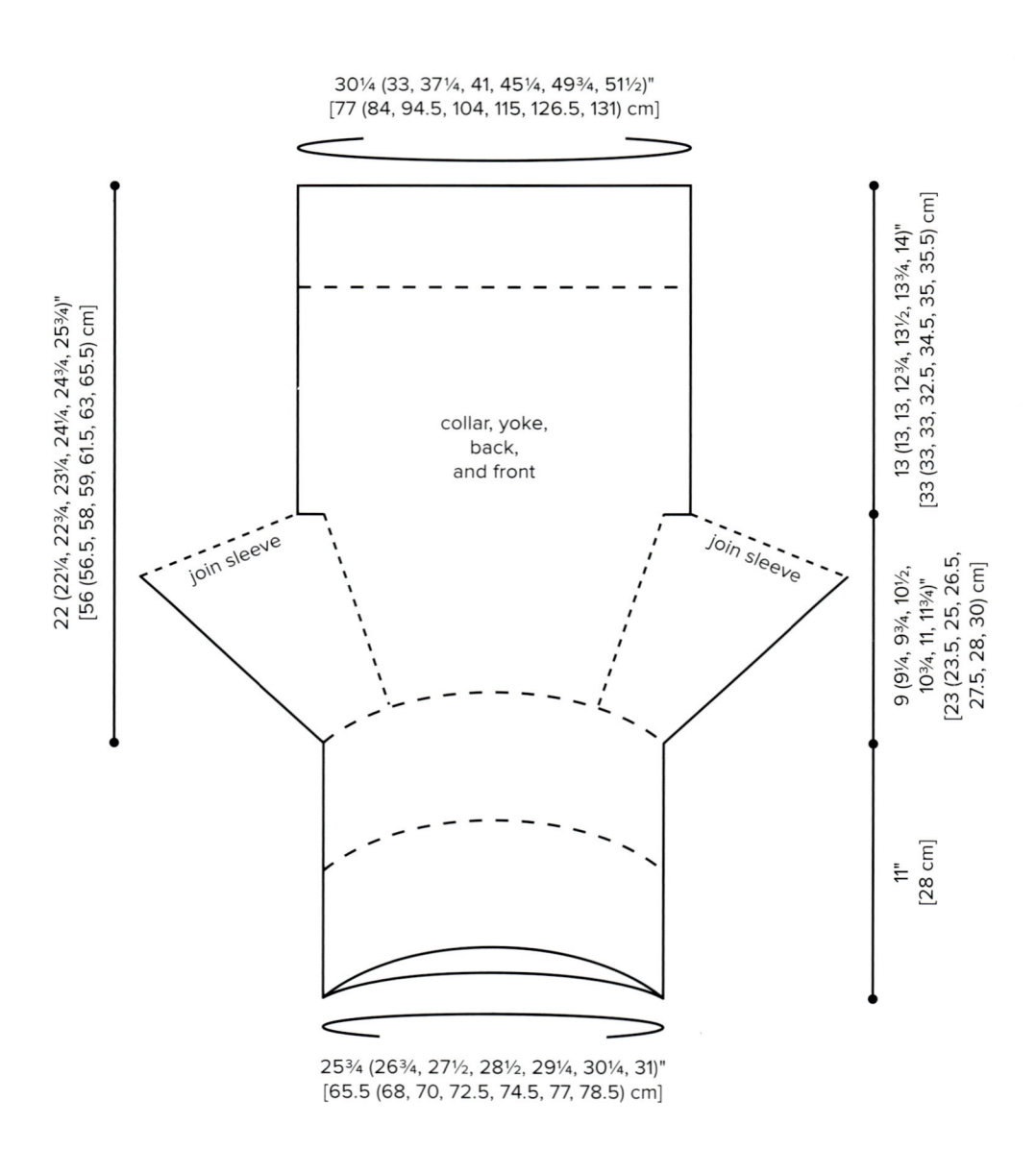

30¼ (33, 37¼, 41, 45¼, 49¾, 51½)"
[77 (84, 94.5, 104, 115, 126.5, 131) cm]

collar, yoke,
back,
and front

join sleeve

join sleeve

22 (22¼, 22¾, 23¼, 24¼, 24¾, 25¾)"
[56 (56.5, 58, 59, 61.5, 63, 65.5) cm]

13 (13, 13, 12¾, 13½, 13¾, 14)"
[33 (33, 33, 32.5, 34.5, 35, 35.5) cm]

9 (9¼, 9¾, 10½,
10¾, 11, 11¾)"
[23 (23.5, 25, 26.5,
27.5, 28, 30) cm]

11"
[28 cm]

25¾ (26¾, 27½, 28½, 29¼, 30¼, 31)"
[65.5 (68, 70, 72.5, 74.5, 77, 78.5) cm]

12½ (14¼, 15, 15, 15, 15, 15)"
[32 (36, 38, 38, 38, 38, 38) cm]

10¾ (11½, 13¼, 13¾, 13¾, 14¼, 14¼)"
[27.5 (29, 33.5, 35, 35, 36, 36) cm]

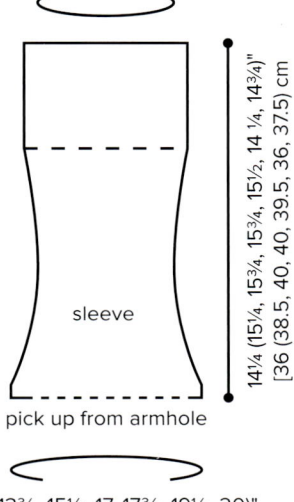

sleeve

14¼ (15¼, 15¾, 15¾, 15½, 14 ¼, 14¾)"
[36 (38.5, 40, 40, 39.5, 36, 37.5) cm]

pick up from armhole

13 (13¾, 15½, 17, 17¾, 19½, 20)"
[33 (35, 39.5, 43, 45, 49.5, 51) cm]

SLEEVES

NOTE: Use your preferred method of working in the rnd when working the Sleeves. Transfer Sleeve sts to needle(s). With RS facing, rejoin yarn at armhole; knit to end, pick up and knit 0 (1, 4, 5, 6, 9, 8) st(s) to center underarm, pm for beginning of rnd, pick up and knit 0 (1, 4, 5, 6, 9, 8) st(s), knit to end—58 (62, 70, 76, 80, 88, 90) sts.
NOTE: You will not pick up from every CO st for the 3 largest sizes. Join for working in the rnd. Knit 4 rnds.

Shape Sleeve

DECREASE RND: Decrease 2 sts this rnd, then every 5 (5, 6, 5, 4, 2, 2) rnds 4 (4, 4, 6, 8, 11, 12) times, as follows: K1, k2tog, knit to last 3 sts, ssk, k1—48 (52, 60, 62, 62, 64, 64) sts remain. Work even for 14 (10, 10, 10, 10, 10, 10) rnds.
INCREASE RND: Increase 2 sts this rnd, then every 5 (5, 8, 9, 7, 18, 18) rnds 3 (5, 3, 2, 2, 1, 1) time(s), as follows: K1, M1-r, knit to last st, M1-l, k1—56 (64, 68, 68, 68, 68, 68) sts. Work even for 1 rnd.
NEXT RND: Change to Seersucker Stitch; work even until 3 vertical repeats of pattern have been completed. BO all sts loosely knitwise.

FINISHING

Fold neck in half to WS at turning rnd and tack down to top of Yoke, being careful not to let sts show on RS. Block as desired.

CHAPTER 2

RIBS

RIBS ARE TYPICALLY alternating columns of knit and purl stitches that create a stretchy, often reversible, texture. The most common types of ribs are those that utilize the same number of knit and purl columns (so you cast on an even number of stitches and then k1, p1 or k2, p2). You can see an example of this method in the 1x1 Rib or 2x2 Rib patterns shown on page 60. But the world of ribs is much richer and more varied than that! In this chapter, I tried to include rib stitch patterns that also showcase fancier treatments like yarnovers, twists, and even horizontal welts. Before choosing a rib for a cuff or even an all-over fabric, give it a test run with a variety of needle sizes to decide which fabric you like best. Some ribs stretch more than others and some, like the Wavy Rib on page 65, are best suited for larger canvases like a scarf or stole. xx

STITCHES

1X1 RIB
2X2 RIB
4-STITCH RIBS
SLIP STITCH RIB
GARTER RIB
DOUBLE GARTER RIB
RIBBED COLUMNS
WAVY RIB
HORIZONTAL WELTS
FARROW RIB
BOBBLE RIB
PIQUÉ RIB

DIAGONAL BROKEN RIB
FUJI RIB
SHADOW RIB
BLANKET RIB
BAMBOO RIB
EMBOSSED MOSS
 STITCH RIB
PUFFY RIB
DOUBLE EYELET RIB

PROJECT

FUJI RIB WRAP

1x1 Rib (FULLY REVERSIBLE)

FLAT

(odd number of sts; 2-row repeat)

ROW 1 (RS): *K1, p1; repeat from * to last st, k1.

ROW 2: P1, *k1, p1; repeat from * to end.

Repeat Rows 1 and 2 for 1x1 Rib Flat.

IN THE ROUND

(even number of sts; 1-rnd repeat)

ALL RNDS: *K1, p1; repeat from * to end.

2x2 Rib (FULLY REVERSIBLE)

FLAT

(multiple of 4 sts + 2; 2 row-repeat)

ROW 1 (RS): *K2, p2; repeat from * to last 2 sts, k2.

ROW 2: P2, *k2, p2; repeat from * to end.

Repeat Rows 1 and 2 for 2x2 Rib Flat.

IN THE ROUND

(multiple of 4 sts; 1-rnd repeat)

ALL RNDS: *K2, p2; repeat from * to end.

4-Stitch Ribs (FULLY REVERSIBLE)

FLAT

(multiple of 8 sts; 1-row repeat)

ROW 1 (RS): *K4, p4; repeat from * to end.

ROW 2: *P4, k4; repeat from * to end.

Repeat Rows 1 and 2 for 4-Stitch Ribs Flat.

IN THE ROUND

(multiple of 8 sts; 2-rnd repeat)

RND 1: *K4, p4; repeat from * to end.

RND 2: *P4, k4; repeat from * to end.

Repeat Rnds 1 and 2 for 4-Stitch Ribs in the round.

Slip Stitch Rib

FLAT

(multiple of 5 sts + 2; 2-row repeat)

NOTE: Pattern begins with a WS row.

ROW 1 (WS): K2, *p3, k2; repeat from * to end.

ROW 2: *P2, k1, slip 1 wyib, k1; repeat from * to last 2 sts, p2.

Repeat Rows 1 and 2 for Slip Stitch Rib Flat.

IN THE ROUND

(multiple of 5 sts; 2-rnd repeat)

RND 1: *K3, p2; repeat from * to end.

RND 2: *K1, slip 1 wyib, k1, p2; repeat from * to end.

Repeat Rnds 1 and 2 for Slip Stitch Rib in the Round.

Garter Rib (TWO-SIDED)

FLAT

(odd number of sts; 2-row repeat)

ROW 1 (RS): *P1, k1; repeat from * to last st, p1.

ROW 2: Knit.

Repeat Rows 1 and 2 for Garter Rib Flat.

IN THE ROUND

(even number of sts; 2-rnd repeat)

RND 1: *P1, k1; repeat from * to end.

RND 2: Purl.

Repeat Rnds 1 and 2 for Garter Rib in the Round.

Double Garter Rib (TWO-SIDED)

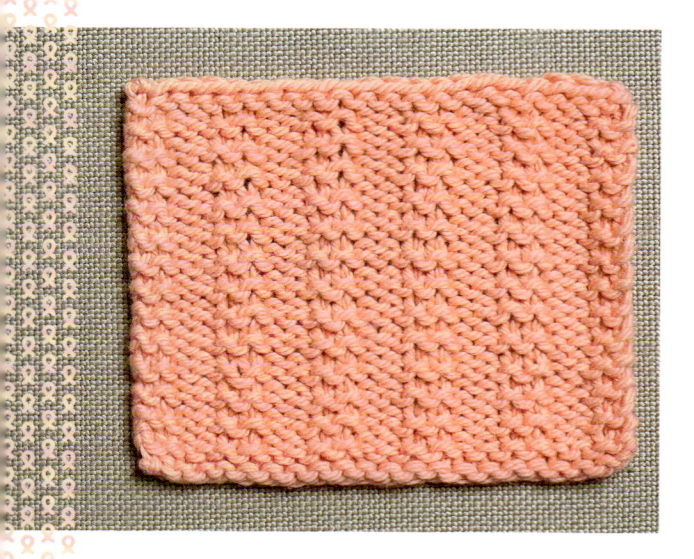

FLAT

(multiple of 4 sts + 2; 2-row repeat)

ROW 1 (RS): *P2, k2; repeat from * to last 2 sts, p2.

ROW 2: Knit.

Repeat Rows 1 and 2 for Double Garter Rib Flat.

IN THE ROUND

(multiple of 4 sts; 2-rnd repeat)

RND 1: *P2, k2; repeat from * to end.

RND 2: Purl.

Repeat Rnds 1 and 2 for Double Garter Rib in the Round.

Ribbed Columns (FULLY REVERSIBLE)

FLAT

(multiple of 6 sts; 8-row repeat)

ROW 1 (RS): *P2, k2, p2; repeat from * to end.

ROWS 2-4: Knit the knit sts and purl the purl sts as they face you.

ROW 5: *P1, k4, p1; repeat from * to end.

ROWS 6-8: Repeat Row 2.

Repeat Rows 1–8 for Ribbed Columns Flat.

IN THE ROUND

(multiple of 6 sts; 8-rnd repeat)

RNDS 1-4: *P2, k2, p2; repeat from * to end.

RNDS 5-8: *P1, k4, p1; repeat from * to end.

Repeat Rnds 1–8 for Ribbed Columns in the Round.

FLAT & IN THE ROUND

8-row/rnd repeat

6-st repeat

Wavy Rib (TWO-SIDED)

FLAT

(multiple of 16 sts + 2; 16-row repeat)

ROW 1 (RS): *K10, p2, k2, p2; repeat from * to last 2 sts, k2.

ROW 2: P2, *[k2, p2] twice, k6, p2; repeat from * to end.

ROWS 3-8: Repeat Rows 1 and 2.

ROW 9: *[K2, p2] twice, k8; repeat from * to last 2 sts, k2.

ROW 10: P2, *k6, [p2, k2] twice, p2; repeat from * to end.

ROWS 11-16: Repeat Rows 9 and 10.

Repeat Rows 1–16 for Wavy Rib Flat.

FLAT

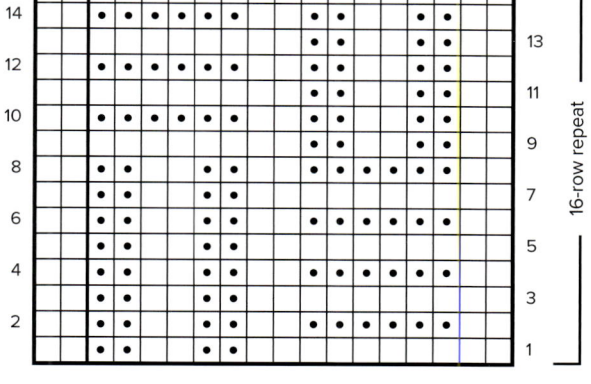

IN THE ROUND

(multiple of 16 sts; 16-rnd repeat)

RND 1: *K10, p2, k2, p2; repeat from * to end.

RND 2: *K2, p6, [k2, p2] twice; repeat from * to end.

RNDS 3-8: Repeat Rnds 1 and 2.

RND 9: *[K2, p2] twice, k8; repeat from * to end.

RND 10: *[K2, p2] twice, k2, p6; repeat from * to end.

RNDS 11-16: Repeat Rnds 9 and 10.

Repeat Rnds 1–16 for Wavy Rib in the Round.

IN THE ROUND

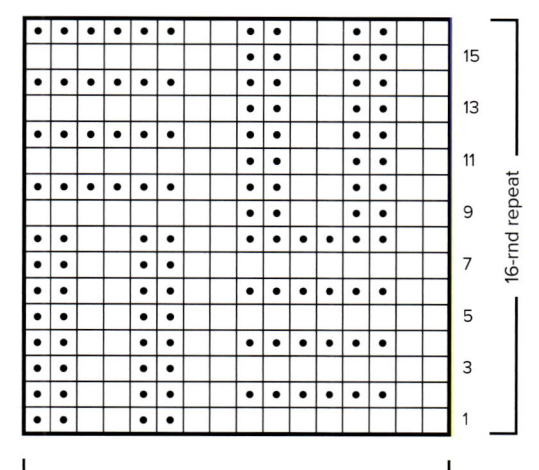

Horizontal Welts (FULLY REVERSIBLE)

FLAT

(any number of sts; 6-row repeat)

ROW 1 (RS): Knit.

ROW 2: Purl.

ROW 3: Knit.

ROWS 4–6: Repeat Rows 1–3.

Repeat Rows 1–6 for Horizontal Welts Flat.

IN THE ROUND

(any number of stitches; 6-rnd repeat)

RNDS 1–3: Knit.

RNDS 4–6: Purl.

Repeat Rnds 1–6 for Horizontal Welts in the Round.

Farrow Rib (FULLY REVERSIBLE)

FLAT

(multiple of 3 sts; 1-row repeat)

ALL ROWS: *K2, p1; repeat from * to end.

IN THE ROUND

(multiple of 3 sts; 2-rnd repeat)

RND 1: *K2, p1; repeat from * to end.

RND 2: *K1, p2; repeat from * to end.

Repeat Rnds 1 and 2 for Farrow Rib in the Round.

Bobble Rib

FLAT

(multiple of 8 sts + 3; 4-row repeat)

MB: Make Bobble (see below).

ROW 1 (RS): *K3, p2, MB, p2; repeat from * to last 3 sts, k3.

ROW 2: P3, *k2, p1, k2, p3; repeat from * to end.

ROWS 3 AND 4: Knit the knit sts and purl the purl sts as they face you.

Repeat Rows 1–4 for Bobble Rib Flat.

IN THE ROUND

(multiple of 8 sts; 4-rnd repeat)

MB: Make Bobble (see below).

RND 1: *K3, p2, MB, p2; repeat from * to end.

RNDS 2–4: *K3, p2, k1, p2; repeat from * to end.

Repeat Rnds 1–4 for Bobble Rib in the Round.

FLAT

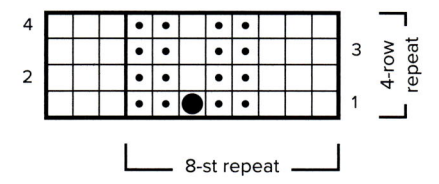

8-st repeat · 4-row repeat

IN THE ROUND

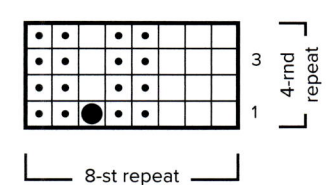

8-st repeat · 4-rnd repeat

● **Make Bobble:** (P1, k1, p1, k1) into same st to increase to 4 sts, pass second, third, then fourth sts one at a time over first st and off needle.

Piqué Rib (TWO-SIDED)

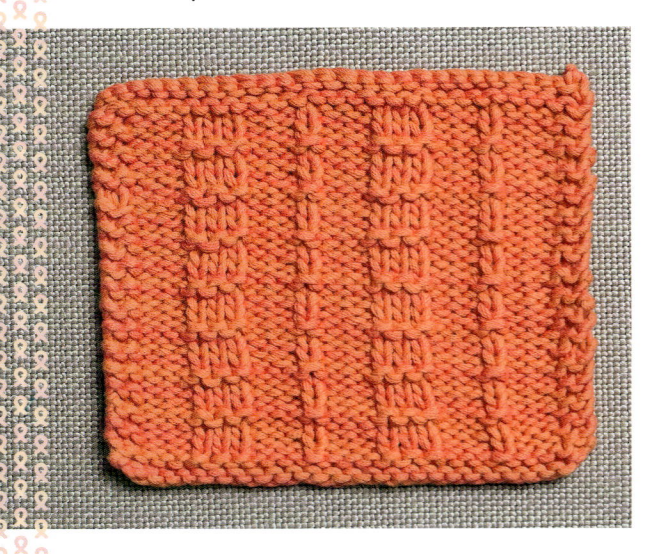

FLAT

(multiple of 10 sts + 3; 4-row repeat)

ROW 1 (RS): *P3, k1, p3, k3; repeat from * to last 3 sts, p3.

ROWS 2 AND 3: Knit the knit sts and purl the purl sts as they face you.

ROW 4: Knit.

Repeat Rows 1–4 for Piqué Rib Flat.

IN THE ROUND

(multiple of 10 sts; 4-rnd repeat)

RNDS 1-3: *P3, k1, p3, k3; repeat from * to end.

RND 4: Purl.

Repeat Rnds 1–4 for Piqué Rib in the Round.

FLAT

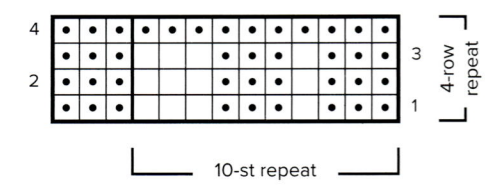

IN THE ROUND

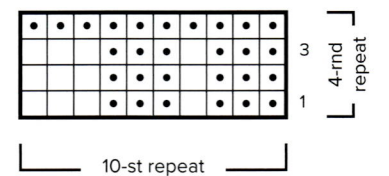

Diagonal Broken Rib (TWO-SIDED)

FLAT

(multiple of 6 sts; 12-row repeat)

ROW 1 (RS): *K4, p2; repeat from * to end.

ROWS 2-4: Knit the knit sts and purl the purl sts as they face you.

ROW 5: K2, *p2, k4; repeat from * to last 4 sts, p2, k2.

ROWS 6-8: Repeat Row 2.

ROW 9: *P2, k4; repeat from * to end.

ROWS 10-12: Repeat Row 2.

Repeat Rows 1–12 for Diagonal Broken Rib Flat.

IN THE ROUND

(multiple of 6 sts; 12-rnd repeat)

RNDS 1-4: *K4, p2; repeat from * to end.

RNDS 5-8: K2, *p2, k4; repeat from * to last 4 sts, p2, k2.

RNDS 9-12: *P2, k4; repeat from * to end.

Repeat Rnds 1–12 for Diagonal Broken Rib in the Round.

FLAT & IN THE ROUND

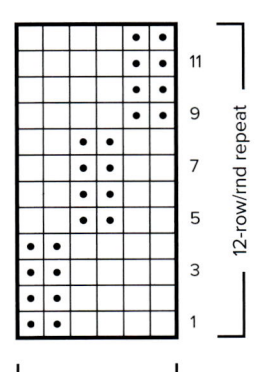

6-st repeat

12-row/rnd repeat

Fuji Rib

FLAT

(multiple of 14 sts + 1; 18-row repeat)

Pkok: See below.

ROW 1: *K1-tbl, p1; repeat from * to last st, k1-tbl.

ROW 2: P1-tbl, *k1, p1-tbl; repeat from * to end.

ROWS 3 AND 4: Repeat Rows 1 and 2.

ROW 5: *[K1-tbl, p1] 3 times, pkok, [p1, k1-tbl] twice, p1; repeat from * to last st, k1-tbl.

ROW 6: P1-tbl, *[k1, p1-tbl] twice, k1, p3, [k1, p1-tbl] 3 times; repeat from * to end.

ROW 7: *[K1-tbl, p1] twice, pkok, k1, pkok, p1, k1-tbl, p1; repeat from * to last st, k1-tbl.

ROW 8: P1-tbl, *k1, p1-tbl, k1, p7, [k1, p1-tbl] twice; repeat from * to end.

ROW 9: *[K1-tbl, p1] twice, k2, pkok, k2, p1, k1-tbl, p1; repeat from * to last st, k1-tbl.

ROW 10: Repeat Row 8.

ROW 11: Repeat Row 7.

ROW 12: Repeat Row 6.

ROW 13: Repeat Row 5.

ROW 14: Repeat Row 2.

ROWS 15-18: Repeat Rows 1 and 2.

Repeat Rows 1–18 for Fuji Rib Flat.

IN THE ROUND

(multiple of 14 sts; 18-rnd repeat)

Pkok: See below.

RNDS 1-4: *K1-tbl, p1; repeat from * to end.

RND 5: *[K1-tbl, p1] 3 times, pkok, [p1, k1-tbl] twice, p1; repeat from * to end.

RND 6: K1-tbl, *[p1, k1-tbl] twice, p1, k3, [p1, k1-tbl] 3 times; repeat from * to end.

RND 7: *[K1-tbl, p1] twice, pkok, k1, pkok, p1, k1-tbl, p1; repeat from * to end.

RND 8: K1-tbl, *p1, k1-tbl, p1, k7, [p1, k1-tbl] twice; repeat from * to end.

RND 9: *[K1-tbl, p1] twice, k2, pkok, k2, p1, k1-tbl, p1; repeat from * to end.

RND 10: Repeat Rnd 8.

RND 11: Repeat Rnd 7.

RND 12: Repeat Rnd 6.

RND 13: Repeat Rnd 5.

RNDS 14-18: Repeat Rnd 1.

Repeat Rnds 1–18 for Fuji Rib in the Round.

FLAT

18-row repeat · 14-st repeat

IN THE ROUND

18-rnd repeat · 14-st repeat

Pkok: Slip third st on left-hand needle over first 2 sts and off needle; k1, yo, k1.

Shadow Rib

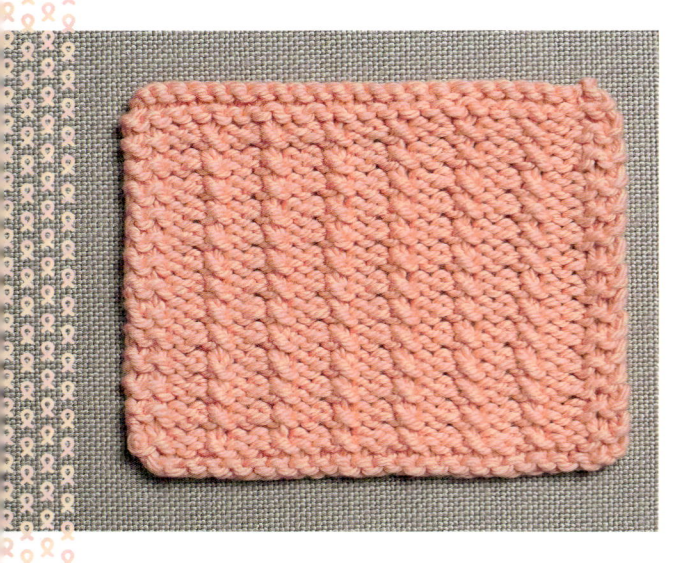

FLAT

(multiple of 3 sts + 2; 2-row repeat)
ROW 1 (RS): *P2, k1-tbl; repeat from * to last 2 sts, p2.
ROW 2: Knit.
Repeat Rows 1 and 2 for Shadow Rib Flat.

IN THE ROUND

(multiple of 3 sts; 2-rnd repeat)
RND 1: P1, *k1-tbl, p2; repeat from * to last 2 sts, k1-tbl, p1.
RND 2: Purl.
Repeat Rnds 1 and 2 for Shadow Rib in the Round.

Blanket Rib

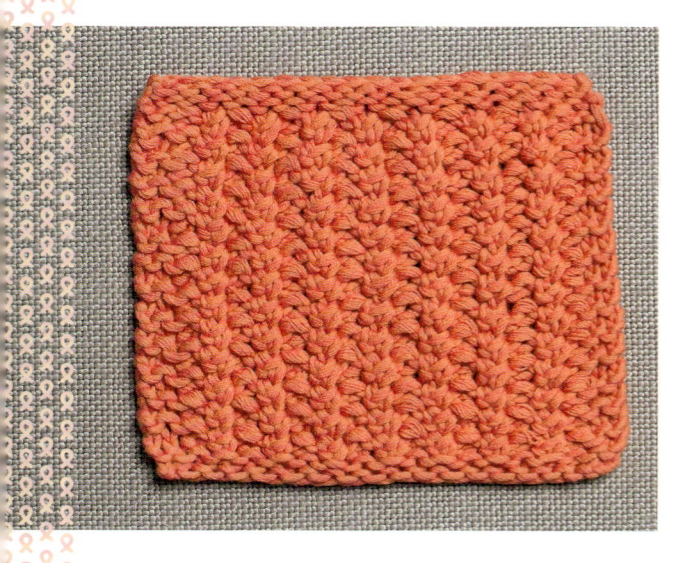

FLAT

(odd number of sts; 2-row repeat)
NOTE: You will double your st count on Row 1; original st count is restored on Row 2.
ROW 1 (RS): *K1-f/b; repeat from * to end.
ROW 2: K2tog, *p2tog, k2tog; repeat from * to end.
Repeat Rows 1 and 2 for Blanket Rib Flat.

IN THE ROUND

(even number of sts; 2-rnd repeat)
NOTE: You will double your st count on Rnd 1; original st count is restored on Rnd 2.
RND 1: *K1-f/b; repeat from * to end.
RND 2: *K2tog, p2tog; repeat from * to end.
Repeat Rnds 1 and 2 for Blanket Rib in the Round.

Bamboo Rib

FLAT

(multiple of 12 sts + 2; 12-row repeat)

ROW 1 (RS): *P2, k4; repeat from * to last 2 sts, p2.

ROWS 2-4: Knit the knit sts and purl the purl sts as they face you.

ROW 5: *P8, k4; repeat from * to last 2 sts, p2.

ROW 6: Repeat Row 2.

ROWS 7-10: Repeat Rows 1–4.

ROW 11: *P2, k4, p6; repeat from * to last 2 sts, p2.

ROW 12: Repeat Row 2.

Repeat Rows 1–12 for Bamboo Rib Flat.

FLAT

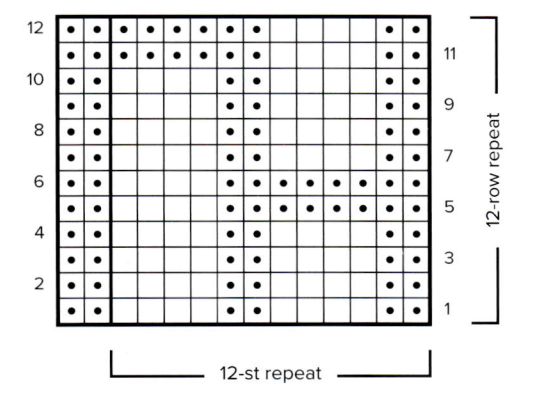

IN THE ROUND

(multiple of 12 sts; 12-rnd repeat)

RNDS 1-4: *P2, k4; repeat from * to end.

RNDS 5 AND 6: *P8, k4; repeat from * to end.

RNDS 7-10: Repeat Rnds 1–4.

RNDS 11 AND 12: P2, *k4, p8; repeat from * to last 10 sts, k4, p6.

Repeat Rnds 1–12 for Bamboo Rib in the Round.

IN THE ROUND

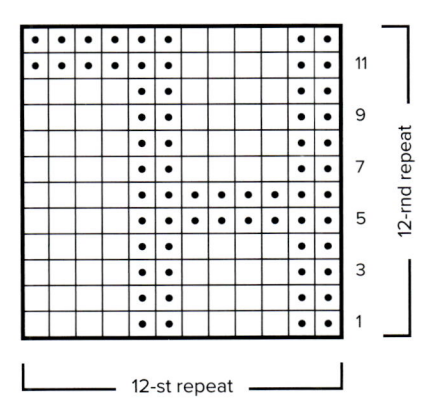

Embossed Moss Stitch Rib (TWO-SIDED)

FLAT

(multiple of 7 sts + 3; 4-row repeat)

ROW 1 (RS): *P3, k1, p1, k2; repeat from * to last 3 sts, p3.

ROW 2: K3, *p2, k1, p1, k3; repeat from * to end.

ROW 3: *P3, k2, p1, k1; repeat from * to last 3 sts, p3.

ROW 4: K3, *p1, k1, p2, k3; repeat from * to end.

Repeat Rows 1–4 for Embossed Moss Stitch Rib Flat.

IN THE ROUND

(multiple of 7 sts; 4-rnd repeat)

RNDS 1 AND 2: *P3, k1, p1, k2; repeat from * to end.

RNDS 3 AND 4: *P3, k2, p1, k1; repeat from * to end.

Repeat Rnds 1–4 for Embossed Moss Stitch Rib in the Round.

FLAT

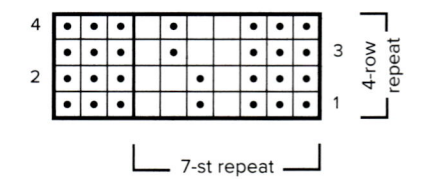

IN THE ROUND

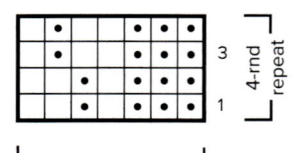

Puffy Rib

FLAT

(multiple of 3 sts + 2; 4-row repeat)

NOTE: You will increase 2 sts per repeat on Row 1; original st count is restored on Row 4.

ROW 1 (RS): *P2, yo, k1, yo; repeat from * to last 2 sts, p2.

ROW 2: K2, *p3, k2; repeat from * to end.

ROW 3: *P2, k3; repeat from * to last 2 sts, p2.

ROW 4: K2, *p3tog, k2; repeat from * to end.

Repeat Rows 1–4 for Puffy Rib Flat.

FLAT

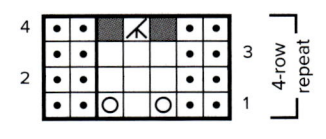

IN THE ROUND

(multiple of 3 sts; 4-rnd repeat)

NOTE: You will increase 2 sts per repeat on Rnd 1; original st count is restored on Rnd 4.

RND 1: *Yo, k1, yo, p2; repeat from * to end.

RNDS 2 AND 3: *K3, p2; repeat from * to end.

RND 4: *K3tog, p2; repeat from * to end.

Repeat Rnds 1–4 for Puffy Rib in the Round.

IN THE ROUND

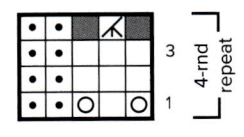

Double Eyelet Rib

BOTTOM-UP FLAT

(multiple of 7 sts + 2; 4-row repeat)
ROW 1 (RS): *P2, k2tog, yo, k1, yo, ssk; repeat from * to last 2 sts, p2.
ROW 2: K2, *p5, k2; repeat from * to end.
ROWS 3 AND 4: Knit the knit sts and purl the purl sts as they face you.
Repeat Rows 1–4 for Double Eyelet Rib Bottom-Up Flat.

BOTTOM-UP FLAT

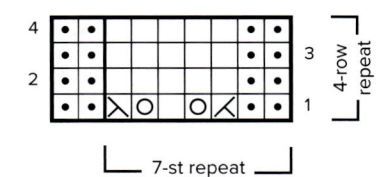

TOP-DOWN FLAT

(multiple of 7 sts + 2; 4-row repeat)
ROW 1 (RS): *P2, k5; repeat from * to last 2 sts, p2.
ROW 2: K2, *p5, k2; repeat from * to end.
ROW 3: *P2, ssk, yo, k1, yo, k2tog; repeat from * to last 2 sts, p2.
ROW 4: Repeat Row 2.
Repeat Rows 1–4 for Double Eyelet Rib Top-Down Flat.

TOP-DOWN FLAT

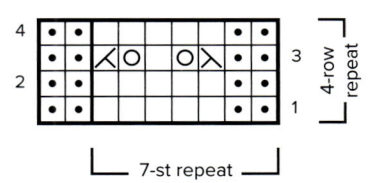

BOTTOM-UP IN THE ROUND

(multiple of 7 sts; 4-rnd repeat)
RND 1: *P2, k2tog, yo, k1, yo, ssk; repeat from * to end.
RNDS 2–4: *P2, k5; repeat from * to end.
Repeat Rnds 1–4 for Double Eyelet Rib Bottom-Up in the Round.

BOTTOM-UP IN THE ROUND

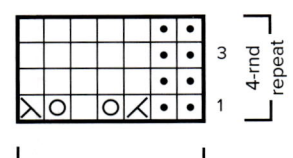

TOP-DOWN IN THE ROUND

(multiple of 7 sts; 4-rnd repeat)
RNDS 1–3: *P2, k5; repeat from * to end.
RND 4: *P2, ssk, yo, k1, yo, k2tog; repeat from * to end.
Repeat Rnds 1–4 for Double Eyelet Rib Top-Down in the Round.

TOP-DOWN IN THE ROUND

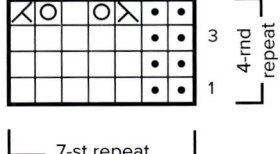

Fuji Rib Wrap

What makes this simple, long rectangle special and cozy are the button closures that allow you to wrap the fabric around yourself however you'd like. If you want, you can also re-create this as a long stole or scarf by omitting the buttons and loops, or play with the number of stitch repeats to make a skinnier scarf. Another idea would be to substitute a stitch pattern using the Stitch Multiple Index on page 282—just make sure to select one that looks good on both sides.

FINISHED MEASUREMENTS

Approximately 9½" (24 cm) wide x 82" (208.5 cm) long, before blocking

Approximately 10" (25.5 cm) wide x 86" (218.5 cm) long, after blocking

YARN

Blue Sky Alpacas Extra (55% baby alpaca, 45% fine merino; 218 yards / 150 grams): 3 hanks #3510 Butter Cream

NEEDLE

One pair straight needles size US 8 (5 mm)

Change needle size if necessary to obtain correct gauge.

NOTIONS

Three ½" (12 mm) buttons; button craft thread or fingering weight yarn in matching color, for button loops; yarn needle

GAUGE

24 sts and 22 rows = 4" (10 cm) in Fuji Pattern, before blocking

23 sts and 21 rows = 4" (10 cm) in Fuji Pattern, after blocking

Pkok: Slip third st on left-hand needle over first 2 sts and off needle; k1, yo, k1.

STITCH PATTERN
Fuji Rib

(multiple of 14 sts + 1; 18-row repeat)

Pkok: See below.

ROW 1: *K1-tbl, p1; repeat from * to last st, k1-tbl.

ROW 2: P1-tbl, *k1, p1-tbl; repeat from * to end.

ROWS 3 AND 4: Repeat Rows 1 and 2.

ROW 5: *[K1-tbl, p1] 3 times, pkok, [p1, k1-tbl] twice, p1; repeat from * to last st, k1-tbl.

ROW 6: P1-tbl, *[k1, p1-tbl] twice, k1, p3, [k1, p1-tbl] 3 times; repeat from * to end.

ROW 7: *[K1-tbl, p1] twice, pkok, k1, pkok, p1, k1-tbl, p1; repeat from * to last st, k1-tbl.

ROW 8: P1-tbl, *k1, p1-tbl, k1, p7, [k1, p1-tbl] twice; repeat from * to end.

ROW 9: *[K1-tbl, p1] twice, k2, pkok, k2, p1, k1-tbl, p1; repeat from * to last st, k1-tbl.

ROW 10: Repeat Row 8.

ROW 11: Repeat Row 7.

ROW 12: Repeat Row 6.

ROW 13: Repeat Row 5.

ROW 14: Repeat Row 2.

ROWS 15-18: Repeat Rows 1 and 2.

Repeat Rows 1–18 for Fuji Rib.

FUJI RIB

14-st repeat

18-row repeat

WRAP

CO 57 sts. Begin Fuji Rib; work even until 25 vertical repeats of pattern have been worked. Wrap should measure approximately 82" (208.5 cm) from beginning. BO all sts in pattern.

FINISHING

Block to measurements.

Overcast Button Loops

Work button loops 2", 5½" and 9" (5 cm, 14 cm, and 23 cm) down from BO edge, along left-hand long edge, as follows: Using yarn needle and button craft thread or fingering weight yarn, bring yarn from back to front through edge st, then take yarn back to WS approximately ¼" (6 mm) away from first st, and draw it through until loop is long enough for button to fit through fit snugly. Bring yarn from back to front through first hoie again and pull until loops are the same length. *Holding yarn to left of needle, insert needle under loops, then over yarn and pull snug, pushing each st tightly against previous st. Repeat from * until you reach opposite edge. Fasten off.

Sew buttons in the same positions at opposite end, along same long edge.

CHAPTER 3

TWISTED, SLIPPED & FANCY

THIS CHAPTER IS SORT OF a "catch-all-that-doesn't-apply" chapter. In other words, the stitch patterns here are those that don't fit neatly into, let's say, a cable chapter, a rib chapter, or a lace chapter. Here, you'll find slipped stitches, looped stitches where you wrap yarn around your thumb to elongate your stitches (see page 88), and even stitches that are knit in the row below. Although some of these stitch patterns are a little unconventional and call for off-the-radar moves that will bring your knitting to a new level, they are all fun to work and carefully curated so that they won't be a drag on your knitting joy (I promise). xx

STITCHES

TUCK STITCH
STAR STITCH
INDIAN CROSS STITCH
CHECKERBOARD BOWS
LOOP STITCH
BLANKET MOSS STITCH
SLIP STITCH HONEYCOMB
SURFACE TWISTS
HONEYCOMB SMOCKING
PUFFY DIAMONDS
SWEDISH CHECK
LOAF PATTERN
TRIPLE-SLIP
  HERRINGBONE
CLUSTER STITCH
POPCORN STITCH

INDIAN PILLAR STITCH
SLIP STITCH MESH
ALTERNATING SLIP
  STITCH
CHECKED BASKET STITCH
TRELLIS STITCH
SWAG STITCH
BOWKNOTS
RAINDROPS
JEWELED BOXES
ZIGZAG CHEVRON
WELTING FANTASTIC

PROJECT

INDIAN PILLAR MITTS

Tuck Stitch

FLAT

(multiple of 4 sts + 3; 8-row repeat)

Tuck st: See below.

ROW 1 (RS): Purl.

ROW 2 AND ALL WS ROWS: Knit.

ROW 3: *P3, tuck st; repeat from * to last 3 sts, p3.

ROW 5: Purl.

ROW 7: P1, *tuck st, p3; repeat from * to last 2 sts, tuck st, p1.

ROW 8: Knit.

Repeat Rows 1–8 for Tuck Stitch Flat.

IN THE ROUND

(multiple of 4 sts; 8-rnd repeat)

Tuck st: See below.

RNDS 1 AND 2: Purl.

RND 3: *P3, tuck st; repeat from * to end.

RNDS 4–6: Purl.

RND 7: P1, *tuck st, p3; repeat from * to last 3 sts, tuck st, p2.

RND 8: Purl.

Repeat Rnds 1–8 for Tuck Stitch in the Round.

FLAT

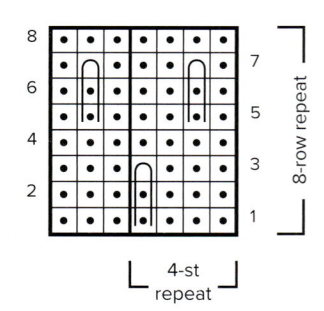

8-row repeat

4-st repeat

IN THE ROUND

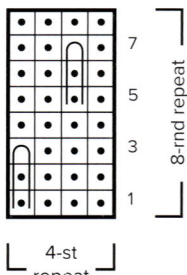

8-rnd repeat

4-st repeat

 Tuck st: On first row/rnd, purl; on second row/rnd, work st as it appears; on third row/rnd, tuck st.

Star Stitch

FLAT

(multiple of 4 sts + 1; 4-row repeat)

Make star: See below.

ROW 1 (RS): Knit.

ROW 2: P1, *make star, p1; repeat from * to end.

ROW 3: Knit.

ROW 4: P3, *make star, p1; repeat from * to last 2 sts, p2.

Repeat Rows 1–4 for Star Stitch Flat.

FLAT

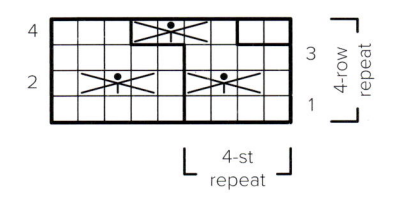

IN THE ROUND

(multiple of 4 sts; 4-rnd repeat)

Make star: See right.

SET-UP RND: Knit.

RND 1: *Make star, k1; repeat from * to end.

RND 2: Knit to end, remove beginning-of-rnd marker, k1, replace marker.

RND 3: *K1, make star; repeat from * to end.

RND 4: Knit to end, reposition beginning-of-rnd marker to before last st; slip last st back to left-hand needle to be worked in make star at beginning of Rnd 1.

Repeat Rnds 1–4 for Star Stitch in the Round.

IN THE ROUND

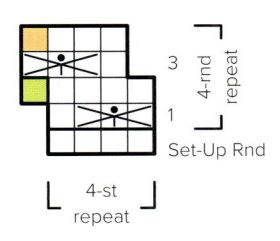

 Make star: When working flat, p3tog, leaving sts on needle, yo, then p3tog into same 3 sts again, slipping sts from left-hand needle. When working in the rnd, work k3tog instead of p3tog.

On Rnd 2, knit to end, remove beginning-of-rnd marker, k1, replace marker.

At end of Rnd 4 only, knit to end, reposition beginning-of-rnd marker to before last st; slip last st back to left-hand needle, to be worked in make star at beginning of Rnd 1.

Indian Cross Stitch (TWO-SIDED)

FRONT   BACK

FLAT

(multiple of 8 sts; 12-row repeat)

NOTE: Do not count sts on Rows 5 and 11; original st count is restored on Rows 6 and 12.

ROWS 1–4: Knit.

ROW 5: K1, *k1, wrapping yarn 4 times; repeat from * to last st, k1.

ROW 6: *Slip 8 sts wyib, dropping all extra wraps, insert left-hand needle into first 4 slipped sts and pass them over second 4 slipped sts, return second 4 sts to left-hand needle and knit all 8 sts in their new positions; repeat from * to end.

ROWS 7–10: Knit.

ROW 11: Repeat Row 5.

ROW 12: Slip 4 sts, dropping all extra wraps, insert left-hand needle into first 2 slipped sts and pass them over second 2 slipped sts, return second 2 sts to left-hand needle and knit all 4 sts in their new positions, *slip 8 sts, dropping extra wraps, then cross and knit these 8 sts as in Row 6; repeat from * to last 4 sts, slip 4 sts, dropping extra wraps, then cross and knit these 4 sts as at beginning of row.

Repeat Rows 1–12 for Indian Cross Stitch Flat.

IN THE ROUND

(multiple of 8 sts; 12-rnd repeat)

NOTE: Do not count sts on Rnds 5 and 11; original st count is restored on Rnds 6 and 12.

RND 1: Knit.

RND 2: Purl.

RNDS 3 AND 4: Repeat Rnds 1 and 2.

RND 5: *K1, wrapping yarn 4 times; repeat from * to end.

RND 6: *Slip 8 sts wyif, dropping all extra wraps, insert left-hand needle into first 4 slipped sts and pass them over second 4 slipped sts, return second 4 sts to left-hand needle and purl all 8 sts in their new positions; repeat from * to end.

RND 7: Knit.

RND 8: Purl.

RNDS 9 AND 10: Repeat Rnds 7 and 8. Remove beginning-of-rnd marker, slip 4 sts to right-hand needle, pm for new beginning of rnd.

RNDS 11 AND 12: Repeat Rnds 5 and 6. Remove beginning-of-rnd marker, slip last 4 sts back to left-hand needle, pm for new beginning of rnd.

Repeat Rnds 1–12 for Indian Cross Stitch in the Round.

Checkerboard Bows

FLAT

(multiple of 16 sts + 9; 16-row repeat)

NOTE: Do not count sts on yo rows; original st count is restored on rows following yo rows. To tie bows, on RS, using spare needle, pull up elongated loop from dropped yos on either side of k1 until k1 is snug. Tie loops together using a square knot.

ROW 1 (RS): Knit.

ROW 2: K4, *[yo] 3 times, k1, [yo] 3 times, k15; repeat from * to last 5 sts, [yo] 3 times, k1, [yo] 3 times, k4.

ROW 3: Knit, dropping all yos. Tie bows.

ROWS 4–7: Repeat Rows 2 and 3.

ROWS 8 AND 9: Knit.

ROW 10: K12, *[yo] 3 times, k1, [yo] 3 times, k15; repeat from * to last 13 sts, [yo] 3 times, k1, [yo] 3 times, k12.

ROW 11: Repeat Row 3.

ROWS 12–15: Repeat Rows 10 and 11.

ROW 16: Knit.

Repeat Rows 1–16 for Checkerboard Bows Flat.

IN THE ROUND

(multiple of 16 sts; 16-rnd repeat)

NOTE: Do not count sts on yo rnds; original st count is restored on rnds following yo rnds. To tie bows, using spare needle, pull up elongated loop from dropped yos on either side of k1 until k1 is snug. Tie loops together using a square knot.

RND 1: Knit.

RND 2: *[Yo] 3 times, p1, [yo] 3 times, p15; repeat from * to end.

RND 3: Knit, dropping all yos. Tie bows.

RNDS 4–7: Repeat Rnds 2 and 3.

RND 8: Purl.

RND 9: Knit.

RND 10: P7, *[yo] 3 times, p1, [yo] 3 times, p15; repeat from * to last 9 sts, [yo] 3 times, p1, [yo] 3 times, p8.

RND 11: Repeat Rnd 3.

RNDS 12–15: Repeat Rnds 10 and 11.

RND 16: Purl.

Repeat Rnds 1–16 for Checkerboard Bows in the Round.

Loop Stitch

FLAT

(any number of sts; 2-row repeat)

NOTE: Pattern begins with a WS row.

ROW 1 (WS): Knit.

ROW 2: *K1, leaving st on left-hand needle, bring yarn to front between needles, around left thumb, then to back, knit the same st again, dropping st from left-hand needle, then pass first st over second st to lock loop in place. Note: To keep loops consistent, leave each loop on thumb while you slip first st over second st.

Repeat Rows 1 and 2 for Loop Stitch Flat.

IN THE ROUND

(any number of sts; 2-rnd repeat)

RND 1: Purl.

RND 2: *K1, leaving st on left-hand needle, bring yarn to front between needles, around left thumb, then to back, knit the same st again, dropping st from left-hand needle, then pass first st over second st to lock loop in place. Note: To keep loops consistent, leave each loop on thumb while you slip first st over second st.

Repeat Rnds 1 and 2 for Loop Stitch in the Round.

Blanket Moss Stitch

FLAT

(odd number of sts; 4-row repeat)

NOTE: You will double the number of sts on Row 1; original st count will be restored on Row 2.

ROW 1 (RS): *K1-f/b; repeat from * to end.

ROW 2: K2tog, *p2tog, k2tog; repeat from * to end.

ROW 3: Repeat Row 1.

ROW 4: P2tog, *k2tog, p2tog; repeat from * to end.

Repeat Rows 1–4 for Blanket Moss Stitch Flat.

IN THE ROUND

(even number of sts; 4-rnd repeat)

NOTE: You will double the number of sts on Rnd 1; original st count will be restored on Rnd 2.

RND 1: *K1-f/b; repeat from * to end.

RND 2: *P2tog, k2tog; repeat from * to end.

RND 3: Repeat Rnd 1.

RND 4: *K2tog, p2tog; repeat from * to end.

Repeat Rnds 1–4 for Blanket Moss Stitch in the Round.

Slip Stitch Honeycomb

FLAT

(odd number of sts; 4-row repeat)

ROW 1 (RS): Knit.

ROW 2: K1, *slip 1 wyib, k1; repeat from * to end.

ROW 3: Knit.

ROW 4: K2, *slip 1 wyib, k1; repeat from * to last st, k1.

Repeat Rows 1–4 for Slip Stitch Honeycomb Flat.

IN THE ROUND

(even number of sts; 4-rnd repeat)

RND 1: Knit.

RND 2: *P1, slip 1 wyif; repeat from * to end.

RND 3: Knit.

RND 4: *Slip 1 wyif, p1; repeat from * to end.

Repeat Rnds 1–4 for Slip Stitch Honeycomb in the Round.

Surface Twists

FLAT

(multiple of 3 sts; 4-row repeat)

ROW 1 (RS): *RT, k1; repeat from * to end.

ROW 2: Purl.

ROW 3: *K1, RT; repeat from * to end.

ROW 4: Purl.

Repeat Rows 1–4 for Surface Twists Flat.

IN THE ROUND

(multiple of 3 sts; 4-rnd repeat)

RND 1: *RT, k1; repeat from * to end.

RND 2: Knit.

RND 3: *K1, RT; repeat from * to end.

RND 4: Knit.

Repeat Rnds 1–4 for Surface Twists in the Round.

Honeycomb Smocking

FLAT

(multiple of 8 sts + 3; 14-row repeat)

Work smocking: See below.

ROW 1 (RS): *P3, k1; repeat from * to last 3 sts, p3.

ROWS 2–6: Knit the knit sts and purl the purl sts as they face you.

ROW 7: *P3, work smocking; repeat from * to last 3 sts, p3.

ROWS 8–10: Repeat Row 2.

ROW 11: P3, k1, *p3, work smocking; repeat from * to last 7 sts, p3, k1, p3.

ROWS 12–14: Repeat Row 2.

Repeat Rows 1–14 for Honeycomb Smocking Flat.

IN THE ROUND

(multiple of 8 sts; 14-rnd repeat)

Work smocking: See below.

RNDS 1–6: *K1, p3; repeat from * to end.

RND 7: *Work smocking, p3; repeat from * to end.

RNDS 8–10: Repeat Rnd 1.

RND 11: K1, *p3, work smocking; repeat from * to last 4 sts, work smocking over next 4 sts and first st of Rnd 12, leaving beginning-of-rnd marker in place.

RND 12: P3, *k1, p3; repeat from * to end.

RNDS 13 AND 14: Repeat Rnd 1.

Repeat Rnds 1–14 for Honeycomb Smocking Flat.

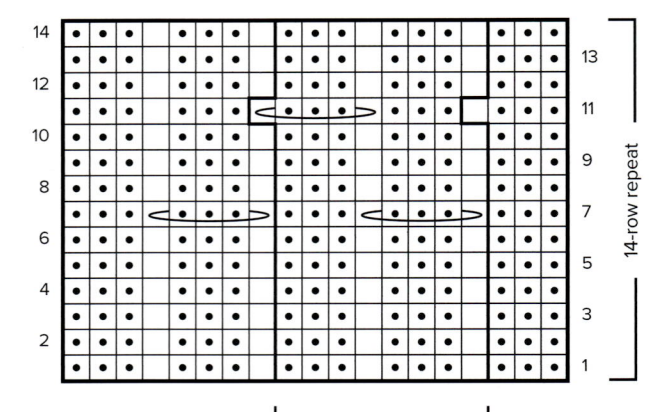

FLAT

8-st repeat

14-row repeat

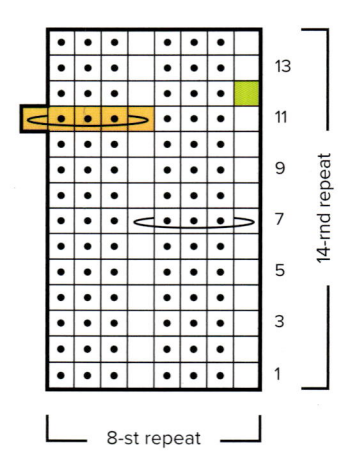

IN THE ROUND

8-st repeat

14-rnd repeat

Work smocking: K1, p3, k1, slip last 5 sts on right-hand needle to cn, hold to front, wrap yarn clockwise around these 5 sts twice, ending wyib, slip these sts back to right-hand needle.

On last repeat of Rnd 11, you will work smocking on last 4 sts of Rnd 11 and first st of Rnd 12; keep beginning-of-rnd marker in place when you work smocking.

On first repeat of Rnd 12, omit this st; it was worked with last 4 sts of Rnd 11. Work as knit st on subsequent repeats.

Puffy Diamonds

FLAT

FLAT

(multiple of 16 sts + 1; 24-row repeat)

Kw2: See below.

ROW 1 (RS): [Kw2] 5 times, *p7, [kw2] 9 times; repeat from * to last 12 sts, p7, [kw2] 5 times.

ROW 2: P5, *k7, p9; repeat from * to last 12 sts, k7, p5.

ROW 3: [Kw2] 4 times, *p9, [kw2] 7 times; repeat from * to last 13 sts, p9, [kw2] 4 times.

ROW 4: P4, *k9, p7; repeat from * to last 13 sts, k9, p4.

ROW 5: [Kw2] 3 times, *p5, kw2, p5, [kw2] 5 times; repeat from * to last 14 sts, p5, kw2, p5, [kw2] 3 times.

ROW 6: P3, *k5, p1, k5, p5; repeat from * to last 14 sts, k5, p1, k5, p3.

ROW 7: [Kw2] twice, *p5, [kw2] 3 times; repeat from * to last 7 sts, p5, [kw2] twice.

ROW 8: P2, *k5, p3; repeat from * to last 7 sts, k5, p2.

ROW 9: *Kw2, p5, [kw2] 5 times, p5; repeat from * to last st, kw2.

ROW 10: P1, *k5, p5, k5, p1; repeat from * to end.

ROW 11: P5, *[kw2] 7 times, p9; repeat from * to last 12 sts, [kw2] 7 times, p5.

ROW 12: K5, *p7, k9; repeat from * to last 12 sts, p7, k5.

ROW 13: P4, *[kw2] 9 times, p7; repeat from * to last 13 sts, [kw2] 9 times, p4.

ROW 14: K4, *p9, k7; repeat from * to last 13 sts, p9, k4.

ROWS 15 AND 16: Repeat Rows 11 and 12.

ROWS 17 AND 18: Repeat Rows 9 and 10.

ROWS 19 AND 20: Repeat Rows 7 and 8.

ROWS 21 AND 22: Repeat Rows 5 and 6.

ROWS 23 AND 24: Repeat Rows 3 and 4.

Repeat Rows 1–24 for Puffy Diamonds Flat.

16-st repeat · 24-row repeat

Kw2: K1, wrapping yarn twice; drop extra wrap on following row.

IN THE ROUND

(multiple of 16 sts; 24-rnd repeat)

Kw2: See below.

RND 1 (RS): [Kw2] 5 times, *p7, [kw2] 9 times; repeat from * to last 11 sts, p7, [kw2] 4 times.

RND 2: K5, *p7, k9; repeat from * to last 11 sts, p7, k4.

RND 3: [Kw2] 4 times, *p9, [kw2] 7 times; repeat from * to last 12 sts, p9, [kw2] 3 times.

RND 4: K4, *p9, k7; repeat from * to last 12 sts, p9, k3.

RND 5: [Kw2] 3 times, *p5, kw2, p5, [kw2] 5 times; repeat from * to last 13 sts, p5, kw2, p5, [kw2] twice.

RND 6: K3, *p5, k1, p5, k5; repeat from * to last 13 sts, p5, k1, p5, k2.

RND 7: [Kw2] twice, *p5, [kw2] 3 times; repeat from * to last 6 sts, p5, kw2.

RND 8: K2, *p5, k3; repeat from * to last 6 sts, p5, k1.

RND 9: *Kw2, p5, [kw2] 5 times, p5; repeat from * to end.

RND 10: *K1, p5, k5, p5; repeat from * to end.

RND 11: P5, *[kw2] 7 times, p9; repeat from * to last 11 sts, [kw2] 7 times, p4.

RND 12: P5, *k7, p9; repeat from * to last 11 sts, k7, p4.

RND 13: P4, *[kw2] 9 times, p7; repeat from * to last 12 sts, [kw2] 9 times, p3.

RND 14: P4, *k9, p7; repeat from * to last 12 sts, k9, p3.

RNDS 15 AND 16: Repeat Rnds 11 and 12.

RNDS 17 AND 18: Repeat Rnds 9 and 10.

RNDS 19 AND 20: Repeat Rnds 7 and 8.

RNDS 21 AND 22: Repeat Rnds 5 and 6.

RNDS 23 AND 24: Repeat Rnds 3 and 4.

Repeat Rnds 1–24 for Puffy Diamonds in the Round.

IN THE ROUND

16-st repeat

24-rnd repeat

Kw2: K1, wrapping yarn twice; drop extra wrap on following rnd.

Swedish Check

FLAT

(multiple of 4 sts + 2; 8-row repeat)

ROW 1 (RS): *K1-tbl; repeat from * to end.

ROW 2: Purl.

ROW 3: *[K1-tbl] twice, p2; repeat from * to last 2 sts, [k1-tbl] twice.

ROW 4: P2, *k2, p2; repeat from * to end.

ROWS 5 AND 6: Repeat Rows 1 and 2.

ROW 7: *P2, [k1-tbl] twice; repeat from * to last 2 sts, p2.

ROW 8: K2, *p2, k2; repeat from * to end.

Repeat Rows 1–8 for Swedish Check Flat.

IN THE ROUND

(multiple of 4 sts; 8-rnd repeat)

RND 1: *K1-tbl; repeat from * to end.

RND 2: Knit.

RND 3: *[K1-tbl] twice, p2; repeat from * to end.

RND 4: *K2, p2; repeat from * to end.

RND 5 AND 6: Repeat Rnds 1 and 2.

RND 7: *P2, [k1-tbl] twice.

RND 8: *P2, k2; repeat from * to end.

Repeat Rnds 1–8 for Swedish Check in the Round.

FLAT

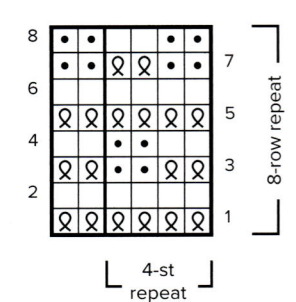

IN THE ROUND

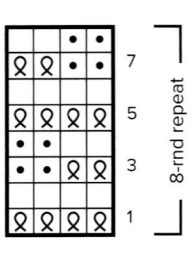

Loaf Pattern

FLAT

(multiple of 8 sts + 7; 12-row repeat)

NOTE: You will increase 2 sts per repeat on Rows 1 and 7; original st count is restored on Rows 6 and 12.

ROW 1 (RS): *P7, [k1, p1, k1] into next st; repeat from * to last 7 sts, p7.

ROW 2: K7, *p3, k7; repeat from * to end.

ROWS 3-5: Knit the knit sts and purl the purl sts as they face you.

ROW 6: K7, *k3tog, k7; repeat from * to end.

ROW 7: P3, *[k1, p1, k1] into next st, p7; repeat from * to last 4 sts, [k1, p1, k1] into next st, k3.

ROW 8: K3, *p3, k7; repeat from * to last 6 sts, p3, k3.

ROWS 9-11: Repeat Row 3.

ROW 12: K3, *k3tog, k7; repeat from * to last 6 sts, p3tog, k3.

Repeat Rows 1–12 for Loaf Pattern Flat.

IN THE ROUND

(multiple of 8 sts; 12-rnd repeat)

NOTE: You will increase 2 sts per repeat on Rnds 1 and 7; original st count is restored on Rnds 6 and 12.

RND 1: *P7, [k1, p1, k1] into next st; repeat from * to end.

RNDS 2-5: *P7, k3; repeat from * to end.

RND 6: *P7, p3tog; repeat from * to end.

RND 7: P3, *[k1, p1, k1] into next st, p7; repeat from * to last 5 sts, [k1, p1, k1] into next st, p4.

RNDS 8-11: P3, *k3, p7; repeat from * to last 7 sts, k3, p4.

RND 12: P3, *p3tog, p7; repeat from * to last 7 sts, p3tog, p4.

Repeat Rnds 1–12 for Loaf Pattern in the Round.

FLAT

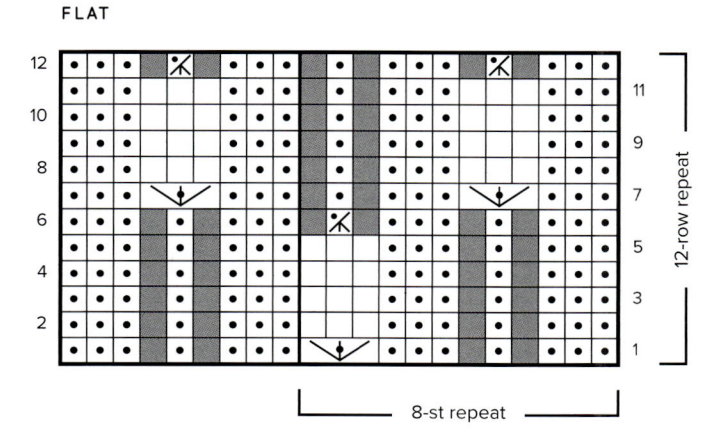

8-st repeat

12-row repeat

IN THE ROUND

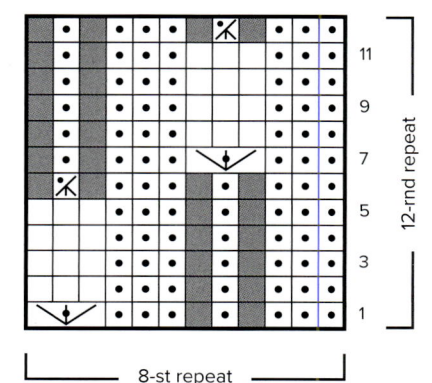

8-st repeat

12-rnd repeat

Triple-Slip Herringbone

FLAT

(multiple of 6 sts + 3; 20-row repeat)

NOTES: A selvage st will be required to anchor slipped sts at beginning and end of rows. Slip all sts purlwise with yarn to RS.

ROW 1 (RS): *Slip 3, k3; repeat from * to last 3 sts; slip 3.

ROW 2: Slip 2, *p3, slip 3; repeat from * to last st, p1.

ROW 3: K2, *slip 3, k3; repeat from * to last st, slip 1.

ROW 4: P3, *slip 3, p3; repeat from * to end.

ROW 5: Slip 1, *k3, slip 3; repeat from * to last 2 sts, k2.

ROW 6: P1, *slip 3, p3; repeat from * to last 2 sts, slip 2.

ROWS 7-10: Repeat Rows 1–4.

ROW 11: Repeat Row 1.

ROW 12: Repeat Row 6.

ROW 13: Repeat Row 5.

ROW 14: Repeat Row 4.

ROW 15: Repeat Row 3.

ROW 16: Repeat Row 2.

ROWS 17-20: Repeat Rows 11–14.

Repeat Rows 1–20 for Triple-Slip Herringbone Flat.

IN THE ROUND

(multiple of 6 sts; 20-rnd repeat)

NOTE: Slip all sts purlwise wyif.

RND 1: *Slip 3, k3; repeat from * to end.

RND 2: K1, *slip 3, k3; repeat from * to last 5 sts, slip 3, k2.

RND 3: K2, *slip 3, k3; repeat from * to last 4 sts, slip 3, k1.

RND 4: *K3, slip 3; repeat from * to end.

RND 5: Slip 1, *k3, slip 3; repeat from * to last 5 sts, k3, slip 2.

RND 6: Slip 2, *k3, slip 3; repeat from * to last 4 sts, k3, slip 1.

RNDS 7-10: Repeat Rnds 1–4.

RND 11: Repeat Rnd 1.

RND 12: Repeat Rnd 6.

RND 13: Repeat Rnd 5.

RND 14: Repeat Rnd 4.

RND 15: Repeat Rnd 3.

RND 16: Repeat Rnd 2.

RNDS 17-20: Repeat Rnds 11–14.

Repeat Rnds 1–20 for Triple-Slip Herringbone in the Round.

FLAT

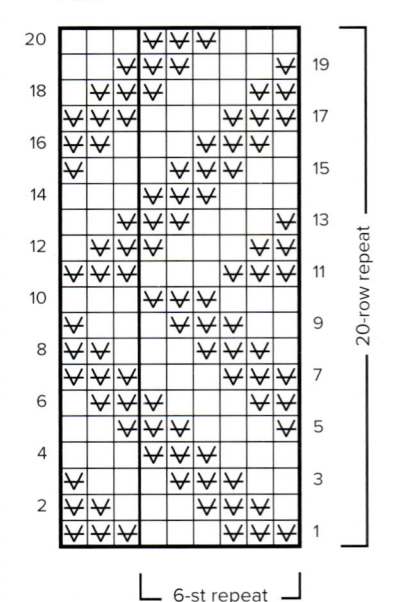

6-st repeat

IN THE ROUND

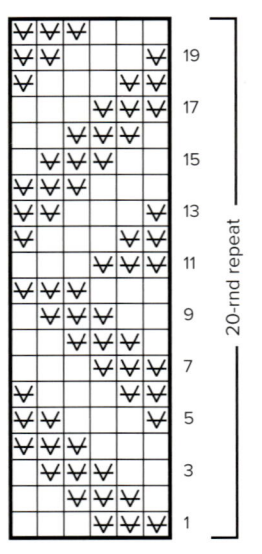

6-st repeat

Cluster Stitch

FLAT

(multiple of 8 sts + 5; 8-row repeat)

Work cluster: See below.

ROW 1 (RS): Knit.

ROW 2 AND ALL WS ROWS: Purl.

ROW 3: *K5, work cluster; repeat from * to last 5 sts, k5.

ROW 5: Knit.

ROW 7: K1, *work cluster, k5; repeat from * to last 4 sts, work cluster, k1.

ROW 8: Purl.

Repeat Rows 1–8 for Cluster Stitch Flat.

IN THE ROUND

(multiple of 8 sts; 8-rnd repeat)

Work cluster: See below.

RND 1: Knit.

RND 2 AND ALL EVEN-NUMBERED RNDS: Knit.

RND 3: *K5, work cluster; repeat from * to end.

RND 5: Knit.

RND 7: *K1, work cluster, k4; repeat from * to end.

RND 8: Knit.

Repeat Rnds 1–8 for Cluster Stitch in the Round.

FLAT

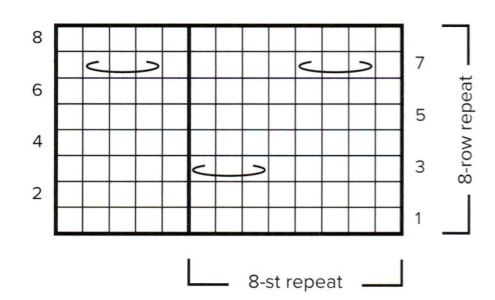

IN THE ROUND

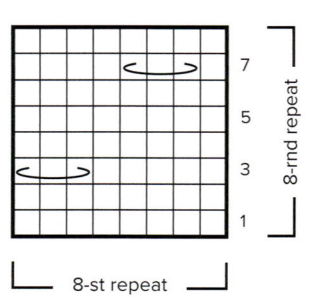

 Work cluster: Slip next 3 sts cn, wrap yarn counterclockwise around these 3 sts 6 times, ending wyib, k3 from cn.

Popcorn Stitch

FLAT

(multiple of 6 sts + 3; 8-row repeat)

MB: Make Bobble (see below).

ROW 1 (RS): Knit.

ROW 2 AND ALL WS ROWS: Purl.

ROW 3: K1, *MB, k5; repeat from * to last 2 sts, MB, k1.

ROW 5: Knit.

ROW 7: K4, *MB, k5; repeat from * to last 5 sts, MB, k4.

ROW 8: Purl.

Repeat Rows 1–8 for Popcorn Stitch flat.

FLAT

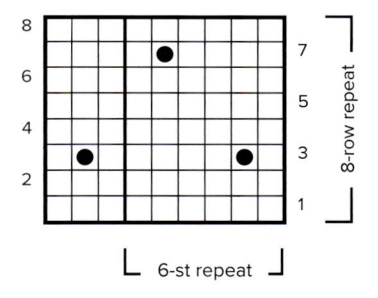

6-st repeat

IN THE ROUND

(multiple of 6 sts; 8-rnd repeat)

MB: Make Bobble (see below).

RND 1: Knit.

RND 2 AND ALL EVEN-NUMBERED RNDS: Knit.

RND 3: *K1, MB, k4; repeat from * to end.

RND 5: Knit.

RND 7: *K4, MB, k1; repeat from * to end.

RND 8: Knit.

Repeat Rnds 1–8 for Popcorn Stitch in the Round.

IN THE ROUND

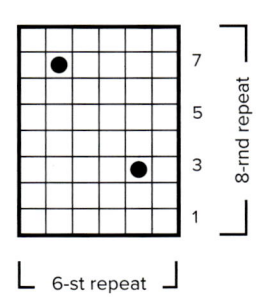

6-st repeat

● **MB:** Make Bobble. [K1, p1, k1] into next st, lift second and third sts over first st.

Indian Pillar Stitch (TWO-SIDED)

FLAT

(multiple of 4 sts + 3; 2-row repeat)

NOTE: This pattern should be worked loosely on large needles.

Make star: P3tog, leaving sts on needle, k2tog into same 3 sts again, then p3tog into same 3 sts again, slipping sts from left-hand needle.

ROW 1 (RS): K2, *make star, k1; repeat from * to last st, k1.

ROW 2: Purl.

Repeat Rows 1 and 2 for Indian Pillar Stitch Flat.

IN THE ROUND

(multiple of 4 sts; 2-rnd repeat)

NOTE: This pattern should be worked loosely on large needles.

Make star: P3tog, leaving sts on needle, k2tog into same 3 sts again, then p3tog into same 3 sts again, slipping sts from left-hand needle.

RND 1: Make star, k1; repeat from * to end.

RND 2: Knit.

Repeat Rnds 1 and 2 for Indian Pillar Stitch in the Round.

FRONT   BACK

Slip Stitch Mesh (TWO-SIDED)

FLAT

(even number of sts; 6-row repeat)

ROW 1 (RS): Purl.

ROW 2: Knit.

ROW 3: K2, *slip 1 wyib, k1; repeat from * to end.

ROW 4: *K1, slip 1 wyif; repeat from * to last 2 sts, k2.

ROW 5: K1, *yo, k2tog; repeat from * to last st, k1.

ROW 6: Purl.

Repeat Rows 1–6 for Slip Stitch Mesh Flat.

IN THE ROUND

(even number of sts; 6-rnd repeat)

RNDS 1 AND 2: Purl.

RND 3: *K1, slip 1 wyib; repeat from * to end.

RND 4: *P1, slip 1 wyib; repeat from * to end.

RND 5: *Yo, k2tog; repeat from * to end.

RND 6: Knit.

Repeat Rnds 1–6 for Slip Stitch Mesh in the Round.

FLAT

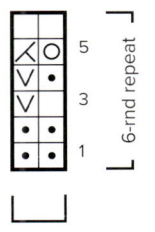

2-st repeat

IN THE ROUND

2-st repeat

Alternating Slip Stitch

FLAT

(multiple of 4 sts + 3; 12-row repeat)

NOTE: Slip all sts purlwise with yarn to WS.

ROW 1 (RS): *K3, slip 1; repeat from * to last 3 sts, k3.

ROW 2: P3, *slip 1, p3; repeat from * to end.

ROWS 3 AND 4: Repeat Rows 1 and 2.

ROW 5: Knit.

ROW 6: K3, *p1, k3; repeat from * to end.

ROW 7: K1, *slip 1, k3; repeat from * to last 2 sts, slip 1, k1.

ROW 8: P1, slip 1, *p3, slip 1; repeat from * to last st, p1.

ROWS 9 AND 10: Repeat Rows 7 and 8.

ROW 11: Knit.

ROW 12: K1, *p1, k3; repeat from * to last 2 sts, p1, k1.

Repeat Rows 1–12 for Alternating Slip Stitch Flat.

FLAT

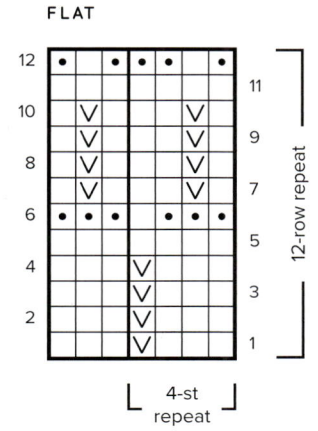

IN THE ROUND

(multiple of 4 sts; 12-rnd repeat)

NOTE: Slip all sts wyib.

RNDS 1-4: *K3, slip 1; repeat from * to end.

RND 5: Knit.

RND 6: *P3, k1; repeat from * to end.

RNDS 7-10: *K1, slip 1, k2; repeat from * to end.

RND 11: Knit.

RND 12: *P1, k1, p2; repeat from * to end.

Repeat Rnds 1–12 for Alternating Slip Stitch in the Round.

IN THE ROUND

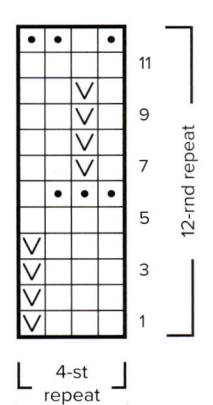

Checked Basket Stitch

FLAT

(multiple of 6 sts + 4; 12-row repeat)

NOTE: Slip all sts purlwise with yarn to WS.

ROW 1 (RS): Knit.

ROW 2: Purl.

ROWS 3–6: K1, *slip 2, k4; repeat from * to last 3 sts, slip 2, k1.

ROWS 7 AND 8: Repeat Rows 1 and 2.

ROW 9: *K4, slip 2; repeat from * to last 4 sts, k4.

ROW 10: K4, *slip 2, k4; repeat from * to end.

ROWS 11 AND 12: Repeat Rows 9 and 10.

Repeat Rows 1–12 for Checked Basket Stitch Flat.

IN THE ROUND

(multiple of 6 sts; 12-rnd repeat)

NOTE: Slip all sts purlwise wyib.

RNDS 1 AND 2: Knit.

RND 3: *K1, slip 2, k3; repeat from * to end.

RND 4: *P1, slip 2, p3; repeat from * to end.

RNDS 5 AND 6: Repeat Rnds 3 and 4.

RNDS 7 AND 8: Knit.

RND 9: *K4, slip 2; repeat from * to end.

RND 10: *P4, slip 2; repeat from * to end.

RNDS 11 AND 12: Repeat Rnds 9 and 10.

Repeat Rnds 1–12 for Checked Basket Stitch in the Round.

FLAT

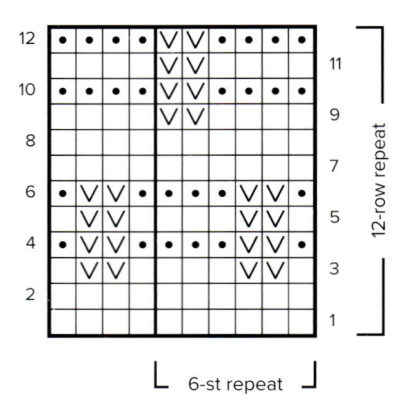

IN THE ROUND

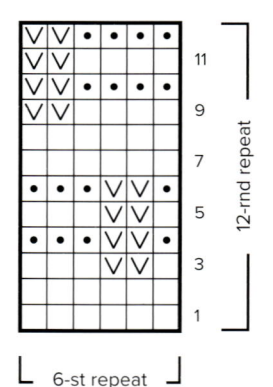

Trellis Stitch

FLAT

(multiple of 6 sts + 5; 12-row repeat)

NOTE: Slip all sts purlwise with yarn to RS.

Catch floats: See below.

ROW 1 (RS): K1, *p3, slip 3; repeat from * to last 4 sts, p3, k1.

ROW 2: P1, k3, *slip 3, k3; repeat from * to last st, p1.

ROW 3: K1, *p3, k3; repeat from * to last 4 sts, p3, k1.

ROW 4: P1, k3, *p3, k3; repeat from * to last st, p1.

ROW 5: *K5, catch floats; repeat from * to last 5 sts, k5.

ROW 6: Repeat Row 3.

ROW 7: P1, *slip 3, p3; repeat from * to last 4 sts, slip 3, p1.

ROW 8: K1, slip 3, *k3, slip 3; repeat from * to last st, k1.

ROW 9: Repeat Row 4.

ROW 10: Repeat Row 3.

ROW 11: K2, *catch floats, k5; repeat from * to last 3 sts, catch floats, k2.

ROW 12: Repeat Row 4.

Repeat Rows 1–12 for Trellis Stitch Flat.

IN THE ROUND

(multiple of 6 sts; 12-rnd repeat)

NOTE: Slip all sts purlwise wyif.

Catch floats: See below.

RNDS 1 AND 2: *P3, slip 3; repeat from * to end.

RNDS 3 AND 4: *P3, k3; repeat from * to end.

RND 5: *K4, catch floats, k1; repeat from * to end.

RND 6: *K3, p3; repeat from * to end.

RNDS 7 AND 8: *Slip 3, p3; repeat from * to end.

RNDS 9 AND 10: Repeat Rnd 6.

RND 11: *K1, catch floats, k4; repeat from * to end.

RND 12: Repeat Rnd 3.

Repeat Rnds 1–12 for Trellis Stitch in the Round.

IN THE ROUND

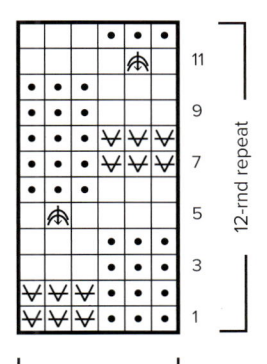

12-rnd repeat

6-st repeat

FLAT

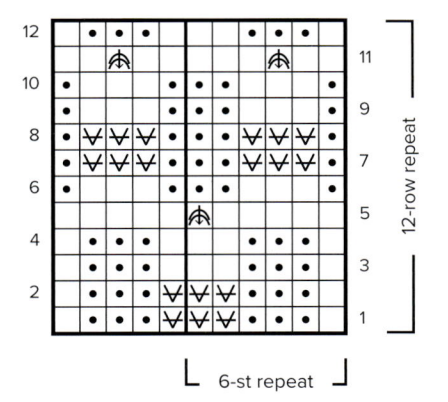

12-row repeat

6-st repeat

 Catch floats: Insert right-hand needle upward under the 2 floats in front of the slipped sts 3 and 4 row/rnds below next st and knit the next st, then lift the 2 floats off over the tip of the right-hand needle.

Swag Stitch

FLAT

(multiple of 5 sts + 2; 6-row repeat)

NOTE: Pattern begins with a WS row.

ROW 1 (WS) AND ALL WS ROWS: Purl.

ROW 2: Knit.

ROWS 4 AND 6: *P2, slip 3 wyif; repeat from * to last 2 sts, p2.

Repeat Rows 1–6 for Swag Stitch Flat.

IN THE ROUND

(multiple of 5 sts; 6-rnd repeat)

RNDS 1–3: Knit.

RND 4: *P2, slip 3 wyif; repeat from * to end.

RND 5: Knit.

RND 6: Repeat Rnd 4.

Repeat Rnds 1–6 for Swag Stitch in the Round.

FLAT

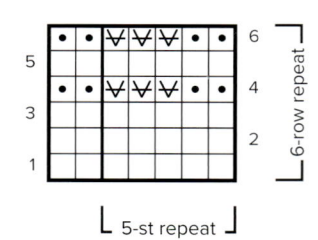

IN THE ROUND

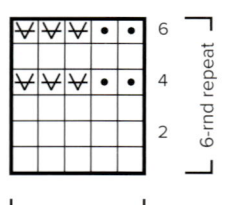

Note: Pattern begins with a WS row.

Bowknots

FLAT

(multiple of 6 sts + 3; 8-row repeat)

NOTE: Pattern begins with a WS row.

ROW 1 (WS): Purl.

ROW 2: Knit.

ROW 3: *K3, p3; repeat from * to last 3 sts, k3.

ROW 4: P1, k1b, p1, *k3, p1, k1b, p1; repeat from * to end.

ROWS 5 AND 6: Repeat Rows 1 and 2.

ROW 7: *P3, k3; repeat from * to last 3 sts, p3.

ROW 8: K3, *p1, k1b, p1, k3; repeat from * to end.

Repeat Rows 1–8 for Bowknots Flat.

FLAT

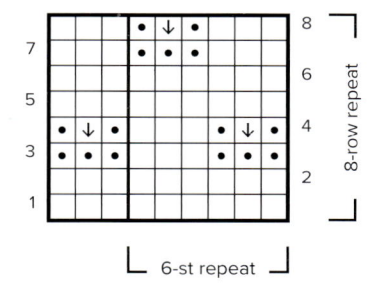

6-st repeat

Note: Pattern begins with a WS row.

IN THE ROUND

(multiple of 6 sts; 8-rnd repeat)

RNDS 1 AND 2: Knit.

RND 3: *P3, k3; repeat from * to end.

RND 4: *P1, k1b, p1, k3; repeat from * to end.

RNDS 5 AND 6: Knit.

RND 7: *K3, p3; repeat from * to end.

RND 8: *K3, p1, k1b, p1; repeat from * to end.

Repeat Rnds 1–8 for Bowknots in the Round.

IN THE ROUND

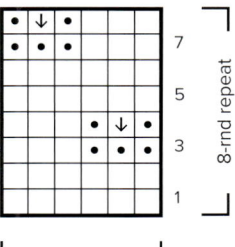

6-st repeat

Raindrops

BOTTOM-UP FLAT

(multiple of 6 sts + 3; 12-row repeat)

ROW 1 (RS): *P4, yo, p2tog; repeat from * to last 3 sts; p3.

ROW 2: Knit.

ROW 3: P4, *k1, p5; repeat from * to last 5 sts, k1, p4.

ROWS 4–6: Knit the knit sts and purl the purl sts as they face you.

ROW 7: P1, *yo, p2tog, p4; repeat from * to last 2 sts, yo, p2tog.

ROW 8: Knit.

ROW 9: P1, *k1, p5; repeat from * to last 2 sts, k1, p1.

ROWS 10–12: Repeat Row 4.

Repeat Rows 1–12 for Raindrops Bottom-Up Flat.

BOTTOM-UP IN THE ROUND

(multiple of 6 sts; 12-rnd repeat)

RND 1: *P4, yo, p2tog; repeat from * to end.

RND 2: Purl.

RNDS 3–6: *P4, k1, p1; repeat from * to end.

RND 7: *P1, yo, p2tog, p3; repeat from * to end.

RND 8: Purl.

RNDS 9–12: *P1, k1, p4; repeat from * to end.

Repeat Rnds 1–12 for Raindrops Bottom-Up in the Round.

TOP-DOWN FLAT

(multiple of 6 sts + 3; 12-row repeat)

NOTE: Pattern begins with a WS row.

ROW 1 (WS): K1, *p1, k5; repeat from * to last 2 sts, p1, k1.

ROWS 2–4: Knit the knit sts and purl the purl sts as they face you.

ROW 5: Knit.

ROW 6: P1, *yo, p2tog, p4; repeat from * to last 2 sts, yo, p2tog.

ROW 7: K4, *p1, k5; repeat from * to last 5 sts, p1, k4.

ROWS 8–10: Repeat Row 2.

ROW 11: Knit.

ROW 12: *P4, yo, p2tog; repeat from * to last 3 sts, p3.

Repeat Rows 1–12 for Raindrops Top-Down Flat.

TOP-DOWN IN THE ROUND

(multiple of 6 sts; 12-rnd repeat)

RNDS 1–4: *P1, k1, p4; repeat from * to end.

RND 5: Purl.

RND 6: *P1, yo, p2tog, p3; repeat from * to end.

RNDS 7–10: *P4, k1, p1; repeat from * to end.

RND 11: Purl.

RND 12: *P4, yo, p2tog; repeat from * to end.

Repeat Rnds 1–12 for Raindrops Top-Down in the Round.

BOTTOM-UP FLAT — 6-st repeat, 12-row repeat

BOTTOM-UP IN THE ROUND — 6-st repeat, 12-rnd repeat

TOP-DOWN FLAT — 6-st repeat, 12-row repeat

TOP-DOWN IN THE ROUND — 6-st repeat, 12-rnd repeat

Note: Pattern begins with a WS row.

Jeweled Boxes

FLAT

(multiple of 7 sts + 1; 10-row repeat)

NOTE: Pattern begins with a WS row. Slip all sts purlwise with yarn to WS.

DSC: Double Slipped Cross (see below).

ROW 1 (WS): P3, *k2, p5; repeat from * to last 5 sts, k2, p3.

ROW 2: Knit.

ROWS 3–6: Repeat Rows 1 and 2.

ROW 7: K2, *slip 1, k2, slip 1, k3; repeat from * to last 6 sts, [slip 1, k2] twice.

ROW 8: K2, *slip 1, k2, slip 1, k3; repeat from * to last 6 sts, [slip 1, k2] twice.

ROW 9: Repeat Row 7.

ROW 10: K2, *DSC, k3; repeat from * to last 6 sts, DSC, k2.

Repeat Rows 1–10 for Jeweled Boxes Flat.

FLAT

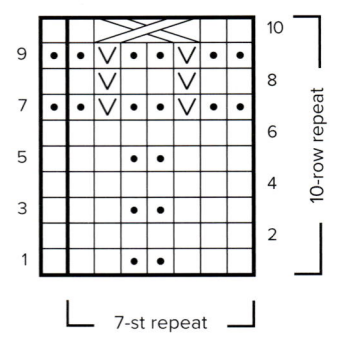

Note: Pattern begins with a WS row.

IN THE ROUND

(multiple of 7 sts; 10-rnd repeat)

NOTE: Slip all sts purlwise wyib.

DSC: Double Slipped Cross (see below).

RND 1: *K3, p2, k2; repeat from * to end.

RND 2: Knit.

RNDS 3–6: Repeat Rnds 1 and 2.

RND 7: *[P2, slip 1] twice, p1; repeat from * to end.

RND 8: *[K2, slip 1] twice, k1; repeat from * to end.

RND 9: Repeat Rnd 7.

RND 10: *K2, DSC, k1; repeat from * to end.

Repeat Rnds 1–10 for Jeweled Boxes in the Round.

IN THE ROUND

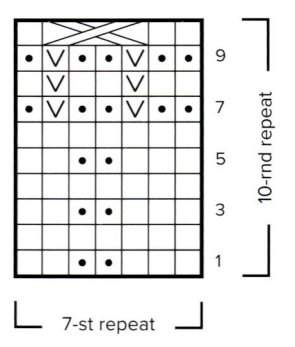

DSC: Double Slipped Cross. Drop first slipped st off needle to front, slip next 2 sts to right-hand needle, drop second slipped st off needle to front, pick up first dropped st with left-hand needle, slip last 2 sts on right-hand needle back to left-hand needle, then pick up second dropped st with right-hand needle and place it on left-hand needle, k4.

Zigzag Chevron

FLAT

(multiple of 14 sts + 2; 2-row repeat)

NOTE: Pattern begins with a WS row.

ROW 1 (WS): Purl.

ROW 2: K1, *k1-f/b, k4, skp, k2tog, k4, k1-f/b; repeat from * to last st, k1.

Repeat Rows 1 and 2 for Zigzag Chevron Flat.

IN THE ROUND

(multiple of 14 sts; 2-rnd repeat)

RND 1: Knit.

RND 2: *K1-f/b, k4, skp, k2tog, k4, k1-f/b; repeat from * to end.

Repeat Rnds 1 and 2 for Zigzag Chevron in the Round.

FLAT

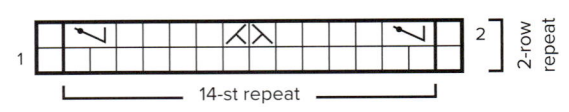

Note: Pattern begins with a WS row.

IN THE ROUND

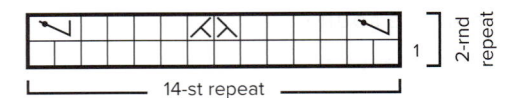

Welting Fantastic

FLAT

(multiple of 11 sts; 10-row repeat)

NOTE: Pattern begins with a WS row.

ROW 1 (WS): Knit.

ROWS 2–5: Knit.

ROW 6: *K2tog, k2, [k1-f/b] twice, k3, ssk; repeat from * to end.

ROW 7: Purl.

ROW 8: Repeat Row 6.

ROWS 9 AND 10: Repeat Rows 7 and 8.

Repeat Rows 1–10 for Welting Fantastic Flat.

IN THE ROUND

(multiple of 11 sts; 10-rnd repeat)

RND 1: Purl.

RND 2: Knit.

RNDS 3 AND 4: Repeat Rows 1 and 2.

RND 5: Purl.

RND 6: *K2tog, k2, [k1-f/b] twice, k3, ssk; repeat from * to end.

RND 7: Knit.

RND 8: Repeat Rnd 6.

RNDS 9 AND 10: Repeat Rnds 7 and 8.

Repeat Rnds 1–10 for Welting Fantastic in the Round.

FLAT & IN THE ROUND

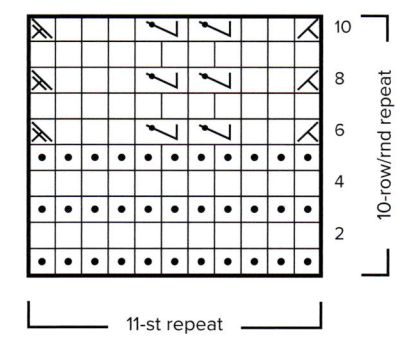

Note: Flat pattern begins with a WS row.

Indian Pillar Mitts

In these fingerless mitts, I incorporated a fun and fancy stitch pattern that runs down the center front. Swapping out another stitch pattern for the top of the mitts is easy: Just choose another in-the-round pattern from this book with stitch multiples that will fit within the top half of stitches on the mittens and you're good to go!

SIZES
Adult Small (Medium, Large)

FINISHED MEASUREMENTS
Approximately 7½ (7¾, 8½)" [19 (19.5, 21.5) cm] hand circumference
Approximately 8½ (8½, 9¼)" [21.5 (21.5, 23.5) cm] long

YARN USED
Blue Sky Alpacas Sport Weight (100% baby alpaca; 110 yards / 50 grams): 2 hanks #505 Taupe

NEEDLES
One set of four double-pointed needles (dpn) size US 3 (3.25 mm)

Change needle size if necessary to obtain correct gauge.

NOTIONS
Stitch markers; waste yarn

GAUGE
24 sts and 32 rows = 4" (10 cm) in Stockinette stitch (St st), washed and blocked

STITCH PATTERNS

1x1 Rib
(even number of sts; 1-rnd repeat)
ALL RNDS: *K1, p1; repeat from * to end.

Indian Pillar Stitch
(multiple of 4 sts; 2-rnd repeat)
Make star: P3tog, leaving sts on needle, k2tog into same 3 sts again, then p3tog into same 3 sts again, slipping sts from left-hand needle.
RND 1: *Make star, k1; repeat from * to end.
RND 2: Knit.
Repeat Rnds 1 and 2 for Indian Pillar Stitch.

RIGHT MITT

CO 44 (46, 50) sts. Divide sts among 3 dpns. Join for working in the rnd, being careful not to twist sts; pm for beginning of rnd. Work 1x1 Rib for 2¾ (2¾, 3)" [7 (7, 7.5) cm].
NEXT RND: Knit to end, rearranging sts so that there are 20 (20, 24) sts on Needle 1 for back of hand.

Shape Thumb Gusset
INCREASE RND 1: *Needle 1:* Work Indian Pillar Stitch to end of needle; *Needle 2:* K2 (2, 4), pm, M1-l, pm, knit to end of needle; *Needle 3:* Knit—45 (47, 51) sts. Work even for 1 rnd, working Indian Pillar Stitch on Needle 1 and St st on Needles 2 and 3.

INCREASE RND 2: Working increased sts in St st, increase 2 sts this rnd, then every 3 rnds until you have 15 (17, 19) sts between markers, as follows: Work to marker, sm, M1-r, knit to marker, M1-l, sm, work to end—59 (63, 69) sts.

NEXT RND: Work to first marker, remove marker, transfer next 15 (17, 19) sts to waste yarn, remove marker, using Backward Loop CO (see Special Techniques, page 280), CO 1 st over gap, knit to end—45 (47, 51) sts remain. Work even until piece measures approximately 7 (7, 7½)" [18 (18, 19) cm] from beginning, ending with Rnd 2 of pattern.

NEXT RND: Change to 1x1 Rib; work even for 9 (9, 11) rnds, decrease 1 st on first rnd—44 (46, 50) sts remain. BO all sts in pattern.

Thumb
Transfer 15 (17, 19) sts from waste yarn to dpns. Rejoin yarn; pick up and knit 1 st from st CO over gap—16 (18, 20) sts. Knit 4 (4, 6) rnds. Change to 1x1 Rib; work 4 (4, 6) rnds. BO all sts in pattern.

LEFT MITT

Work as for Right Mitt to beginning of Thumb Gusset.

Shape Thumb Gusset
INCREASE RND 1: *Needle 1:* Work Indian Pillar Stitch to end of needle; *Needle 2:* Knit; *Needle 3:* Knit to last 2 (2, 4) sts, pm, M1-l, pm, knit to end—45 (47, 51) sts. Complete as for Right Mitt.

CHAPTER 4
CABLES

CABLING, WHICH IS SIMPLY the technique of crossing one group of stitches over another group of stitches, adds a lot of textural interest to knitted fabric. Although making cables isn't typically thought of as a beginner's technique, it is easier to execute than one would think, and the effect is unmistakably dramatic. Many of the cables in this chapter are made up of knit stitches on a Reverse Stockinette Stitch background, but there are also others that create an all-over cabled fabric like the Fractured Lattice on page 139 or Checkerboard Cables on page 125. Whichever cable you choose to knit, understand that cables draw the fabric in width-wise; therefore, more stitches are required to make a given width. So, if you want to insert cables into a sweater pattern that is composed of knit stitches, take this into account and add extra stitches accordingly. **xx**

HOW TO MAKE MIRRORED CABLES

If you've ever seen a sweater or vest with columns of cables, you'll notice many times that there will be a centered, main cable flanked by mirrored, smaller cables. If you want your cables to be mirrored—in other words, you want one to twist to the right and the other one to twist to the left—just switch the position of the cable needle. For example, if you want a right-crossed cable instead of one that crosses to the left, hold your stitches to the back of the work instead of the front, and vice versa.

STITCHES

WISHBONE RIBBED CABLE
INTERLOCKING RINGS
CHECKERBOARD CABLES
SLIPPED 3-STITCH CABLE
LITTLE PEARLS
NESTLED DIAMONDS
CLIMBING FRAME
CROSSED V-STITCH
PLAITED CABLE
CABLE FABRIC
FRACTURED LATTICE
WHEAT CABLE
WICKERWORK PATTERN
LONG AND LEAN CABLES
TELESCOPE LATTICE
REVERSIBLE 4-STITCH
  CABLES

CABLE TEXTURE
NARROW CROSS AND
  TWIST
SAUSAGE CABLE
ROUND CABLE
FOLDED CABLE
GULL STITCH
STACKED CABLES
CABLE AND LADDER
KNOTTED CABLE
CLAW PATTERN
12-STITCH PLAIT

PROJECT

WOVEN TAFFY TOQUE

Wishbone Ribbed Cable (TWO-SIDED)

BOTTOM-UP FLAT

(multiple of 16 sts; 10-row repeat)

ROW 1: P1, *k2, p2; repeat from * to last 3 sts, k2, p1.

ROWS 2-4: Knit the knit sts and purl the purl sts as they face you.

ROW 5: *Slip 4 sts to cn, hold to back, p1, k2, p1, [p1, k2, p1] from cn, slip 4 sts to cn, hold to front, p1, k2, p1, [p1, k2, p1] from cn; repeat from * to end.

ROW 6: K1, *p2, k2; repeat from * to last 3 sts, p2, k1.

ROWS 7-10: Repeat Row 2.

Repeat Rows 1–10 for Wishbone Ribbed Cable Bottom-Up Flat.

BOTTOM-UP IN THE ROUND

(multiple of 16 sts; 10-rnd repeat)

RNDS 1-4: P1, *k2, p2; repeat from * to last 3 sts, k2, p1.

RND 5: *Slip 4 sts to cn, hold to back, p1, k2, p1, [p1, k2, p1] from cn, slip 4 sts to cn, hold to front, p1, k2, p1, [p1, k2, p1] from cn; repeat from * to end.

RNDS 6-10: Repeat Rnd 1.

Repeat Rnds 1–10 for Wishbone Ribbed Cable Bottom-Up in the Round.

TOP-DOWN FLAT

(multiple of 16 sts; 10-row repeat)

ROW 1: P1, *k2, p2; repeat from * to last 3 sts, k2, p1.

ROWS 2-4: Knit the knit sts and purl the purl sts as they face you.

ROW 5: *Slip 4 sts to cn, hold to front, p1, k2, p1, [p1, k2, p1] from cn, slip 4 sts to cn, hold to back, p1, k2, p1, [p1, k2, p1] from cn; repeat from * to end.

ROW 6: K1, *p2, k2; repeat from * to last 3 sts, p2, k1.

ROWS 7-10: Repeat Row 2.

Repeat Rows 1–10 for Wishbone Ribbed Cable Top-Down Flat.

TOP-DOWN IN THE ROUND

(multiple of 16 sts; 10-rnd repeat)

RNDS 1-4: P1, *k2, p2; repeat from * to last 3 sts, k2, p1.

RND 5: * Slip 4 sts to cn, hold to front, p1, k2, p1, [p1, k2, p1] from cn, slip 4 sts to cn, hold to back, p1, k2, p1, [p1, k2, p1] from cn; repeat from * to end.

RNDS 6-10: Repeat Rnd 1.

Repeat Rnds 1–10 for Wishbone Ribbed Cable in the Top-Down in the Round.

BOTTOM-UP FLAT & IN THE ROUND

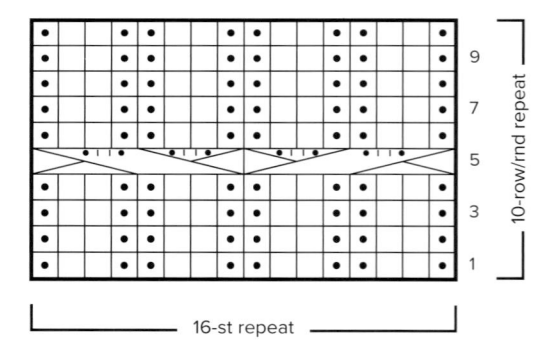

16-st repeat

10-row/rnd repeat

TOP-DOWN FLAT & IN THE ROUND

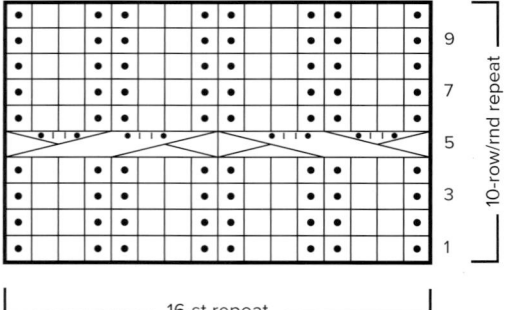

16-st repeat

10-row/rnd repeat

Slip 4 sts to cn, hold to back, p1, k2, p1, [p1, k2, p1] from cn.

Slip 4 sts to cn, hold to front, p1, k2, p1, [p1, k2, p1] from cn.

Interlocking Rings

FLAT

(multiple of 10 sts; 32-row repeat)

ROW 1 (RS): *P3, k4, p3; repeat from * to end.

ROW 2 AND ALL WS ROWS: Knit the knit sts and purl the purl sts as they face you.

ROW 3: *P3, C4F, p3; repeat from * to end.

ROW 5: *P2, 2/1 RC-p, 2/1 LC-p, p2; repeat from * to end.

ROW 7: *P1, 2/1 RC-p, p2, 2/1 LC-p, p1; repeat from * to end.

ROW 9: *2/1 RC-p, p4, 2/1 LC-p; repeat from * to end.

ROW 11: K2, *p6, C4F; repeat from * to last 8 sts, p6, k2.

ROW 13: K2, *p6, k4; repeat from * to last 8 sts, p6, k2.

ROWS 15 AND 17: Repeat Rows 11 and 13.

ROW 19: Repeat Row 11.

ROW 21: *2/1 LC-p, p4, 2/1 RC-p; repeat from * to end.

ROW 23: *P1, 2/1 LC-p, p2, 2/1 RC-p, p1; repeat from * to end.

ROW 25: *P2, 2/1 LC-p, 2/1 RC-p, p2; repeat from * to end.

ROW 27: *P3, C4F, p3; repeat from * to end.

ROWS 29 AND 31: Repeat Rows 1 and 3.

ROW 32: Repeat Row 2.

Repeat Rows 1–32 for Interlocking Rings Flat.

FLAT

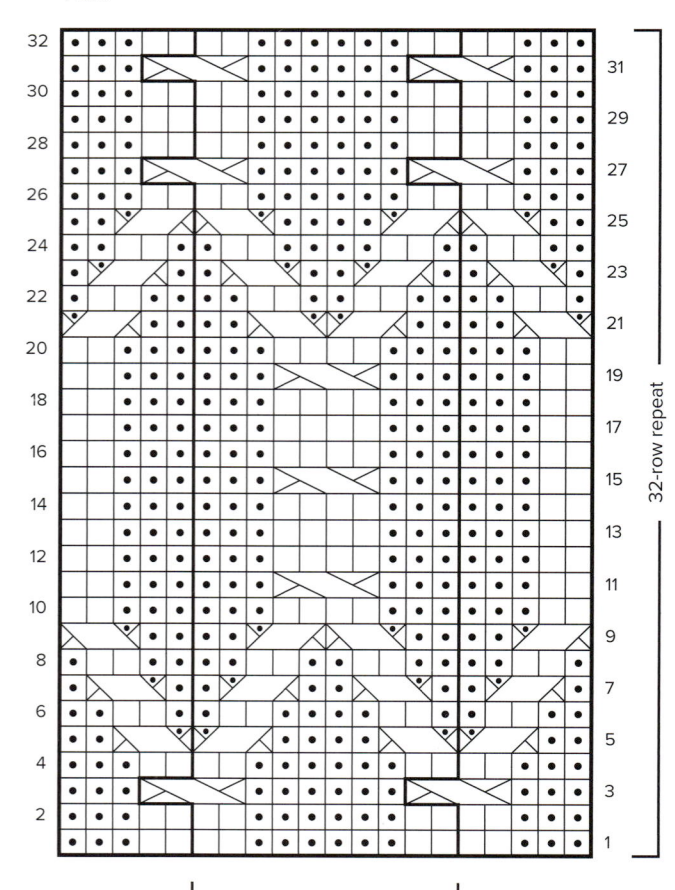

10-st repeat

32-row repeat

IN THE ROUND

(multiple of 10 sts; 32-rnd repeat)

SET-UP RND 1: *K2, p6, k2; repeat from * to end.

SET-UP RND 2 AND ALL EVEN-NUM-BERED RNDS: Knit the knit sts and purl the purl sts as they face you.

SET-UP RND 3: Remove beginning-of-rnd marker, slip 2 sts, place marker, *p6, C4F; repeat from * to end. Reposition beginning-of-rnd marker to center of last 4 sts.

RND 5: *2/1 LC-p, p4, 2/1 RC-p; repeat from * to end.

RND 7: *P1, 2/1 LC-p, p2, 2/1 RC-p, p1; repeat from * to end.

RND 9: *P2, 2/1 LC-p, 2/1 RC-p, p2; repeat from * to end.

RND 11: *P3, C4F, p3; repeat from * end.

RND 13: *P3, k4, p3; repeat from * to end.

RNDS 15 AND 17: Repeat Rnds 11 and 13.

RND 19: Repeat Rnd 11.

RND 21: *P2, 2/1 RC-p, 2/1 LC-p, p2; repeat from * to end.

RND 23: *P1, 2/1 RC-p, p2, 2/1 LC-p, p1; repeat from * to end.

RND 25: *2/1 RC-p, p4, 2/1 LC-p; repeat from * to end.

RND 27: Remove beginning-of-rnd marker, slip 2 sts, place marker, *p6, C4F; repeat from * to end. Leave marker in place.

RND 29: *P6, k4; repeat from * to end.

RND 31: *P6, C4F; repeat from * to end.

RNDS 33 AND 35: Repeat Rnds 29 and 31. After last repeat on Rnd 35, reposition beginning-of-rnd marker to center of last 4 sts.

RND 36: Repeat Set-Up Rnd 2.

Repeat Rnds 5–36 for Interlocking Rings in the Round.

IN THE ROUND

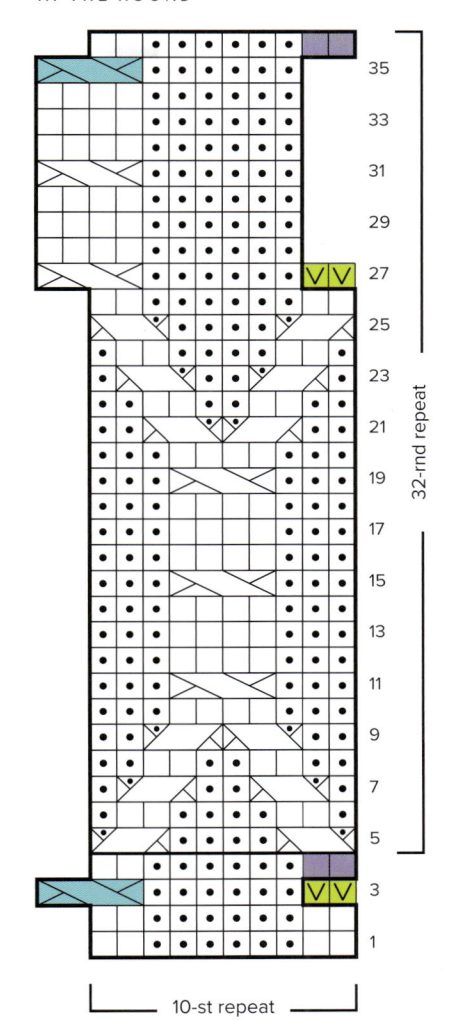

10-st repeat

32-rnd repeat

 On first repeat of Rnds 3 and 27 only, remove beginning-of-rnd marker, slip these 2 sts, place marker. Omit these sts on subsequent repeats.

After last repeat of Rnds 3 and 35, reposition beginning-of-rnd marker to center of these 4 sts.

On first repeat of Rnds 4 and 36 only, omit these 2 sts; they were worked in cable at end of previous rnd. Work as knit sts on subsequent repeats.

FRONT

BACK

Checkerboard Cables (TWO-SIDED)

BOTTOM-UP FLAT

(multiple of 16 sts; 16-row repeat)
ROW 1 (RS): *P8, k8; repeat from * to end.
ROWS 2-6: Repeat Row 1.
ROW 7: *P8, C8F.
ROW 8: Repeat Row 1.
ROWS 9-14: *K8, p8; repeat from * to end.
ROW 15: *C8F, p8; repeat from * to end.
ROW 16: Repeat Row 9.
Repeat Rows 1–16 for Checkerboard Cables Bottom-Up Flat.

BOTTOM-UP IN THE ROUND

(multiple of 16 sts; 16-rnd repeat)
RNDS 1-6: *P8, k8; repeat from * to end.
RND 7: *P8, C8F; repeat from * to end.
RND 8: Repeat Rnd 1.
RNDS 9-14: *K8, p8; repeat from * to end.
RND 15: *C8F, p8; repeat from * to end.
RND 16: Repeat Rnd 9.
Repeat Rnds 1–16 for Checkerboard Cables Bottom-Up
in the Round.

TOP-DOWN FLAT

(multiple of 16 sts; 16-row repeat)
NOTE: Pattern begins with a WS row.
ROW 1 (WS): *P8, k8; repeat from * to end.
ROW 2: *P8, C8F; repeat from * to end.
ROWS 3-8: Repeat Row 1.
ROW 9: *K8, p8; repeat from * to end.
ROW 10: *C8F, p8; repeat from * to end.
ROWS 11-16: Repeat Row 9.
Repeat Rows 1–16 for Checkerboard Cables Top-Down Flat.

TOP-DOWN IN THE ROUND

(multiple of 16 sts; 16-rnd repeat)
RND 1: *P8, k8; repeat from * to end.
RND 2: *P8, C8F; repeat from * to end.
RNDS 3-8: Repeat Rnd 1.
RND 9: *K8, p8; repeat from * to end.
RND 10: *C8F, p8; repeat from * to end.
RNDS 11-16: Repeat Rnd 9.
Repeat Rnds 1–16 for Checkerboard Cables Top-Down
in the Round.

BOTTOM-UP FLAT & IN THE ROUND

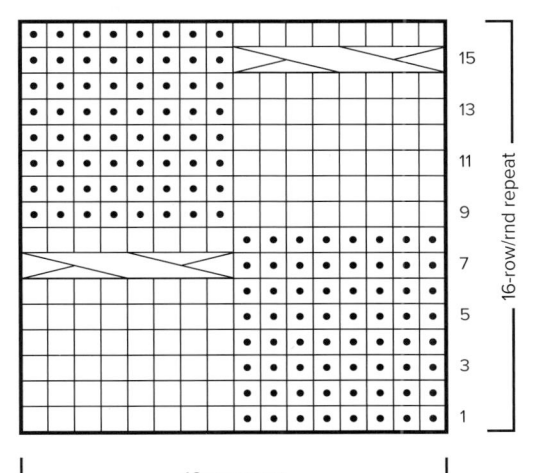

16-row/rnd repeat

16-st repeat

TOP-DOWN FLAT & IN THE ROUND

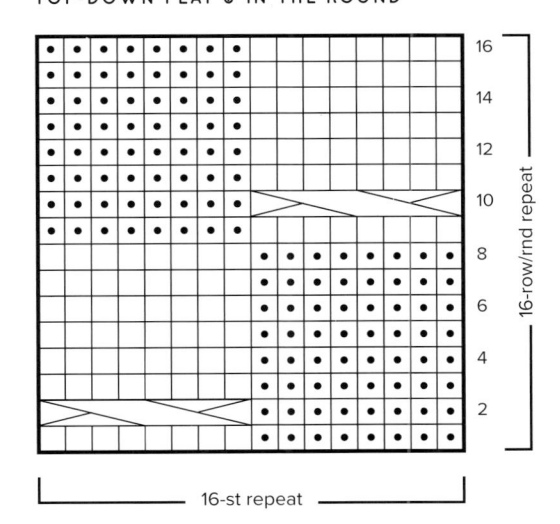

16-row/rnd repeat

16-st repeat

Note: Flat Chart begins with a WS row.

Slipped 3-Stitch Cable

FLAT

(panel of 3 sts worked on a background of Rev St st; 4-row repeat)

ROW 1 (RS): Slip 1, k2.

ROW 2: P2, slip 1.

ROW 3: 1/2 LC.

ROW 4: Purl.

Repeat Rows 1–4 for Slipped 3-Stitch Cable Flat.

IN THE ROUND

(panel of 3 sts worked on a background of Rev St st; 4-rnd repeat)

RNDS 1 AND 2: Slip 1, k2.

RND 3: 1/2 LC.

RND 4: Knit.

Repeat Rnds 1–4 for Slipped 3-Stitch Cable in the Round.

FLAT & IN THE ROUND

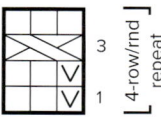

Little Pearls

FLAT

(panel of 4 sts worked on a background of Rev St st; 4-row repeat)

ROW 1 (RS): LC, RC.

ROW 2: Purl.

ROW 3: RC, LC.

ROW 4: Purl.

Repeat Rows 1–4 for Little Pearls Flat.

IN THE ROUND

(panel of 4 sts worked on a background of Rev St st; 4-rnd repeat)

RND 1: LC, RC.

RND 2: Knit.

RND 3: RC, LC.

RND 4: Knit.

Repeat Rnds 1–4 for Little Pearls in the Round.

FLAT & IN THE ROUND

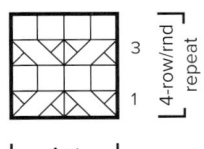

3

1

4-row/rnd repeat

4-st panel

Nestled Diamonds

BOTTOM-UP FLAT

(multiple of 18 sts; 32-row repeat)

RSC: Right Slipped Cross (see below).

LSC: Left Slipped Cross (see below).

ROW 1 (RS): *K5, [RSC] twice, [LSC] twice, k5; repeat from * to end.

ROW 2 AND ALL WS ROWS: Purl.

ROW 3: *K4, [RSC] twice, k2, [LSC] twice, k4; repeat from * to end.

ROW 5: *K3, [RSC] twice, k4, [LSC] twice, k3; repeat from * to end.

ROW 7: *K2, [RSC] twice, k6, [LSC] twice, k2; repeat from * to end.

ROW 9: *K1, RSC, k1, LSC, k6, RSC, k1, LSC, k1; repeat from * to end.

ROW 11: *RSC, k3, LSC, k4, RSC, k3, LSC; repeat from * to end.

ROW 13: *LSC, k4, LSC, k2, RSC, k4, RSC; repeat from * to end.

ROW 15: *K1, LSC, k4, LSC, RSC, k4, RSC, k1; repeat from * to end.

ROW 17: *[LSC] twice, k10, [RSC] twice; repeat from * to end.

ROW 19: *K1, [LSC] twice, k8, [RSC] twice, k1; repeat from * to end.

ROW 21: *K2, [LSC] twice, k6, [RSC] twice, k2; repeat from * to end.

ROW 23: *K3, [LSC] twice, k4, [RSC] twice, k3; repeat from * to end.

ROW 25: *K3, RSC, k1, LSC, k2, RSC, k1, LSC, k3; repeat from * to end.

ROW 27: *K2, RSC, k3, LSC, RSC, k3, LSC, k2; repeat from * to end.

ROW 29: *K1, RSC, k4, RSC, LSC, k4, LSC, k1; repeat from * to end.

ROW 31: *RSC, k4, RSC, k2, LSC, k4, LSC; repeat from * to end.

ROW 32: Repeat Row 2.

Repeat Rows 1–32 for Nestled Diamonds Bottom-Up Flat.

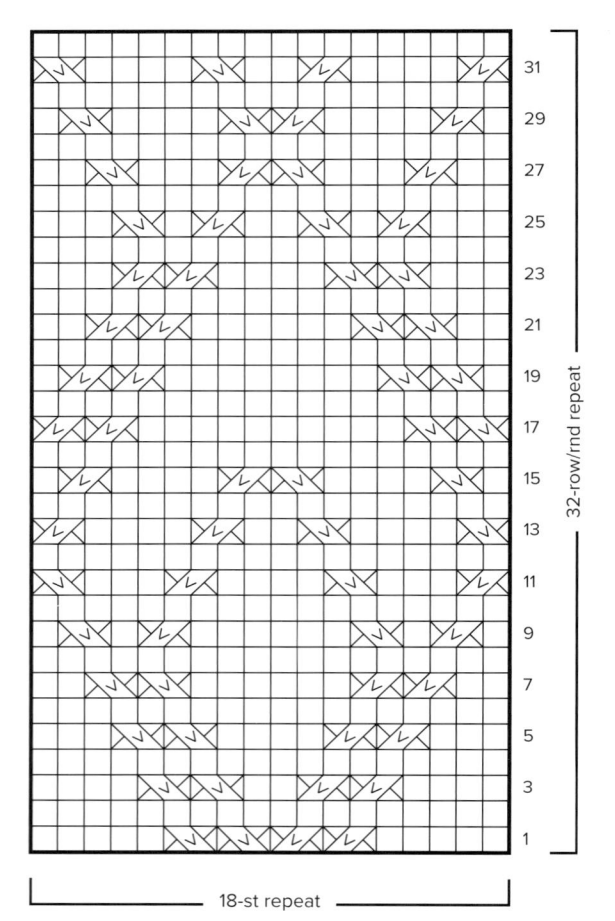

18-st repeat

32-row/rnd repeat

 RSC: Right Slipped Cross. Slip 1 st to cn, hold to back, slip 1, k1 from cn.

LSC: Left Slipped Cross. Slip 1 st to cn, hold to front, k1, slip 1 from cn. To work without a cn, insert needle from back to front between first and second sts and knit into front of second st (leaving st on left-hand needle), slip first st to right-hand needle, then drop second st from left-hand needle.

Nestled Diamonds (CONT'D)

BOTTOM-UP IN THE ROUND

(multiple of 18 sts; 32-rnd repeat)

RSC: Right Slipped Cross (see opposite).
LSC: Left Slipped Cross (see opposite).
RND 1: *K5, [RSC] twice, [LSC] twice, k5; repeat from * to end.
RND 2 AND ALL EVEN-NUMBERED RNDS: Knit.
RND 3: *K4, [RSC] twice, k2, [LSC] twice, k4; repeat from * to end.
RND 5: *K3, [RSC] twice, k4, [LSC] twice, k3; repeat from * to end.
RND 7: *K2, [RSC] twice, k6, [LSC] twice, k2; repeat from * to end.
RND 9: *K1, RSC, k1, LSC, k6, RSC, k1, LSC, k1; repeat from * to end.
RND 11: *RSC, k3, LSC, k4, RSC, k3, LSC; repeat from * to end.
RND 13: *LSC, k4, LSC, k2, RSC, k4, RSC; repeat from * to end.
RND 15: *K1, LSC, k4, LSC, RSC, k4, RSC, k1; repeat from * to end.
RND 17: *[LSC] twice, k10, [RSC] twice; repeat from * to end.
RND 19: *K1, [LSC] twice, k8, [RSC] twice, k1; repeat from * to end.
RND 21: *K2, [LSC] twice, k6, [RSC] twice, k2; repeat from * to end.
RND 23: *K3, [LSC] twice, k4, [RSC] twice, k3; repeat from * to end.
RND 25: *K3, RSC, k1, LSC, k2, RSC, k1, LSC, k3; repeat from * to end.
RND 27: *K2, RSC, k3, LSC, RSC, k3, LSC, k2; repeat from * to end.
RND 29: *K1, RSC, k4, RSC, LSC, k4, LSC, k1; repeat from * to end.
RND 31: *RSC, k4, RSC, k2, LSC, k4, LSC; repeat from * to end.
RND 32: Repeat Rnd 2.
Repeat Rnds 1–32 for Nestled Diamonds Bottom-Up in the Round.

TOP-DOWN FLAT

(multiple of 18 sts; 32-row repeat)

RSC: Right Slipped Cross (see opposite).
LSC: Left Slipped Cross (see opposite).
ROW 1 (RS): *LSC, k4, LSC, k2, RSC, k4, RSC; repeat from * to end.
ROW 2 AND ALL WS ROWS: Purl.
ROW 3: *K1, LSC, k4, LSC, RSC, k4, RSC, k1; repeat from * to end.
ROW 5: *K2, LSC, k3, RSC, LSC, k3, RSC, k2; repeat from * to end.
ROW 7: *K3, LSC, k1, RSC, k2, LSC, k1, RSC, k3; repeat from * to end.
ROW 9: *K3, [RSC] twice, k4, [LSC] twice, k3; repeat from * to end.
ROW 11: *K2, [RSC] twice, k6, [LSC] twice, k2; repeat from * to end.
ROW 13: *K1, [RSC] twice, k8, [LSC] twice, k1; repeat from * to end.
ROW 15: *[RSC] twice, k10, [LSC] twice; repeat from * to end.
ROW 17: *K1, RSC, k4, RSC, LSC, k4, LSC, k1; repeat from * to end.
ROW 19: *RSC, k4, RSC, k2, LSC, k4, LSC; repeat from * to end.
ROW 21: *LSC, k3, RSC, k4, LSC, k3, RSC; repeat from * to end.
ROW 23: *K1, LSC, k1, RSC, k6, LSC, k1, RSC, k1; repeat from * to end.
ROW 25: *K2, [LSC] twice, k6, [RSC] twice, k2; repeat from * to end.
ROW 27: *K3, [LSC] twice, k4, [RSC] twice, k3; repeat from * to end.
ROW 29: *K4, R, [LSC] twice, k2, [RSC] twice, k4; repeat from * to end.
ROW 31: *K5, [LSC] twice, [RSC] twice, k5; repeat from * to end.
ROW 32: Repeat Row 2.
Repeat Rows 1–32 for Nestled Diamonds Top-Down Flat.

TOP-DOWN IN THE ROUND

(multiple of 18 sts; 32-rnd repeat)

RSC: Right Slipped Cross (see below).

LSC: Left Slipped Cross (see below).

RND 1: *LSC, k4, LSC, k2, RSC, k4, RSC; repeat from * to end.

RND 2 AND ALL EVEN-NUMBERED RNDS: Knit.

RND 3: *K1, LSC, k4, LSC, RSC, k4, RSC, k1; repeat from * to end.

RND 5: *K2, LSC, k3, RSC, LSC, k3, RSC, k2; repeat from * to end.

RND 7: *K3, LSC, k1, RSC, k2, LSC, k1, RSC, k3; repeat from * to end.

RND 9: *K3, [RSC] twice, k4, [LSC] twice, k3; repeat from * to end.

RND 11: *K2, [RSC] twice, k6, [LSC] twice, k2; repeat from * to end.

RND 13: *K1, [RSC] twice, k8, [LSC] twice, k1; repeat from * to end.

RND 15: *[RSC] twice, k10, [LSC] twice; repeat from * to end.

RND 17: *K1, RSC, k4, RSC, LSC, k4, LSC, k1; repeat from * to end.

RND 19: *RSC, k4, RSC, k2, LSC, k4, LSC; repeat from * to end.

RND 21: *LSC, k3, RSC, k4, LSC, k3, RSC; repeat from * to end.

RND 23: *K1, LSC, k1, RSC, k6, LSC, k1, RSC, k1; repeat from * to end.

RND 25: *K2, [LSC] twice, k6, [RSC] twice, k2; repeat from * to end.

RND 27: *K3, [LSC] twice, k4, [RSC] twice, k3; repeat from * to end.

RND 29: *K4, R, [LSC] twice, k2, [RSC] twice, k4; repeat from * to end.

RND 31: *K5, [LSC] twice, [RSC] twice, k5; repeat from * to end.

RND 32: Repeat Rnd 2.

Repeat Rnds 1–32 for Nestled Diamonds Top-Down in the Round.

TOP-DOWN FLAT & IN THE ROUND

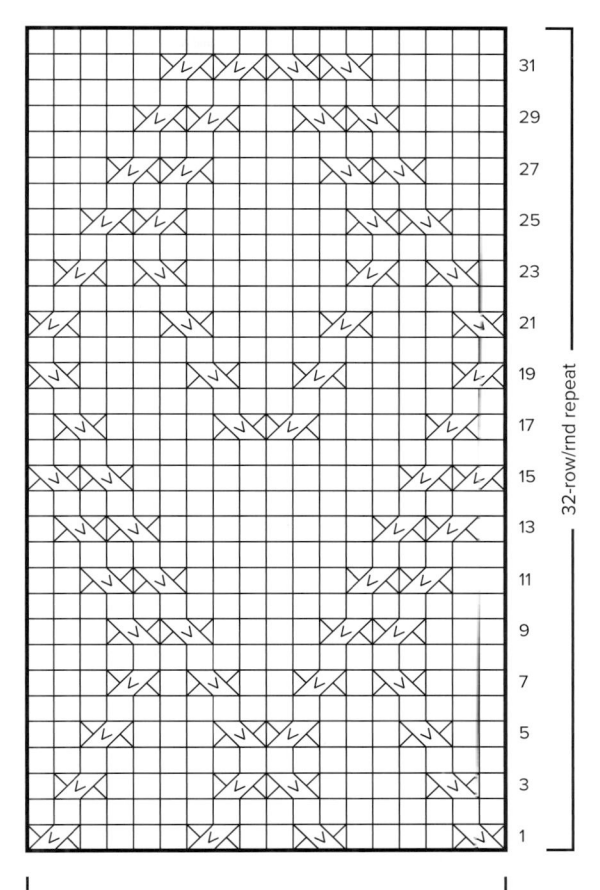

18-st repeat

32-row/rnd repeat

 RSC: Right Slipped Cross. Slip 1 st to cn, hold to back, slip 1, k1 from cn.

LSC: Left Slipped Cross. Slip 1 st to cn, hold to front, k1, slip 1 from cn. To work without a cn, insert needle from back to front between first and second sts and knit into front of second st (leaving st on left-hand needle), slip first st to right-hand needle, then drop second st from left-hand needle.

Climbing Frame

BOTTOM-UP FLAT

(multiple of 10 sts; 4-row repeat)

ROW 1 (RS): Knit.

ROW 2: K4, p2, *k8, p2; repeat from * to last 4 sts, k4.

ROW 3: K3, RC, LC, *k6, RC, LC; repeat from * to last 3 sts, k3.

ROW 4: Purl.

Repeat Rows 1–4 for Climbing Frame Bottom-Up Flat.

BOTTOM-UP FLAT & IN THE ROUND

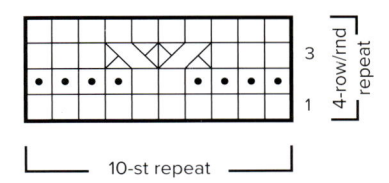

10-st repeat

BOTTOM-UP IN THE ROUND

(multiple of 10 sts; 4-rnd repeat)

RND 1: Knit.

RND 2: P4, k2, *p8, k2; repeat from * to last 4 sts, p4.

RND 3: K3, RC, LC, *k6, RC, LC; repeat from * to last 3 sts, k3.

RND 4: Knit.

Repeat Rnds 1–4 for Climbing Frame Bottom-Up in the Round.

TOP-DOWN FLAT

(multiple of 10 sts; 4-row repeat)

ROW 1 (RS): Knit.

ROW 2: Purl.

ROW 3: K3, *LC, RC, k6; repeat from * to last 7 sts, LC, RC, k3.

ROW 4: K4, *p2, k8; repeat from * to last 6 sts, p2, k4.

Repeat Rows 1–4 for Climbing Frame Top-Down Flat.

TOP-DOWN FLAT

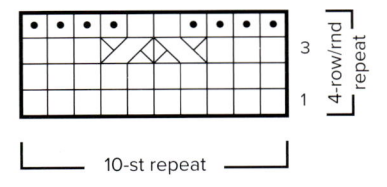

10-st repeat

TOP-DOWN IN THE ROUND

(multiple of 10 sts; 4-rnd repeat)

RNDS 1 AND 2: Knit.

RND 3: K3, LC, RC, *k6, LC, RC; repeat from * to last 3 sts, k3.

RND 4: P4, k2, *p8, k2; repeat from * to last 4 sts, p4.

Repeat Rnds 1–4 for Climbing Frame Top-Down in the Round.

Crossed V-Stitch

BOTTOM-UP FLAT

(panel of 15 sts worked on a background of Rev St st; 14-row repeat)

NOTE: Pattern begins with a WS row.

ROW 1 (WS): K5, p2, k1, p2, k5.

ROW 2: P5, slip 3 sts to cn, hold to back, k2, slip last st from cn back to left-hand needle, p1, k2 from cn, p5.

ROW 3: Repeat Row 1.

ROW 4: P4, 2/1 RC-p, k1, 2/1 LC-p, p4.

ROW 5 AND ALL FOLLOWING WS ROWS: Knit the knit sts and purl the purl sts as they face you.

ROW 6: P3, 2/1 RC-p, k1, p1, k1, 2/1 LC-p, p3.

ROW 8: P2, 2/1 RC-p, [k1, p1] twice, k1, 2/1 LC-p, p2.

ROW 10: P1, 2/1 RC-p, [k1, p1] 3 times, k1, 2/1 LC-p, p1.

ROW 12: 2/1 RC-p, [k1, p1] 4 times, k1, 2/1 LC-p.

ROW 14: K2, p3, k2, p1, k2, p3, k2.

Repeat Rows 1–14 for Crossed V-Stitch Bottom-Up Flat.

BOTTOM-UP FLAT & IN THE ROUND

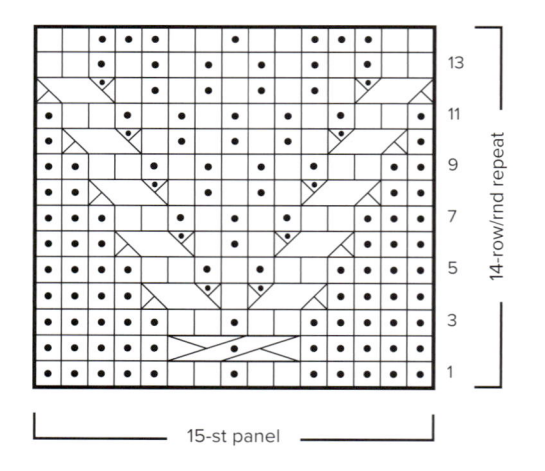

13

11

9

14-row/rnd repeat

7

5

3

1

15-st panel

Note: Flat pattern begins with a WS row.

 Slip 3 sts to cn, hold to back, k2, slip last st from cn back to left-hand needle, p1, k2 from cn.

BOTTOM-UP IN THE ROUND

(panel of 15 sts worked on a background of Rev St st; 14-rnd repeat)

RND 1: P5, k2, p1, k2, p5.

RND 2: P5, slip 3 sts to cn, hold to back, k2, slip last st from cn back to left-hand needle, p1, k2 from cn, p5.

RND 3: Repeat Rnd 1.

RND 4: P4, 2/1 RC-p, k1, 2/1 LC-p, p4.

RND 5 AND ALL FOLLOWING ODD-NUMBERED RNDS: Knit the knit sts and purl the purl sts as they face you.

RND 6: P3, 2/1 RC-p, k1, p1, k1, 2/1 LC-p, p3.

RND 8: P2, 2/1 RC-p, [k1, p1] twice, k1, 2/1 LC-p, p2.

RND 10: P1, 2/1 RC-p, [k1, p1] 3 times, k1, 2/1 LC-p, p1.

RND 12: 2/1 RC-p, [k1, p1] 4 times, k1, 2/1 LC-p.

RND 14: K2, p3, k2, p1, k2, p3, k2.

Repeat Rnds 1–14 for Crossed V-Stitch Bottom-Up in the Round.

TOP-DOWN FLAT

(panel of 15 sts worked on a background of Rev St st; 14-row repeat)

NOTE: Pattern begins with a WS row.

ROW 1 (RS): K2, p3, k2, p1, k2, p3, k2.

ROW 2: P2, [k1, p1] 5 times, k1, p2.

ROW 3: 2/1 LC-p, [k1, p1] 4 times, k1, 2/1 RC-p.

ROW 4: K1, p2, [k1, p1] 4 times, k1, p2, k1.

ROW 5: P1, 2/1 LC-p, [k1, p1] 3 times, k1, 2/1 RC-p, p1.

ROW 6: K2, p2, [k1, p1] 3 times, k1, p2, k2.

ROW 7: P2, 2/1 LC-p, [k1, p1] twice, k1, 2/1 RC-p, p2.

ROW 8: K3, p2, [k1, p1] twice, k1, p2, k3.

ROW 9: P3, 2/1 LC-p, k1, p1, k1, 2/1 RC-p, p3.

ROW 10: K4, p2, k1, p1, k1, p2, k4.

ROW 11: P4, 2/1 LC-p, k1, 2/1 RC-p, p4.

ROW 12: K5, p2, k1, p2, k5.

ROW 13: P5, slip 3 sts to cn, hold to back, k2, slip last st from cn back to left-hand needle, p1, k2, p5.

ROW 14: Repeat Row 12.

Repeat Rows 1–14 for Crossed V-Stitch Top-Down Flat.

TOP-DOWN IN THE ROUND

(panel of 15 sts worked on a background of Rev St st; 14-rnd repeat)

RND 1: K2, p3, k2, p1, k2, p3, k2.

RND 2: K2, [p1, k1] 5 times, p1, k2.

RND 3: 2/1 LC-p, [k1, p1] 4 times, k1, 2/1 RC-p.

RND 4: P1, k2, [p1, k1] 4 times, p1, k2, p1.

RND 5: P1, 2/1 LC-p, [k1, p1] 3 times, k1, 2/1 RC-p, p1.

RND 6: P2, k2, [p1, k1] 3 times, p1, k2, p2.

RND 7: P2, 2/1 LC-p, [k1, p1] twice, k1, 2/1 RC-p, p2.

RND 8: P3, k2, [p1, k1] twice, p1, k2, p3.

RND 9: P3, 2/1 LC-p, k1, p1, k1, 2/1 RC-p, p3.

RND 10: P4, k2, p1, k1, p1, k2, p4.

RND 11: P4, 2/1 LC-p, k1, 2/1 RC-p, p4.

RND 12: P5, k2, p1, k2, p5.

RND 13: P5, slip 3 sts to cn, hold to back, k2, slip last st from cn back to left-hand needle, p1, k2, p5.

RND 14: Repeat Rnd 12.

Repeat Rnds 1–14 for Crossed V-Stitch Top-Down in the Round.

TOP-DOWN FLAT & IN THE ROUND

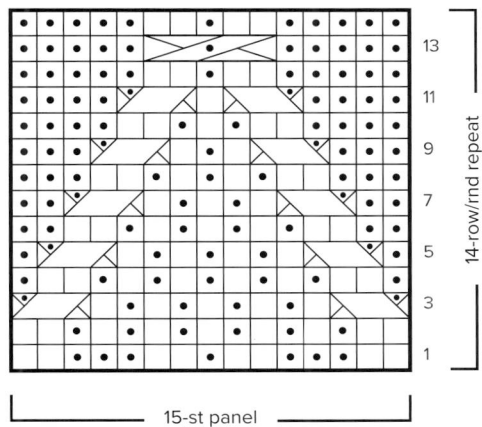

14-row/rnd repeat

15-st panel

Note: Flat pattern begins with a WS row.

 Slip 3 sts to cn, hold to back, k2, slip last st from cn back to left-hand needle, p1, k2 from cn.

Plaited Cable

BOTTOM-UP FLAT

(panel of 15 sts worked on a background of Rev St st; 14-row repeat)

ROW 1 (RS): Knit

ROW 2 AND ALL WS ROWS: Purl.

ROW 3: C10B, k5.

ROWS 5, 7, 9, AND 11: Knit.

ROW 13: K5, C10F.

ROW 14: Purl.

Repeat Rows 1–14 for Plaited Cable Bottom-Up Flat.

BOTTOM-UP IN THE ROUND

(panel of 15 sts worked on a background of Rev St st; 14-rnd repeat)

RNDS 1 AND 2: Knit.

RND 3: C10B, k5.

RNDS 4–12: Knit.

RND 13: K5, C10F.

RND 14: Knit.

Repeat Rnds 1–14 for Plaited Cable Bottom-Up in the Round.

TOP-DOWN FLAT

(panel of 15 sts worked on a background of Rev St st; 14-row repeat)

ROW 1 (RS): Knit

ROW 2 AND ALL WS ROWS: Purl.

ROW 3: C10F, k5.

ROWS 5, 7, 9, AND 11: Knit.

ROW 13: K5, C10B.

ROW 14: Purl.

Repeat Rows 1–14 for Plaited Cable Top-Down Flat.

TOP-DOWN IN THE ROUND

(panel of 15 sts worked on a background of Rev St st; 14-rnd repeat)

RNDS 1 AND 2: Knit.

RND 3: C10F, k5.

RNDS 4–12: Knit.

RND 13: K5, C10B.

RND 14: Knit.

Repeat Rnds 1–14 for Plaited Cable Top-Down in the Round.

BOTTOM-UP FLAT & IN THE ROUND

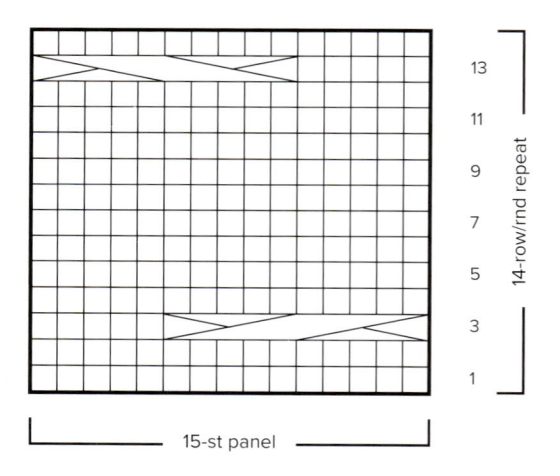

15-st panel

TOP-DOWN FLAT & IN THE ROUND

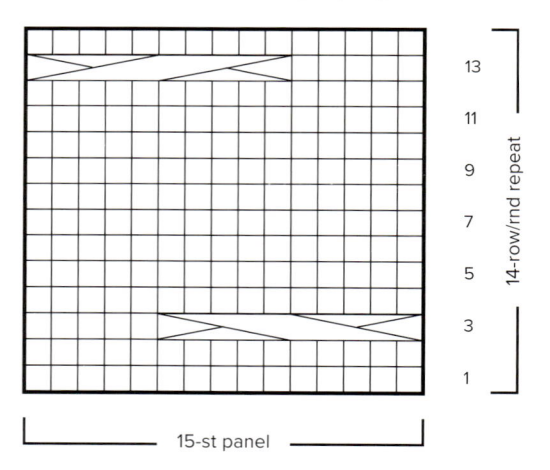

15-st panel

Cable Fabric

FLAT

(multiple of 6 sts; 8-row repeat)

ROW 1 (RS): Knit.

ROW 2 AND ALL WS ROWS: Purl.

ROW 3: *K2, C4B; repeat from * to end.

ROW 5: Knit.

ROW 7: *C4F, k2; repeat from * to end.

ROW 8: Purl.

Repeat Rows 1–8 for Cable Fabric Flat.

IN THE ROUND

(multiple of 6 sts; 8-rnd repeat)

RND 1: Knit.

RND 2 AND ALL EVEN-NUMBERED RNDS: Knit.

RND 3: *K2, C4B; repeat from * to end.

RND 5: Knit.

RND 7: *C4F, k2; repeat from * to end.

RND 8: Knit.

Repeat Rnds 1–8 for Cable Fabric in the Round.

FLAT & IN THE ROUND

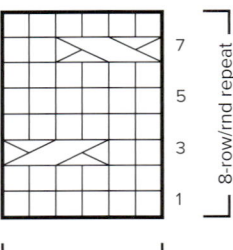

Fractured Lattice

FLAT

(multiple of 8 sts; 8-row repeat)

ROW 1 (RS): *LC, k2, LC, RC; repeat from * to end.

ROW 2 AND ALL WS ROWS: Purl.

ROW 3: K1, *LC, k2, RC, k2; repeat from * to last last 7 sts, LC, k2, RC, k1.

ROW 5: *RC, LC, RC, k2; repeat from * to end.

ROW 7: K3, *LC, k2, RC, k2; repeat from * to last 5 sts, LC, k3.

ROW 8: Purl.

Repeat Rows 1–8 for Fractured Lattice Flat.

FLAT

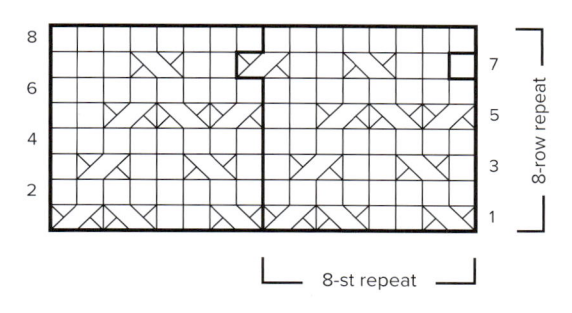

8-row repeat

8-st repeat

IN THE ROUND

(multiple of 8 sts; 8-rnd repeat)

RND 1: *LC, k2, LC, RC; repeat from * to end.

RND 2 AND ALL EVEN-NUMBERED RNDS: Knit.

RND 3: *K1, LC, k2, RC, k2, k1; repeat from * to end.

RND 5: *RC, LC, RC, k2; repeat from * to end.

RND 7: K3, *LC, k2, RC, k2; repeat from * to last 5 sts, LC, k2, work RC on last st of Rnd 7 and first st of Rnd 8, leaving beginning-of-rnd marker in place.

RND 8: Knit.

Repeat Rnds 1–8 for Fractured Lattice in the Round.

IN THE ROUND

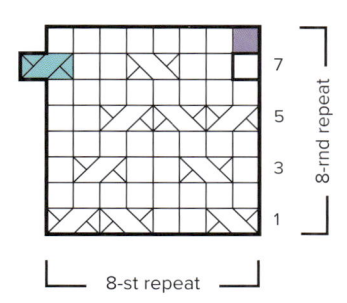

8-rnd repeat

8-st repeat

 On last repeat of Rnd 7, work RC on last st of Rnd 7 and first st of Rnd 8, leaving beginning-of-rnd marker in place.

 On first repeat of Rnd 8, omit this st; it was worked with last st of Rnd 7. Work as knit st on subsequent repeats.

Wheat Cable

BOTTOM-UP FLAT

(panel of 16 sts worked on a background of St st; 16-row repeat)

ROW 1 (RS): K4, C4B, C4F, k4.

ROW 2 AND ALL WS ROWS: Purl.

ROW 3: K2, C4B, k4, C4F, k2.

ROW 5: [C4B] twice, [C4F] twice.

ROW 7: Repeat Row 3.

ROW 9: Repeat Row 5.

ROW 11: Repeat Row 3.

ROW 13: Repeat Row 1.

ROW 15: Knit.

ROW 16: Purl.

Repeat Rows 1–16 for Wheat Cable Bottom-Up Flat.

BOTTOM-UP IN THE ROUND

(panel of 16 sts worked on a background of St st; 16-rnd repeat)

RND 1: K4, C4B, C4F, k4.

RND 2 AND ALL EVEN-NUMBERED RNDS: Knit.

RND 3: K2, C4B, k4, C4F, k2.

RND 5: [C4B] twice, [C4F] twice.

RND 7: Repeat Rnd 3.

RND 9: Repeat Rnd 5.

RND 11: Repeat Rnd 3.

RND 13: Repeat Rnd 1.

RNDS 15 AND 16: Knit.

Repeat Rnds 1–16 for Wheat Cable Bottom-Up in the Round.

TOP-DOWN FLAT

(panel of 16 sts worked on a background of St st; 16-row repeat)

ROW 1 (RS): Knit.

ROW 2 AND ALL WS ROWS: Purl.

ROW 3: K4, C4F, C4B, k4.

ROW 5: K2, C4F, k4, C4B, k2.

ROW 7: [C4F] twice, [C4B] twice.

ROW 9: Repeat Row 5.

ROW 11: Repeat Row 7.

ROW 13: Repeat Row 5.

ROW 15: Repeat Row 3.

ROW 16: Purl.

Repeat Rows 1–16 for Wheat Cable Top-Down Flat.

TOP-DOWN IN THE ROUND

(panel of 16 sts worked on a background of St st; 16-rnd repeat)

RND 1: Knit

RND 2 AND ALL EVEN-NUMBERED RNDS: Knit.

RND 3: K4, C4F, C4B, k4.

RND 5: K2, C4F, k4, C4B, k2.

RND 7: [C4F] twice, [C4B] twice.

RND 9: Repeat Rnd 5.

RND 11: Repeat Rnd 7.

RND 13: Repeat Rnd 5.

RND 15: Repeat Rnd 3.

RND 16: Purl.

Repeat Rnds 1–16 for Wheat Cable Top-Down in the Round.

BOTTOM-UP FLAT & IN THE ROUND

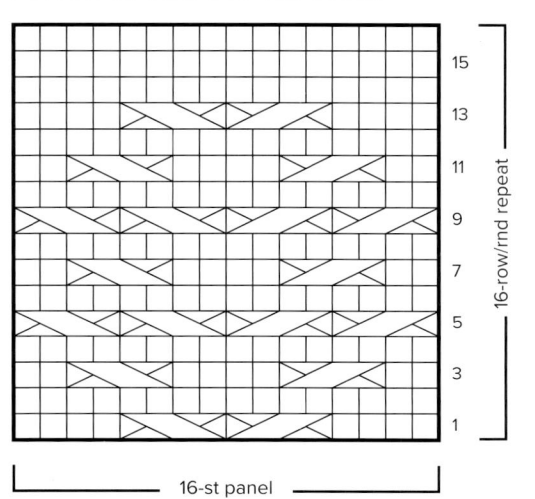

16-row/rnd repeat

16-st panel

TOP-DOWN FLAT & IN THE ROUND

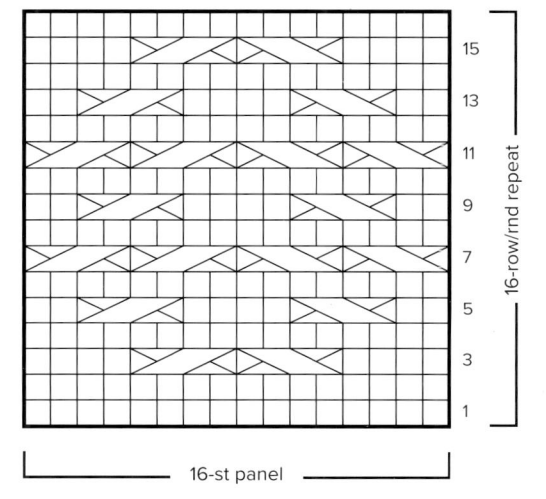

16-row/rnd repeat

16-st panel

Wickerwork Pattern

IN THE ROUND

(multiple of 8 sts; 12-rnd repeat)

RND 1: *K1, p2, k2, p2, k1; repeat from * to end.

RND 2: *K1, p1, RC, LC, p1, k1; repeat from * to end.

RND 3: *K1, p1, k1, p2, k1, p1, k1; repeat from * to end.

RND 4: *K1, RC, p2, LC, k1; repeat from * to end.

RND 5: *K2, p4, k2; repeat from * to end.

RND 6: Knit.

RND 7: *K1, p2, k2, p2, k1; repeat from * to end.

RND 8: *LC, p1, k2, p1, RC; repeat from * to end.

RND 9: *P1, k1, p1, k2, p1, k1, p1; repeat from * to end.

RND 10: *P1, LC, k2, RC, p1; repeat from * to end.

RND 11: *P2, k4, p2; repeat from * to end.

RND 12: Knit.

Repeat Rnds 1–12 for Wickerwork Pattern in the Round.

FLAT

(multiple of 8 sts; 12-row repeat)

NOTE: Pattern begins with a WS row.

ROW 1 (WS): P1, *k2, p2; repeat from * to last 3 sts, k2, p1.

ROW 2: *K1, p1, RC, LC, p1, k1; repeat from * to end.

ROW 3: *P1, k1, p1, k2, p1, k1, p1; repeat from * to end.

ROW 4: *K1, RC, p2, LC, k1; repeat from * to end.

ROW 5: P2, *k4, p4; repeat from * last 6 sts, k4, p2.

ROW 6: Knit.

ROW 7: Repeat Row 1.

ROW 8: *LC, p1, k2, p1, RC; repeat from * to end.

ROW 9: *K1, p1, k1, p2, k1, p1, k1; repeat from * to end.

ROW 10: *P1, LC, k2, RC, p1; repeat from * to end.

ROW 11: K2, *p4, k4; repeat from * to last 6 sts, p4, k2.

ROW 12: Knit.

Repeat Rows 1–12 for Wickerwork Pattern Flat.

FLAT & IN THE ROUND

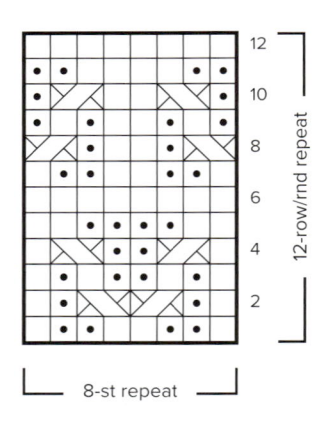

12-row/rnd repeat

8-st repeat

Note: Flat pattern begins with a WS row.

Long and Lean Cables

FLAT

(panel of 9 sts worked on a background of Rev St st; 28-row repeat)

ROW 1 (RS): C4B, p1, C4F.

ROWS 2–4: Knit the knit sts and purl the purl sts as they face you.

ROW 5: C4F, p1, C4B.

ROWS 6–8: Repeat Row 2.

ROW 9: Repeat Row 1.

ROWS 10–24: Repeat Row 2.

ROW 25: Repeat Row 5:

ROWS 26–28: Repeat Row 2.

Repeat Rows 1–28 for Long and Lean Cables Flat.

IN THE ROUND

(panel of 9 sts worked on a background of Rev St st; 28-rnd repeat)

RND 1: C4B, p1, C4F.

RNDS 2–4: K4, p1, k4.

RND 5: C4F, p1, CFB.

RNDS 6–8: Repeat Rnd 2.

RND 9: Repeat Rnd 1.

RNDS 10–24: Repeat Rnd 2.

RND 25: Repeat Rnd 5.

RNDS 26–28: Repeat Rnd 2.

Repeat Rnds 1–28 for Long and Lean Cables in the Round.

FLAT & IN THE ROUND

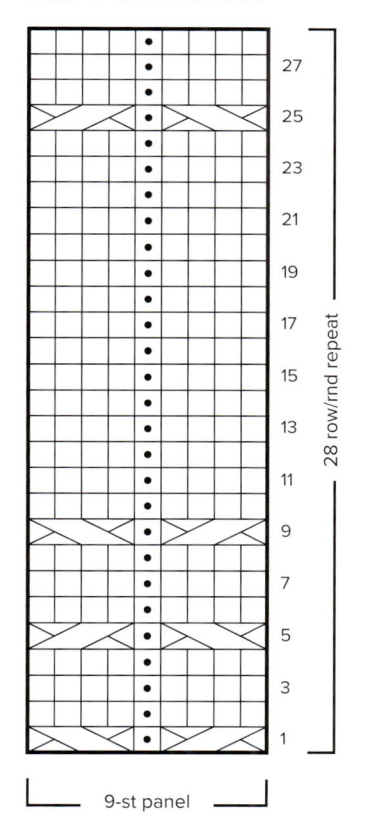

9-st panel

28 row/rnd repeat

Telescope Lattice

BOTTOM-UP FLAT

(multiple of 12 sts + 2; 8-row repeat)

ROW 1 (RS): Knit.

ROW 2 AND ALL WS ROWS: Purl.

ROW 3: K1, *C4B, k4, C4F; repeat from * to last st, k1.

ROW 5: Knit.

ROW 7: K3, *C4F, C4B, k4; repeat from * to last 11 sts, C4F, C4B, k3.

ROW 8: Purl.

Repeat Rows 1–8 for Telescope Lattice Bottom-Up Flat.

BOTTOM-UP FLAT

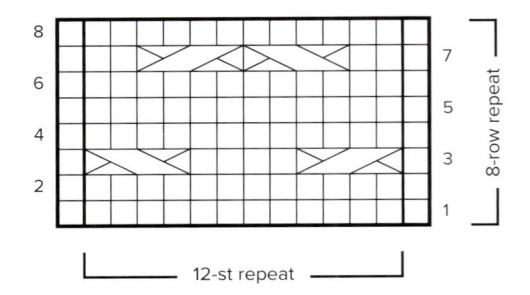

TOP-DOWN FLAT

(multiple of 12 sts + 2; 8-row repeat)

ROW 1 (RS): Knit.

ROW 2 AND ALL WS ROWS: Purl.

ROW 3: K3, *C4B, C4F, k4; repeat from * to last 11 sts, C4B, C4F, k3.

ROW 5: Knit.

ROW 7: K1, *C4F, k4, C4B; repeat from * to last st, k1.

ROW 8: Purl.

Repeat Rows 1–8 for Telescope Lattice Top-Down Flat.

TOP-DOWN FLAT

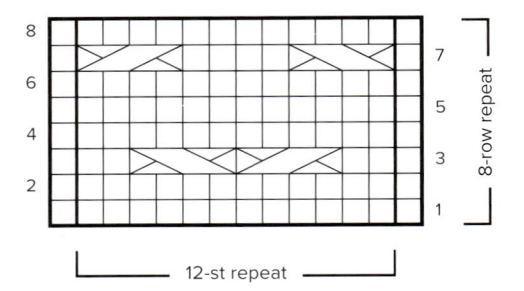

BOTTOM-UP IN THE ROUND

(multiple of 12 sts, 8-rnd repeat)

RNDS 1 AND 2: Knit.

RND 3: *C4B, k4, C4F; repeat from * to end.

RNDS 4–6: Knit.

RND 7: *K2, C4F, C4B, k2; repeat from * to end.

RND 8: Knit.

Repeat Rnds 1–8 for Telescope Lattice Bottom-Up in the Round.

BOTTOM-UP IN THE ROUND

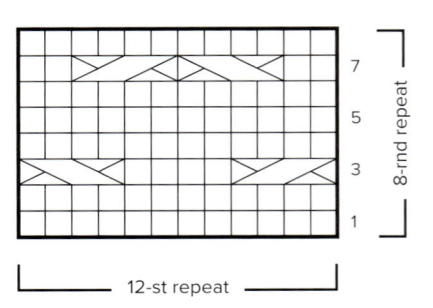

TOP-DOWN IN THE ROUND

(multiple of 12 sts, 8-rnd repeat)

RNDS 1 AND 2: Knit.

RND 3: *K2, C4B, C4F, k2; repeat from * to end.

RNDS 4–6: Knit.

RND 7: *C4F, k4, C4B; repeat from * to end.

RND 8: Knit.

Repeat Rnds 1–8 for Telescope Lattice Top-Down in the Round.

TOP-DOWN IN THE ROUND

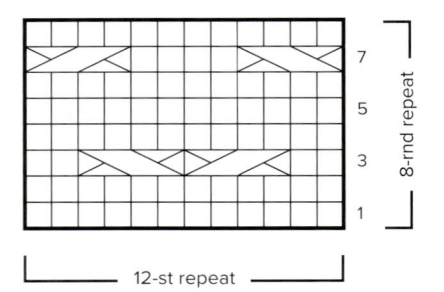

FRONT

BACK

Reversible 4-Stitch Cables (TWO-SIDED)

FLAT

(multiple of 8 sts + 4; 4-row repeat)

C4B-p: Cable 4 Back, purled (see below).

ROW 1 (RS): *K4, C4B-p; repeat from * to last 4 sts, k4.

ROW 2: Knit the knit sts and purl the purl sts as they face you.

ROW 3: *C4F, p4; repeat from * to last 4 sts, C4F.

ROW 4: Repeat Row 2.

Repeat Rows 1–4 for Reversible 4-Stitch Cables Flat.

IN THE ROUND

(multiple of 8 sts; 4-rnd repeat)

C4B-p: Cable 4 Back, purled (see below).

RND 1: *K4, C4B-p; repeat from * to end.

RND 2: *K4, p4; repeat from * to end.

RND 3: *C4F, p4; repeat from * to end.

RND 4: Repeat Rnd 2.

Repeat Rnds 1–4 for Reversible 4-Stitch Cables in the Round.

FLAT

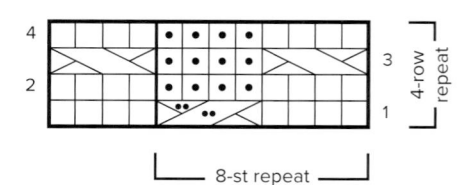

IN THE ROUND

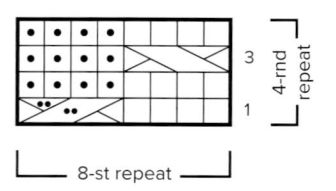

 C4B-p: Cable 4 Back, purled. Slip 2 sts to cn, hold to back, p2, p2 from cn.

Cable Texture

FLAT

(multiple of 6 sts + 2; 6-row repeat)

ROW 1 (RS): Knit.

ROW 2: Purl.

ROW 3: Knit.

ROW 4: K2, *p4, k2; repeat from * to end.

ROW 5: *P2, C4F; repeat from * to last 2 sts, p2.

ROW 6: Purl.

Repeat Rows 1–6 for Cable Texture Flat.

IN THE ROUND

(multiple of 6 sts: 6-rnd repeat)

RNDS 1–3: Knit.

RND 4: *P2, k4; repeat from * to end.

RND 5: *P2, C4F; repeat from * to end.

RND 6: Knit.

Repeat Rnds 1–6 for Cable Texture in the Round.

FLAT

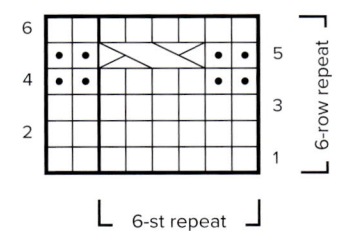

IN THE ROUND

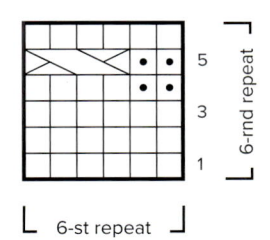

Narrow Cross and Twist

BOTTOM-UP FLAT

(panel of 12 sts worked on a background of Rev St st; 12-row repeat)

ROW 1 (RS): C4F, p4, C4B.

ROW 2 AND ALL WS ROWS: Knit the knit sts and purl the purl sts as they face you.

ROW 3: K2, 2/1 LC-p, p2, 2/1 RC-p, k2.

ROW 5: K2, p1, 2/1 LC-p, 2/1 RC-p, p1, k2.

ROW 7: K2, p2, C4B, p2, k2.

ROW 9: K2, p1, 2/1 RC-p, 2/1 LC-p, p1, k2.

ROW 11: K2, 2/1 RC-p, p2, 2/1 LC-p, k2.

ROW 12: Repeat Row 2.

Repeat Rows 1–12 for Narrow Cross and Twist Bottom-Up Flat.

TOP-DOWN FLAT

(panel of 12 sts worked on a background of Rev St st; 12-row repeat)

ROW 1 (RS): C4B, p4, C4F.

ROW 2: Knit the knit sts and purl the purl sts as they face you.

ROW 3: K2, 2/1 LC-p, p2, 2/1 RC-p, k2.

ROW 5: K2, p1, 2/1 LC-p, 2/1 RC-p, p1, k2.

ROW 7: K2, p2, C4B, p2, k2.

ROW 9: K2, p1, 2/1 RC-p, 2/1 LC-p, p1, k2.

ROW 11: K2, 2/1 RC-p, p2, 2/1 LC-p, k2.

ROW 12: Repeat Row 2.

Repeat Rows 1–12 for Narrow Cross and Twist Top-Down Flat.

BOTTOM-UP IN THE ROUND

(panel of 12 sts worked on a background of Rev St st; 12-rnd repeat)

RND 1: C4F, p4, C4B.

RND 2 AND ALL EVEN-NUMBERED RNDS: Knit the knit sts and purl the purl sts as they face you.

RND 3: K2, 2/1 LC-p, p2, 2/1 RC-p, k2.

RND 5: K2, p1, 2/1 LC-p, 2/1 RC-p, p1, k2.

RND 7: K2, p2, C4B, p2, k2.

RND 9: K2, p1, 2/1 RC-p, 2/1 LC-p, p1, k2.

RND 11: K2, 2/1 RC-p, p2, 2/1 LC-p, k2.

RND 12: Repeat Rnd 2.

Repeat Rnds 1–12 for Narrow Cross and Twist Bottom-Up in the Round.

TOP-DOWN IN THE ROUND

(panel of 12 sts worked on a background of Rev St st; 12-rnd repeat)

RND 1: C4B, p4, C4F.

RND 2: Knit the knit sts and purl the purl sts as they face you.

RND 3: K2, 2/1 LC-p, p2, 2/1 RC-p, k2.

RND 5: K2, p1, 2/1 LC-p, 2/1 RC-p, p1, k2.

RND 7: K2, p2, C4B, p2, k2.

RND 9: K2, p1, 2/1 RC-p, 2/1 LC-p, p1, k2.

RND 11: K2, 2/1 RC-p, p2, 2/1 LC-p, k2.

RND 12: Repeat Rnd 2.

Repeat Rnds 1–12 for Narrow Cross and Twist Top-Down in the Round.

BOTTOM-UP FLAT & IN THE ROUND

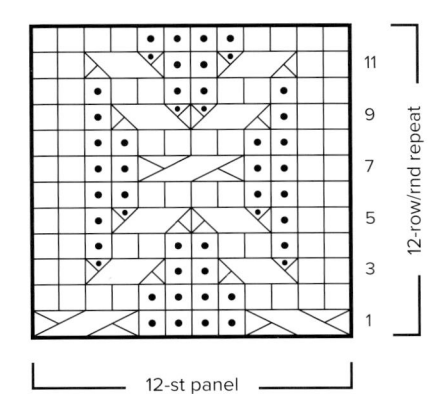

12-row/rnd repeat

12-st panel

TOP-DOWN FLAT & IN THE ROUND

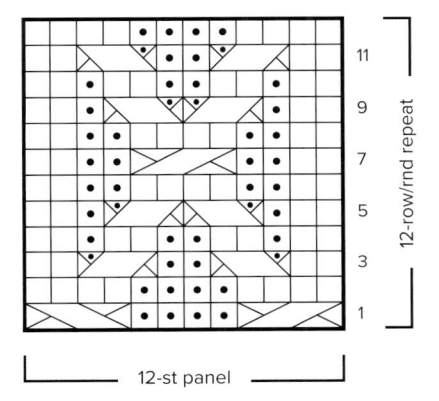

12-row/rnd repeat

12-st panel

Sausage Cable

FLAT

(panel of 8 sts worked on a background of Rev St st; 20-row repeat)

NOTE: You will decrease 2 sts on Rows 11 and 13; original st count is restored on Rows 17 and 19.

ROW 1 (RS): K2, C4F, k2.

ROW 2 AND ALL WS ROWS: Purl.

ROW 3: Knit.

ROW 5: Repeat Row 1.

ROW 7: Repeat Row 3.

ROW 9: Repeat Row 1.

ROW 11: K2, k2tog, ssk, k2.

ROW 13: K1, ssk, k2tog, k1.

ROW 15: C4B.

ROW 17: K1, M1-l, k2, M1-l, k1.

ROW 19: [K2, M1-l] twice, k2.

ROW 20: Purl.

Repeat Rows 1–20 for Sausage Cable Flat.

IN THE ROUND

(panel of 8 sts worked on a background of Rev St st; 20-rnd repeat)

NOTE: You will decrease 2 sts on Rnds 11 and 13; original st count is restored on Rnds 17 and 19.

RND 1: K2, C4F, k2.

RND 2 AND ALL EVEN-NUMBERED RNDS: Purl.

RND 3: Knit.

RND 5: Repeat Rnd 1.

RND 7: Repeat Rnd 3.

RND 9: Repeat Rnd 1.

RND 11: K2, k2tog, ssk, k2.

RND 13: K1, ssk, k2tog, k1.

RND 15: C4B.

RND 17: K1, M1-l, k2, M1-l, k1.

RND 19: [K2, M1-l] twice, k2.

RND 20: Purl.

Repeat Rnds 1–20 for Sausage Cable in the Round.

FLAT & IN THE ROUND

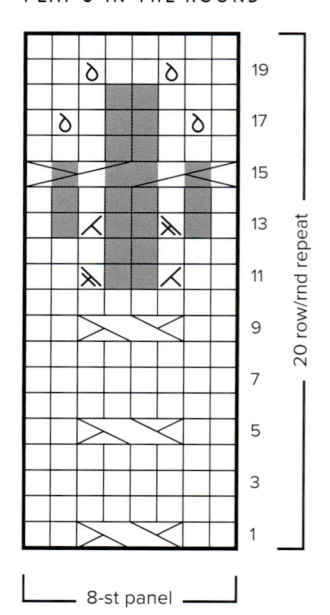

8-st panel

20 row/rnd repeat

C4B

Round Cable

FLAT

(panel of 8 sts worked on a background of Rev St st; 12-row repeat)

2/2 RC-p: 2 over 2 Right Cross, purled (see below).
2/2 LC-p: 2 over 2 Left Cross, purled (see below).
ROW 1 (RS): P2, k4, p2.
ROWS 2-4: Knit the knit sts and purl the purl sts as they face you.
ROW 5: 2/2 RC-p, 2/2 LC-p.
ROWS 6-10: Repeat Row 2.
ROW 11: 2/2 LC-p, 2/2 RC-p.
ROW 12: Repeat Row 2.
Repeat Rows 1–12 for Round Cable Flat.

IN THE ROUND

(panel of 8 sts worked on a background of Rev St st; 12-rnd repeat)

2/2 RC-p: 2 over 2 Right Cross, purled (see below).
2/2 LC-p: 2 over 2 Left Cross, purled (see below).
RNDS 1-4: P2, k4, p2.
RND 5: 2/2 RC-p, 2/2 LC-p.
RNDS 6-10: K2, p4, k2.
RND 11: 2/2 LC-p, 2/2 RC-p.
RND 12: Repeat Rnd 1.
Repeat Rnds 1–12 for Round Cable in the Round.

FLAT & IN THE ROUND

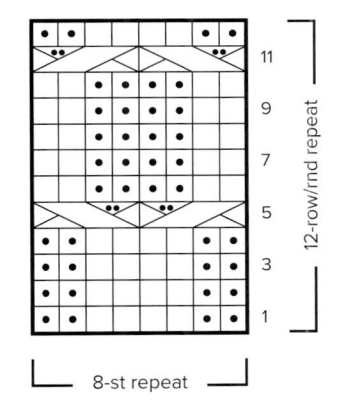

12-row/rnd repeat

8-st repeat

 **2/2 RC-p:** 2 over 2 Right Cross, purled. Slip 2 sts to cn, hold to back, k2, p2 from

 **2/2 LC-p:** 2 over 2 Left Cross, purled. Slip 2 sts to cn, hold to front, p2, k2 from cn.

Folded Cable

BOTTOM-UP FLAT

(panel of 6 sts worked on a background of Rev St st; 12-row repeat)

ROW 1 (RS): Knit.

ROW 2 AND ALL WS ROWS: Purl.

ROW 3: Knit.

ROWS 5, 7, AND 9: 1/2 LC, 1/2 RC.

ROW 11: Knit.

ROW 12: Purl.

Repeat Rows 1–12 for Folded Cable Bottom-Up Flat.

TOP-DOWN FLAT

(panel of 6 sts worked on a background of Rev St st; 12-row repeat)

ROW 1 (RS): Knit.

ROW 2 AND ALL WS ROWS: Purl.

ROW 3: Knit.

ROWS 5, 7, AND 9: 1/2 RC, 1/2 LC.

ROW 11: Knit.

ROW 12: Purl.

Repeat Rows 1–12 for Folded Cable Top-Down Flat.

BOTTOM-UP IN THE ROUND

(panel of 6 sts worked on a background of Rev St st; 12-rnd repeat)

RNDS 1–4: Knit.

RND 5: 1/2 LC, 1/2 RC.

RND 6: Knit.

RNDS 7–10: Repeat Rnds 5 and 6.

RNDS 11 AND 12: Knit.

Repeat Rnds 1–12 for Folded Cable Bottom-Up in the Round.

TOP-DOWN IN THE ROUND

(panel of 6 sts worked on a background of Rev St st; 12-rnd repeat)

RNDS 1–4: Knit.

RND 5: 1/2 RC, 1/2 LC.

RND 6: Knit.

RNDS 7–10: Repeat Rnds 5 and 6.

RNDS 11 AND 12: Knit.

Repeat Rnds 1–12 for Folded Cable Top-Down in the Round.

BOTTOM-UP FLAT & IN THE ROUND

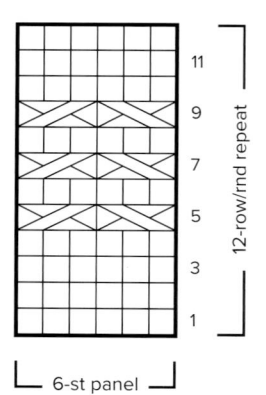

6-st panel

TOP-DOWN FLAT & IN THE ROUND

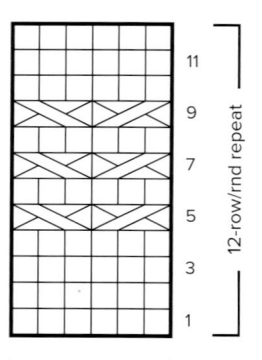

6-st panel

Gull Stitch

BOTTOM-UP FLAT

(panel of 6 sts worked on a background of Rev St st; 4-row repeat)

ROW 1 (RS): K2, slip 2 wyib, k2.

ROW 2: P2, slip 2 wyif, p2.

ROW 3: 1/2 RC, 1/2 LC.

ROW 4: Purl.

Repeat Rows 1–4 for Gull Stitch Bottom-Up Flat.

TOP-DOWN FLAT

(panel of 6 sts worked on a background of Rev St st; 4-row repeat)

ROW 1 (RS): K2, slip 2 wyib, k2.

ROW 2: P2, slip 2 wyif, p2.

ROW 3: 1/2 LC, 1/2 RC.

ROW 4: Purl.

Repeat Rows 1–4 for Gull Stitch Top-Down Flat.

BOTTOM-UP IN THE ROUND

(panel of 6 sts on a background of Rev St st; 4-rnd repeat)

RNDS 1 AND 2: K2, slip 2 wyib, k2.

RND 3: 1/2 RC, 1/2 LC.

RND 4: Knit.

Repeat Rnds 1–4 for Gull Stitch Bottom-Up in the Round.

TOP-DOWN IN THE ROUND

(panel of 6 sts on a background of Rev St st; 4-rnd repeat)

RNDS 1 AND 2: K2, slip 2 wyib, k2.

RND 3: 1/2 LC, 1/2 RC.

RND 4: Knit.

Repeat Rnds 1–4 for Gull Stitch Top-Down in the Round.

BOTTOM-UP FLAT & IN THE ROUND

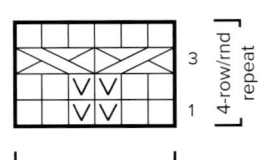

TOP-DOWN FLAT & IN THE ROUND

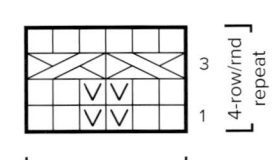

Stacked Cables

FLAT

(panel of 12 sts worked on a background of Rev St st; 12-row repeat)

ROW 1 (RS): C6B, C6F.

ROW 2 AND ALL WS ROWS: Purl.

ROWS 3, 5, 7, AND 9: K4, yo, k2tog, ssk, yo, k4.

ROW 11: Knit.

ROW 12: Purl.

Repeat Rows 1–12 for Stacked Cables Flat.

IN THE ROUND

(panel of 12 sts worked on a background of Rev St st; 12-rnd repeat)

RND 1: C6B, C6F.

RND 2 AND ALL EVEN-NUMBERED RNDS: Knit.

RNDS 3, 5, 7, AND 9: K4, yo, k2tog, ssk, yo, k4.

RNDS 11 AND 12: Knit.

Repeat Rnds 1–12 for Stacked Cables in the Round.

FLAT & IN THE ROUND

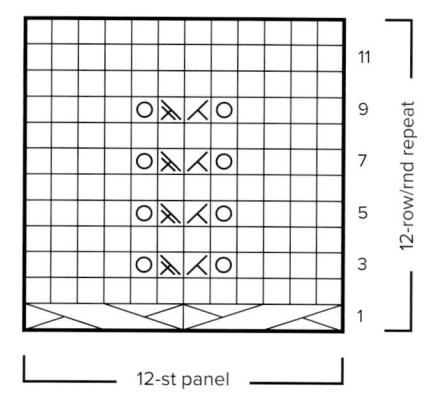

Cable and Ladder

BOTTOM-UP FLAT

(multiple of 14 sts + 1; 8-row repeat)
ROW 1 (RS): K1, *ssk, yo, k12; repeat from * to end.
ROW 2 AND ALL WS ROWS: K1, *p2tog, yo, p11, k1;
repeat from * to end.
ROW 3: K1, *ssk, yo, C6B, k6; repeat from * to end.
ROW 5: Repeat Row 1.
ROW 7: K1, *ssk, yo, k3, C6F, k3; repeat from * to end.
ROW 8: Repeat Row 2.
Repeat Rows 1–8 for Cable and Ladder Bottom-Up Flat.

BOTTOM-UP FLAT

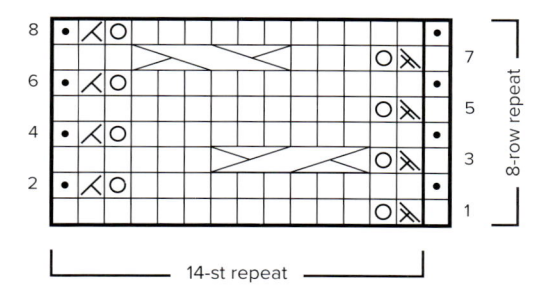

14-st repeat · 8-row repeat

TOP-DOWN FLAT

(multiple of 14 sts + 1; 8-row repeat)
ROW 1 (RS): *K12, yo, ssk; repeat from * to last st, k1.
ROW 2 AND ALL WS ROWS: K1, *p11, yo, p2tog, k1;
repeat from * to end.
ROW 3: *K3, C6F, k3, yo, ssk; repeat from * to last st,
k1.
ROW 5: Repeat Row 1.
ROW 7: *K6, C6B, yo, ssk; repeat from * to last st, k1.
ROW 8: Repeat Row 2.
Repeat Rows 1–8 for Cable and Ladder Top-Down Flat.

TOP-DOWN FLAT

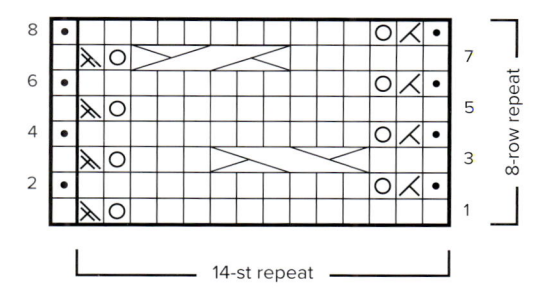

14-st repeat · 8-row repeat

BOTTOM-UP IN THE ROUND

(multiple of 14 sts; 8-rnd repeat)
RND 1: *K1, ssk, yo, k11; repeat from * to end.
RND 2 AND ALL EVEN-NUMBERED RNDS: *P1, k11, yo,
k2tog; repeat from * to end.
RND 3: *K1, ssk, yo, C6B, k5; repeat from * to end.
RND 5: Repeat Rnd 1.
RND 7: *K1, ssk, yo, k3, C6F, k2; repeat from * to end.
RND 8: Repeat Rnd 2.
Repeat Rnds 1–8 for Cable and Ladder Bottom-Up in the
Round.

BOTTOM-UP IN THE ROUND

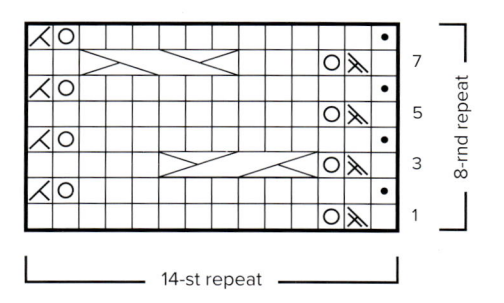

14-st repeat · 8-rnd repeat

TOP-DOWN IN THE ROUND

(multiple of 14 sts; 8-rnd repeat)
RND 1 (RS): *K12, yo, ssk; repeat from * end.
RND 2 AND ALL EVEN-NUMBERED RNDS: *P1, k2tog,
yo, p11; repeat from * to end.
RND 3: *K3, C6F, k3, yo, ssk; repeat from * to end.
RND 5: Repeat Rnd 1.
RND 7: *K6, C6B, yo, ssk; repeat from * to end.
RND 8: Repeat Rnd 2.
Repeat Rnds 1–8 for Cable and Ladder Top-Down in the
Round.

TOP-DOWN IN THE ROUND

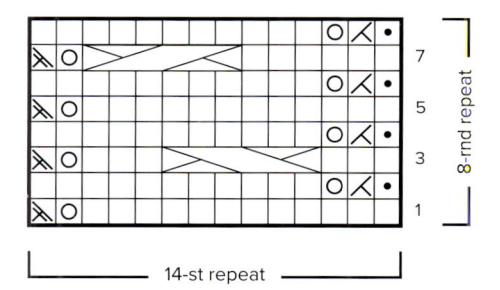

14-st repeat · 8-rnd repeat

Knotted Cable

FLAT

(panel of 6 sts worked on a background of Rev St st; 10-row repeat)

2/2/2 CC: 2 over 2 over 2 Centered Cross (see below).

ROW 1 (RS): K2, p2, k2.

ROW 2: Knit the knit sts and purl the purl sts as they face you.

ROW 3: 2/2/2 CC.

ROWS 4–10: Repeat Row 2.

Repeat Rows 1–10 for Knotted Cable Flat.

IN THE ROUND

(panel of 6 sts worked on a background of Rev St st; 10-rnd repeat)

2/2/2 CC: 2 over 2 over 2 Centered Cross (see below).

RNDS 1 AND 2: K2, p2, k2.

RND 3: 2/2/2 CC.

RNDS 4–10: Repeat Rnd 1.

Repeat Rnds 1–10 for Knotted Cable in the Round.

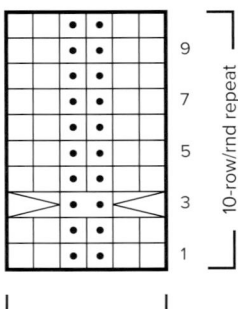

6-st panel

10-row/rnd repeat

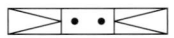

2/2/2 CC: 2 over 2 over 2 Centered Cross. Slip next 4 sts to cn, hold to front, k2 sts from left-hand needle, slip 2 purl sts from cn back to left-hand needle, pass cn with 2 remaining knit sts to back of work, p2 from left-hand needle, then k2 from cn.

Claw Pattern

BOTTOM-UP FLAT

(panel of 8 sts worked on a background of Rev St st;
4-row repeat)

ROW 1 (RS): Knit.

ROW 2: Purl.

ROW 3: C4F, C4B.

ROW 4: Purl.

Repeat Rows 1–4 for Claw Pattern Bottom-Up Flat.

BOTTOM-UP IN THE ROUND

(panel of 8 sts worked on a background of Rev St st;
4-rnd repeat)

RNDS 1 AND 2: Knit.

RND 3: C4F, C4B.

RND 4: Knit.

Repeat Rnds 1–4 for Claw Pattern Bottom-Up in the
Round.

BOTTOM-UP FLAT & IN THE ROUND

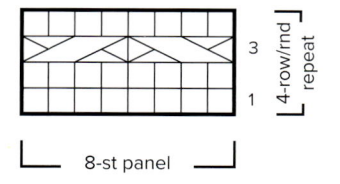

8-st panel

TOP-DOWN FLAT

(panel of 8 sts worked on a background of Rev St st;
4-row repeat)

ROW 1 (RS): Knit.

ROW 2: Purl.

ROW 3: C4B, C4F.

ROW 4: Purl.

Repeat Rows 1–4 for Claw Pattern Top-Down Flat.

TOP-DOWN FLAT & IN THE ROUND

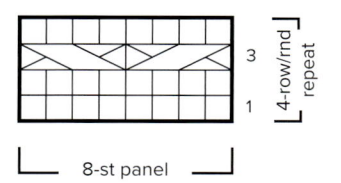

8-st panel

TOP-DOWN IN THE ROUND

(panel of 8 sts worked on a background of Rev St st;
4-rnd repeat)

RNDS 1 AND 2: Knit.

RND 3: C4B, C4F.

RND 4: Knit.

Repeat Rnds 1–4 for Claw Pattern Top-Down in the
Round.

12-Stitch Plait

BOTTOM-UP FLAT

(panel of 12 sts worked on a background of Rev St st; 12-row repeat)

ROW 1 (RS): Knit.
ROW 2 AND ALL WS ROWS: Purl.
ROW 3: C8F, k4.
ROWS 5 AND 7: Knit.
ROW 9: K4, C8B.
ROW 11: Knit.
ROW 12: Purl.
Repeat Rows 1–12 for 12-Stitch Plait Bottom-Up Flat.

TOP-DOWN FLAT

(panel of 12 sts worked on a background of Rev St st; 12-row repeat)

ROW 1 (RS): Knit.
ROW 2 AND ALL WS ROWS: Purl.
ROW 3: C8B, k4.
ROWS 5 AND 7: Knit.
ROW 9: K4, C8F.
ROW 11: Knit.
ROW 12: Purl.
Repeat Rows 1–12 for 12-Stitch Plait Top-Down Flat.

BOTTOM-UP IN THE ROUND

(panel of 12 sts worked on a background of Rev St st; 12-rnd repeat)

RNDS 1 AND 2: Knit.
RND 3: C8F, k4.
RNDS 4–8: Knit.
RND 9: K4, C8B.
RNDS 10–12: Knit.
Repeat Rnds 1–12 for 12-Stitch Plait Bottom-Up in the Round.

TOP-DOWN IN THE ROUND

(panel of 12 sts worked on a background of Rev St st; 12-rnd repeat)

RNDS 1 AND 2: Knit.
RND 3: C8B, k4.
RNDS 4–8: Knit.
RND 9: K4, C8F.
RNDS 10–12: Knit.
Repeat Rnds 1–12 for 12-Stitch Plait Top-Down in the Round.

BOTTOM-UP FLAT & IN THE ROUND

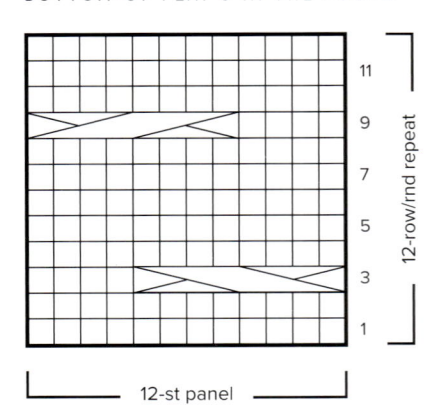

12-st panel

TOP-DOWN FLAT & IN THE ROUND

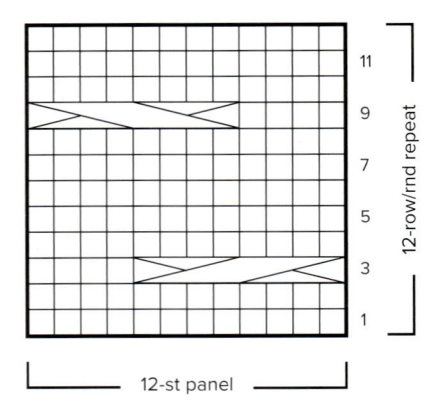

12-st panel

Woven Taffy Toque

You can work caps from the top down or from the bottom up. In this case, I designed this hat to be worked from the bottom up to the crown. Why? I felt I needed to get comfortable with the cables before I decided how to incorporate the crown shaping. Caps like this are a fun and quick knit—try your hand at this one and see if you can sub other cables on the fly.

SIZE
To fit average adult

FINISHED MEASUREMENTS
Approximately 20" (51 cm) circumference x 10½" (26.5 cm) tall

YARN
Blue Sky Alpacas Worsted Hand Dyes (50% royal alpaca / 50% merino; 100 yards / 100 grams): 2 hanks #2008 Light Pink

NEEDLES
One set of five double-pointed needles size US 9 (5.5 mm)

One 16" (40.5 cm) long circular needle size US 8 (5 mm)

One 16" (40.5 cm) long circular needle size US 9 (5.5 mm)

Change needle size if necessary to obtain correct gauge.

NOTIONS
Stitch markers (including 1 in unique color for beginning of rnd); cable needle

GAUGE
19 sts and 30 rows = 4" (10 cm) in Cable Fabric, using larger needles, washed and blocked

STITCH PATTERNS

Rib Pattern
(multiple of 6 sts; 1-rnd repeat)
ALL RNDS: K2, *p2, k4; repeat from * to last 4 sts, p2, k2.

Cable Fabric
(multiple of 6 sts; 8-rnd repeat)
RND 1: *K2, C4B; repeat from * to end.
RND 2 AND ALL EVEN-NUMBERED RNDS: Knit.
RND 3: Knit.
RND 5: *C4F, k2; repeat from * to end.
RNDS 7 AND 8: Knit.
Repeat Rnds 1–8 for Cable Fabric.

TOQUE

Using smaller circular needle, CO 96 sts. Join for working in the rnd, being careful not to twist sts; pm in unique color for beginning of rnd. Begin Rib Pattern; work even for 10 rnds.

Change to larger circular needle and Cable Fabric. Work Rnds 1–8 four times, then Rnds 1–5 once. Piece should measure approximately 6¾" (17 cm) from the beginning.

CABLE FABRIC

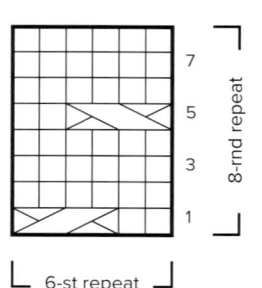

6-st repeat

SHAPE CROWN

NOTE: Change to dpns when necessary for number of sts on needle.
RND 1: [Ssk, k4, pm, k6, pm] 8 times, omitting final pm—88 sts remain.
RND 2: Knit.
RND 3: *C4F, k1, sm, C4F, k2, sm; repeat from * to end.
RND 4: *K5, sm, ssk, k4, sm; repeat from * to end—80 sts remain.
RND 5: Knit.
RND 6: *C4F, k1, sm; repeat from * to end.
RND 7: *K3, ssk, sm, k5, sm; repeat from * to end—72 sts remain.
RND 8: Knit.
RND 9: *C4F, sm, C4F, k1, sm; repeat from * to end.
RND 10: *K4, sm, k3, ssk, sm; repeat from * to end—64 sts remain.
RND 11: *K4, remove marker, k4, sm; repeat from * to end. There are now 8 remaining sections with 8 sts in each section.
RND 12: *K3, LC, k1, ssk; repeat from * to end—56 sts remain.
RND 13: *K4, LC, k1, sm; repeat from * to end.
RND 14: *Knit to 2 sts before marker, ssk, sm; repeat from * to end—48 sts remain.
RND 15: Knit.
RNDS 16–23: Repeat Rnds 14 and 15, removing markers on final rnd—16 sts remain.
Cut yarn, thread tail through remaining sts, pull tight, and fasten off to WS. Block as desired.

CHAPTER 5

LACE

MANY KNITTERS ADMIRE lace knitting but put off learning how to make it themselves because of the perceived difficulty. This is a shame because knitting lace is much simpler than it appears! In fact, I find most lace patterns to be easier than cables, and only very few are what I'd consider difficult. In this chapter, I've included lace patterns that have alternating "working" rows and "resting" rows (where all you have to do is purl or knit), knitted lace where all rows or rounds have patterning, lace panels, and patterns that are composed of eyelets only. If you're concerned that you may make a mistake in your knitting, take out a little knitter's insurance by adding a "lifeline." To create a lifeline, thread a length of dental floss or any smooth yarn that is finer than the one you're using for your project through a tapestry needle and run it through all the loops on your knitting needle after you have completed a row or round (if possible, a "resting" row or round). Then, if you make a mistake that you can't correct in place, all you have to do is unravel down to the lifeline, put the stitches back on the needle, and start over from there. Most knitters who like to use lifelines insert a new one after they've completed a vertical repeat of their stitch pattern and remove the one below it after the new one is secured. **x x**

STITCHES

FEATHER AND FAN
CROSSHATCH LACE
FERN GROTTO LACE
PARACHUTE LACE
QUADRUPLE DIAMOND
  LACE
BRICKLAYER'S LACE
LUCINA SHELL LACE
MILADY'S FAN
FISH SCALE LACE
PAGODA LACE
GOTHIC ARCHES
ENGLISH LACE
FAGGOTING AND FANCY
  RIB
MINIATURE LEAVES
GATE PATTERN

CABLE TWIST LACE
KIMONO LACE
WAVY LACE
OSTRICH PLUMES
PINECONE LADDER
FLORAL MESH LACE
YARN-OVER CABLE
JAPANESE FOLIAGE
VERTICAL OPENWORK
  STRIPES
TRAVELING RIBEED
  EYELETS
SHETLAND EYELETS
HERRINGBONE LACE

PROJECT

BLOSSOM CAMI

Feather and Fan

FLAT

(multiple of 17 sts; 4-row repeat)

ROW 1 (RS): Knit.

ROW 2: Purl.

ROW 3: *[K2tog] 3 times, [yo, k1] 5 times, yo, [ssk] 3 times; repeat from * to end.

ROW 4: Knit.

Repeat Rows 1–4 for Feather and Fan Flat.

IN THE ROUND

(multiple of 17 sts; 4-rnd repeat)

RNDS 1 AND 2: Knit.

RND 3: *[K2tog] 3 times, [yo, k1] 5 times, yo, [ssk] 3 times; repeat from * to end.

RND 4: Purl.

Repeat Rnds 1–4 for Feather and Fan in the Round.

FLAT & IN THE ROUND

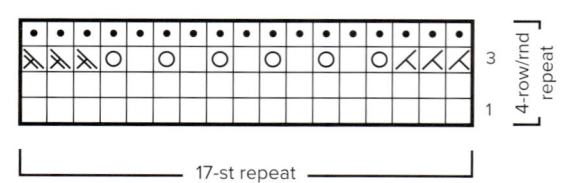

Crosshatch Lace

FLAT

(multiple of 10 sts + 2; 10-row repeat)

ROW 1 (RS): *K8, k2tog, yo; repeat from * to last 2 sts, k2.

ROW 2: P3, *yo, p2tog, p8; repeat from * to last 9 sts, yo, p2tog, p7.

ROW 3: K6, *k2tog, yo, k8; repeat from * to last 6 sts, k2tog, yo, k4.

ROW 4: P5, *yo, p2tog, p8; repeat from * to last 7 sts, yo, p2tog, p5.

ROW 5: K1, *yo, ssk, k1, k2tog, yo, k5; repeat from * to last st, k1.

ROW 6: *P8, ssp, yo; repeat from * to last 2 sts, p2.

ROW 7: K3, *yo, ssk, k8; repeat from * to last 9 sts, yo, ssk, k7.

ROW 8: P6, *ssp, yo, p8; repeat from * to last 6 sts, ssp, yo, p4.

ROW 9: K5, *yo, ssk, k8; repeat from * to last 7 sts, yo, ssk, k5.

ROW 10: P1, *yo, p2tog, p1, ssp, yo, p5; repeat from * to last st, p1.

Repeat Rows 1–10 for Cross Hatch Lace Flat.

IN THE ROUND

(multiple of 10 sts; 10-rnd repeat)

RND 1: K7, *k2tog, yo, k8; repeat from * to last 3 sts, k2tog, yo, k1.

RND 2: K6, *k2tog, yo, k8; repeat from * to last 4 sts, k2tog, yo, k2.

RND 3: K5, *k2tog, yo, k8; repeat from * to last 5 sts, k2tog, yo, k3.

RND 4: K4, *k2tog, yo, k8; repeat from * to last 6 sts, k2tog, yo, k4.

RND 5: *Yo, ssk, k1, k2tog, yo, k5; repeat from * to end.

RND 6: K1, *yo, ssk, k8; repeat from * to last 9 sts, yo, ssk, k7.

RND 7: K2, *yo, ssk, k8; repeat from * to last 8 sts, yo, ssk, k6.

RND 8: K3, *yo, ssk, k8; repeat from * to last 7 sts, yo, ssk, k5.

RND 9: K4, *yo, ssk, k8; repeat from * to last 6 sts, yo, ssk, k4.

RND 10: *K5, yo, ssk, k1, k2tog, yo; repeat from * to end.

Repeat Rnds 1–10 for Cross Hatch Lace in the Round.

FLAT

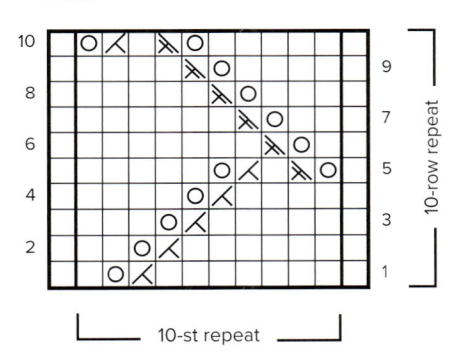

IN THE ROUND

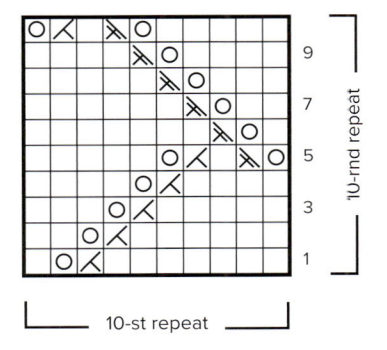

Fern Grotto Lace

BOTTOM-UP FLAT

(panel of 21 sts + 1 worked on a background of St st; 6-row repeat)

ROW 1 (RS): *K1, yo, k3, ssk, k10, k2tog, k3, yo; repeat from * to last st, k1.

ROW 2: P1, *p1, yo, p3, p2tog, p8, ssp, p3, yo, p2; repeat from * to end.

ROW 3: *K3, yo, k3, ssk, k6, k2tog, k3, yo, k2; repeat from * to last st, k1.

ROW 4: P1, *p3, yo, p3, p2tog, p4, ssp, p3, yo, p4; repeat from * to end.

ROW 5: *K5, yo, k3, ssk, k2, k2tog, k3, yo, k4; repeat from * to last st, k1.

ROW 6: P1, *p5, yo, p3, p2tog, ssp, p3, yo, p6; repeat from * to end.

Repeat Rows 1–6 for Fern Grotto Lace Bottom-Up Flat.

BOTTOM-UP FLAT

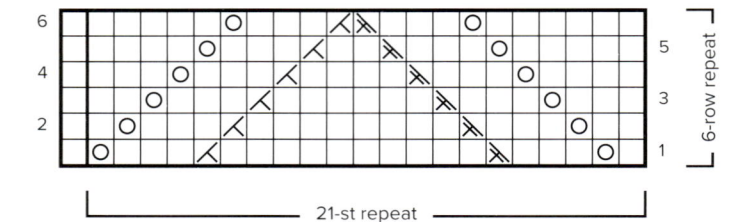

BOTTOM-UP IN THE ROUND

(panel of 21 sts worked on a background of St st; ; 6-rnd repeat)

RND 1: *K1, yo, k3, ssk, k10, k2tog, k3, yo; repeat from * to end.

RND 2: *K2, yo, k3, ssk, k8, k2tog, k3, yo, k1; repeat from * to end.

RND 3: *K3, yo, k3, ssk, k6, k2tog, k3, yo, k2; repeat from * to end.

RND 4: *K4, yo, k3, ssk, k4, k2tog, k3, yo, k3; repeat from * to end.

RND 5: *K5, yo, k3, ssk, k2, k2tog, k3, yo, k4; repeat from * to end.

RND 6: *K6, yo, k3, ssk, k2tog, k3, yo, k5; repeat from * to end.

Repeat Rnds 1–6 for Fern Grotto Lace Bottom-Up in the Round.

BOTTOM-UP IN THE ROUND

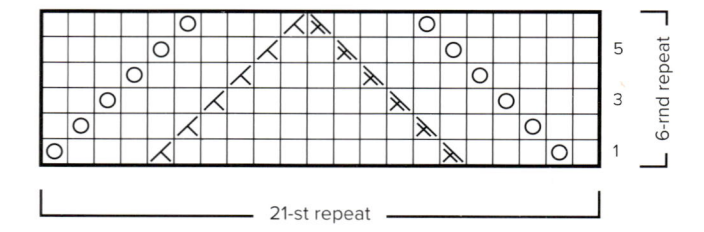

Fern Grotto Lace (CONT'D)

TOP-DOWN IN THE ROUND

(panel of 21 sts worked on a background of St st; 6-rnd repeat)

RND 1: *K5, k2tog, k3, yo, k1, yo, k3, ssk, k5; repeat from * to end.

RND 2: *K4, k2tog, k3, yo, k3, yo, k3, ssk, k4; repeat from * to end.

RND 3: *K3, k2tog, k3, yo, k5, yo, k3, ssk, k3; repeat from * to end.

RND 4: *K2, k2tog, k3, yo, k7, yo, k3, ssk, k2; repeat from * to end.

RND 5: *K1, k2tog, k3, yo, k9, yo, k3, ssk, k1; repeat from * to end.

RND 6: *K2tog, k3, yo, k11, yo, k3, ssk; repeat from * to end.

Repeat Rnds 1–6 for Fern Grotto Lace Top-Down in the Round.

TOP-DOWN FLAT

(panel of 21 sts + 2 worked on a background of St st; 6-row repeat)

ROW 1 (RS): K1, *k5, k2tog, k3, yo, k1, yo, k3, ssk, k5; repeat from * to last st, k1.

ROW 2: P1, *p4, ssp, p3, yo, p3, yo, p3, p2tog, p4; repeat from * to last st, p1.

ROW 3: K1, *k3, k2tog, k3, yo, k5, yo, k3, ssk, k3; repeat from * to last st, k1.

ROW 4: P1, *p2, ssp, p3, yo, p7, yo, p3, p2tog, p2; repeat from * to last st, p1.

ROW 5: K1, *k1, k2tog, k3, yo, k9, yo, k3, ssk, k1; repeat from * to last st, k1.

ROW 6: P1, *ssp, p3, yo, p11, yo, p3, p2tog; repeat from * to last st, p1.

Repeat Rows 1–6 for Fern Grotto Lace Top-Down Flat.

TOP-DOWN FLAT

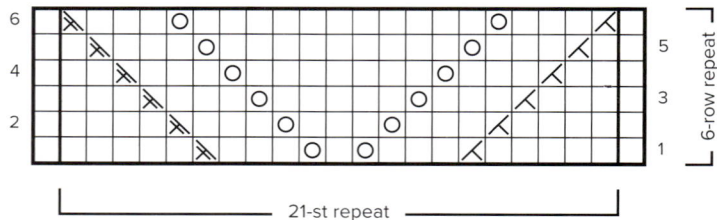

21-st repeat · 6-row repeat

TOP-DOWN IN THE ROUND

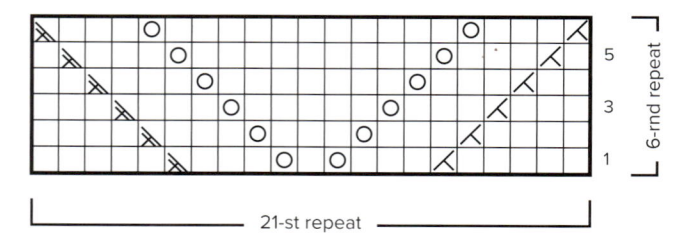

21-st repeat · 6-rnd repeat

Parachute Lace

FLAT

(multiple of 6 sts + 1; 8-row repeat)

ROW 1 (RS): *P1, k2, yo, ssk, k1; repeat from * to last st, p1.

ROW 2 AND ALL WS ROWS: Knit the knit sts and purl the purl sts as they face you; purl all yos.

ROW 3: *P1, k2, yo, k2tog, k1; repeat from * to last st, p1.

ROW 5: *P1, yo, k1, s2kp2, k1, yo; repeat from * to last st, p1.

ROW 7: *P1, k1, yo, s2kp2, k1; repeat from * to last st, p1.

ROW 8: Repeat Row 2.

Repeat Rows 1–8 for Parachute Lace Flat.

FLAT

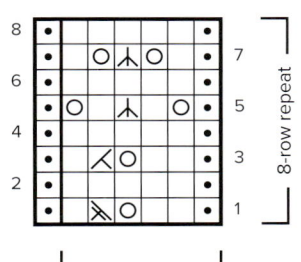

6-st repeat

IN THE ROUND

(multiple of 6 sts; 8-rnd repeat)

RND 1: *P1, k2, yo, ssk, k1; repeat from * to end.

RND 2 AND ALL EVEN-NUMBERED RNDS: Knit the knit sts and purl the purl sts as they face you; knit all yos.

RND 3: *P1, k2, yo, k2tog, k1; repeat from * to end.

RND 5: *P1, yo, k1, s2kp2, k1, yo; repeat from * to end.

RND 7: *P1, k1, yo, s2kp2, yo, k1; repeat from * to end.

RND 8: Repeat Rnd 2.

Repeat Rnds 1–8 for Parachute Lace in the Round.

IN THE ROUND

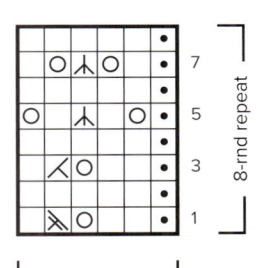

6-st repeat

Quadruple Diamond Lace

FLAT

(panel of 17 sts worked on a background of St st; 28-row repeat)

ROW 1: K6, k2tog, yo, k1, yo, ssk, k6.

ROW 2 AND ALL WS ROWS: Purl.

ROW 3: K5, k2tog, yo, k3, yo, ssk, k5.

ROW 5: K4, [k2tog, yo] twice, k1, [yo, ssk] twice, k4.

ROW 7: K3, k2tog, yo, k2, yo, sk2p, yo, k2, yo, ssk, k3.

ROW 9: K2, k2tog, yo, k1, yo, ssk, k3, k2tog, yo, k1, yo, ssk, k2.

ROW 11: K1, k2tog, yo, k3, yo, ssk, k1, k2tog, yo, k3, yo, ssk, k1.

ROW 13: K2tog, yo, k1, k2tog, yo, k2, yo, sk2p, yo, k2, yo, ssk, k1, yo, ssk.

ROW 15: K1, yo, ssk, k3, k2tog, yo, k1, yo, ssk, k3, k2tog, yo, k1.

ROW 17: K2, yo, ssk, k1, k2tog, yo, k3, yo, ssk, k1, k2tog, yo, k2.

ROW 19: K3, yo, sk2p, yo, k2tog, yo, k1, yo, ssk, yo, k3tog, yo, k3.

ROW 21: K4, yo, ssk, k1, yo, sk2p, yo, k1, k2tog, yo, k4.

ROW 23: K5, yo, ssk, k3, k2tog, yo, k5.

ROW 25: K6, yo, ssk, k1, k2tog, yo, k6.

ROW 27: K7, yo, sk2p, yo, k7.

ROW 28: Purl.

Repeat Rows 1–28 for Quadruple Diamond Lace Flat.

NOTE: In swatch, pattern was worked as follows: Rows 15–28, Rows 1–28, then Rows 1–12.

IN THE ROUND

(panel of 17 sts worked on a background of St st; 28-rnd repeat)

RND 1: K6, k2tog, yo, k1, yo, ssk, k6.

RND 2 AND ALL EVEN-NUMBERED RNDS: Knit.

RND 3: K5, k2tog, yo, k3, yo, ssk, k5.

RND 5: K4, [k2tog, yo] twice, k1, [yo, ssk] twice, k4.

RND 7: K3, k2tog, yo, k2, yo, sk2p, yo, k2, yo, ssk, k3.

RND 9: K2, k2tog, yo, k1, yo, ssk, k3, k2tog, yo, k1, yo, ssk, k2.

RND 11: K1, k2tog, yo, k3, yo, ssk, k1, k2tog, yo, k3, yo, ssk, k1.

RND 13: K2tog, yo, k1, k2tog, yo, k2, yo, sk2p, yo, k2, yo, ssk, k1, yo, ssk.

RND 15: K1, yo, ssk, k3, k2tog, yo, k1, yo, ssk, k3, k2tog, yo, k1.

RND 17: K2, yo, ssk, k1, k2tog, yo, k3, yo, ssk, k1, k2tog, yo, k2.

RND 19: K3, yo, sk2p, yo, k2tog, yo, k1, yo, ssk, yo, k3tog, yo, k3.

RND 21: K4, yo, ssk, k1, yo, sk2p, yo, k1, k2tog, yo, k4.

RND 23: K5, yo, ssk, k3, k2tog, yo, k5.

RND 25: K6, yo, ssk, k1, k2tog, yo, k6.

RND 27: K7, yo, sk2p, yo, k7.

RND 28: Knit.

Repeat Rnds 1–28 for Quadruple Diamond Lace in the Round.

FLAT & IN THE ROUND

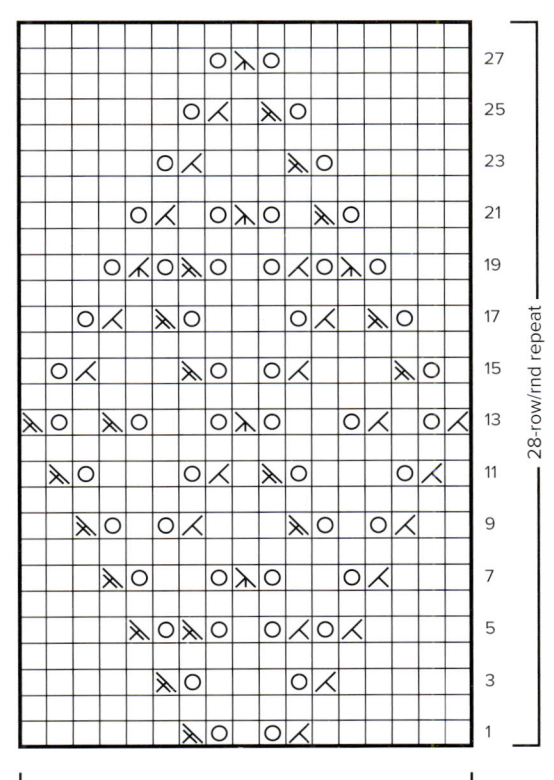

27, 25, 23, 21, 19, 17, 15, 13, 11, 9, 7, 5, 3, 1

28-row/rnd repeat

17-st panel

Bricklayer's Lace

FLAT

(multiple of 12 sts + 4; 12-row repeat)

ROW 1 (RS): K2, *k2, yo, ssk, k3, k2tog, yo, k3; repeat from * to last 2 sts, k2.

ROW 2 AND ALL WS ROWS: Purl.

ROW 3: K2, *k3, yo, ssk, k1, k2tog, yo, k1, yo, ssk, k1; repeat from * to last 2 sts, k2.

ROW 5: K2, *k4, yo, sk2p, yo, k3, yo, ssk; repeat from * to last 2 sts, k2.

ROW 7: K1, yo, *ssk, k3, k2tog, yo, k5, yo; repeat from to last 3 sts, ssk, k1.

ROW 9: K2, *yo, ssk, k1, k2tog, yo, k4, k2tog, yo, k1; repeat from * to last 2 sts, yo, ssk.

ROW 11: K2, *k1, yo, sk2p, yo, k4, k2tog, yo, k2; repeat from * to last 2 sts, k2.

ROW 12: Purl.

Repeat Rows 1–12 for Bricklayer's Lace Flat.

IN THE ROUND

(multiple of 12 sts; 12-rnd repeat)

RND 1: *K2, yo, ssk, k3, k2tog, yo, k3; repeat from * to end.

RND 2: Knit.

RND 3: *K3, yo, ssk, k1, k2tog, yo, k1, yo, ssk, k1; repeat from * to end.

RND 4: Knit.

RND 5: *K4, yo, sk2p, yo, k3, yo, ssk; repeat from * to end.

RND 6: Knit to last st, reposition beginning-of-rnd marker to before last st.

RND 7: *Ssk, k3, k2tog, yo, k5, yo; repeat from * to end.

RND 8: Knit.

RND 9: *Yo, ssk, k1, k2tog, yo, k4, k2tog, yo, k1; repeat from * to end.

RND 10: Knit.

RND 11: *K1, yo, sk2p, yo, k4, k2tog, yo, k2; repeat from * to end.

RND 12: Knit.

Repeat Rnds 1–12 for Bricklayer's Lace in the Round.

FLAT

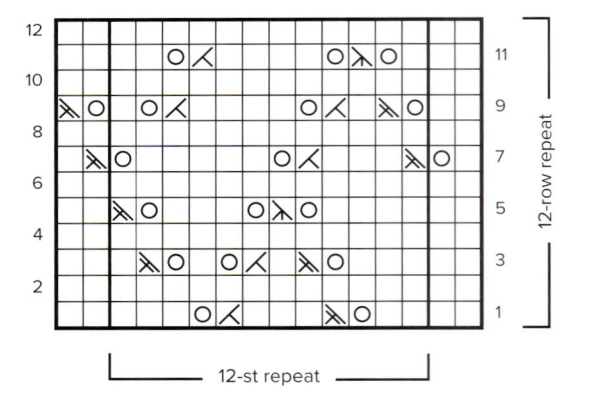

12-row repeat

12-st repeat

IN THE ROUND

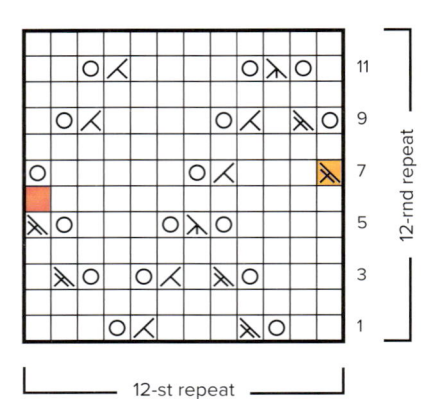

12-rnd repeat

12-st repeat

On Rnd 6 only, end rnd 1 st before beginning-of-rnd marker; reposition beginning-of-rnd marker to before final st of rnd.

On first repeat of Rnd 7 only, work ssk on what was last st of Rnd 6 and first st of Rnd 7; beginning-of-rnd marker should be before this ssk.

Lucina Shell Lace

FLAT

(multiple of 9 sts + 3; 8-row repeat)

NOTE: You will increase 2 sts per repeat on Rows 1, 3, and 5; original st count is restored on Row 7.

K4tog: Knit 4 sts together (see below).

Ssssk: See below.

ROW 1 (RS): K2, *yo, k8, yo, k1; repeat from * to last st, k1.

ROW 2: K3, *p8, k3; repeat from * to end.

ROW 3: K3, *yo, k8, yo, k3; repeat from * to end.

ROW 4: K4, *p8, k5; repeat from * to last 12 sts, p8, k4.

ROW 5: K4, *yo, k8, yo, k5; repeat from * to last 12 sts, yo, k8, yo, k4.

ROW 6: K5, *p8, k7; repeat from * to last 13 sts, p8, k5.

ROW 7: K5, *ssssk, k4tog, k7; repeat from * to last 13 sts, ssssk, k4tog, k5.

ROW 8: Knit.

Repeat Rows 1–8 for Lucina Shell Lace Flat.

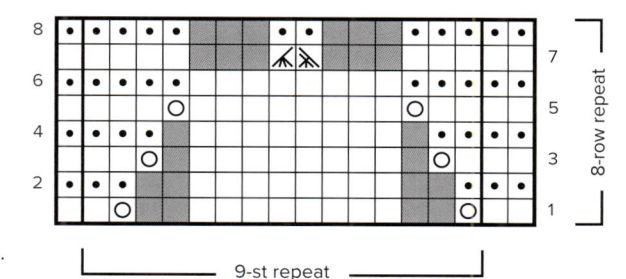

FLAT

9-st repeat / 8-row repeat

IN THE ROUND

(multiple of 9 sts; 8-row repeat)

NOTE: You will increase 2 sts per repeat on Rnds 1, 3, and 5; original st count is restored on Rnd 7.

K4tog: Knit 4 sts together (see right).

Ssssk: See right.

RND 1: *K1, yo, k8, yo; repeat from * to end.

RND 2: *P2, k8, p1; repeat from * to end.

RND 3: K2, *yo, k8, yo, k3; repeat from * to last 9 sts, yo, k8, yo, k1.

RND 4: P3, *k8, p5; repeat from * to last 10 sts, k8, p2.

RND 5: K3, *yo, k8, yo, k5; repeat from * to last 10 sts, yo, k8, yo, k2.

RND 6: P4, *k8, p7; repeat from * to last 11 sts, k8, p3.

RND 7: K4, *ssssk, k4tog, k7; repeat from * to last 11 sts, ssssk, k4tog, k3.

RND 8: Purl.

Repeat Rnds 1–8 for Lucina Shell Lace In the Round.

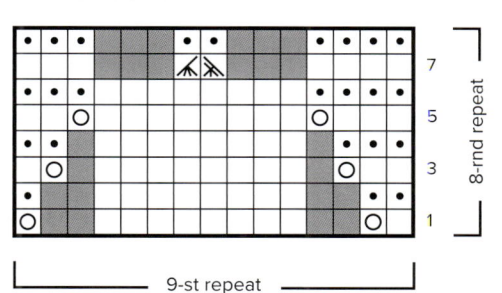

IN THE ROUND

9-st repeat / 8-rnd repeat

Ssssk: Slip next 4 stitches to right-hand needle one at a time knitwise; return them to left-hand needle one at a time in their new orientation; knit them together through back loops.

K4tog: Knit 4 sts together—3 decreased.

Milady's Fan

BOTTOM-UP FLAT

(panel of 23 sts worked on a background of St st; 24-row repeat)

ROW 1 (RS): K9, k2tog, yo, k1, yo, ssk, k9.

ROW 2: Purl.

ROW 3: K8, k2tog, yo, k3, yo, ssk, k8.

ROW 4: Purl.

ROW 5: K7, [k2tog, yo] twice, k1, [yo, ssk] twice, k7.

ROW 6: Purl.

ROW 7: K6, [k2tog, yo] twice, k3, [yo, ssk] twice, k6.

ROW 8: Purl.

ROW 9: K5, [k2tog, yo] 3 times, k1, [yo, ssk] 3 times, k5.

ROW 10: P4, ssp, yo, p11, yo, p2tog, p4.

ROW 11: K3, k2tog, yo, k1, [k2tog, yo] twice, k3, [yo, ssk] twice, k1, yo, ssk, k3.

ROW 12: P2, ssp, yo, p15, yo, p2tog, p2.

ROW 13: K1, k2tog, yo, k2, [k2tog, yo] 3 times, k1, [yo, ssk] 3 times, k2, yo, ssk, k1.

ROW 14: Ssp, yo, p2, ssp, yo, p11, yo, p2tog, p2, yo, p2tog.

ROWS 15 AND 16: Repeat Rows 11 and 12.

ROW 17: Repeat Row 9.

ROW 18: P4, ssp, yo, p11, yo, p2tog, p4.

ROW 19: Repeat Row 7.

ROW 20: Purl.

ROW 21: K10, yo, sk2p, yo, k10.

ROW 22: Purl.

ROW 23: Knit.

ROW 25: Purl.

Repeat Rows 1–24 for Milady's Fan Bottom-Up Flat.

BOTTOM-UP IN THE ROUND

(panel of 23 sts worked on a background of St st; 24-rnd repeat)

RND 1: K9, k2tog, yo, k1, yo, ssk, k9.

RND 2: Knit.

RND 3: K8, k2tog, yo, k3, yo, ssk, k8.

RND 4: Knit.

RND 5: K7, [k2tog, yo] twice, k1, [yo, ssk] twice, k7.

RND 6: Knit.

RND 7: K6, [k2tog, yo] twice, k3, [yo, ssk] twice, k6.

RND 8: Knit.

RND 9: K5, [k2tog, yo] 3 times, k1, [yo, ssk] 3 times, k5.

RND 10: K4, k2tog, yo, k11, yo, ssk, k4.

RND 11: K3, k2tog, yo, k1, [k2tog, yo] twice, k3, [yo, ssk] twice, k1, yo, ssk, k3.

RND 12: K2, k2tog, yo, k15, yo, ssk, k2.

RND 13: K1, k2tog, yo, k2, [k2tog, yo] 3 times, k1, [yo, ssk] 3 times, k2, yo, ssk, k1.

RND 14: K2tog, yo, k2, k2tog, yo, k11, yo, ssk, k2, yo, ssk.

RNDS 15 AND 16: Repeat Rnds 11 and 12.

RND 17: Repeat Rnd 9.

RND 18: K4, k2tog, yo, k11, yo, ssk, k4.

RND 19: Repeat Rnd 7.

RND 20: Knit.

RND 21: K10, yo, sk2p, yo, k10.

RNDS 22–24: Knit.

Repeat Rnds 1–24 for Milady's Fan Bottom-Up in the Round.

BOTTOM-UP FLAT & IN THE ROUND

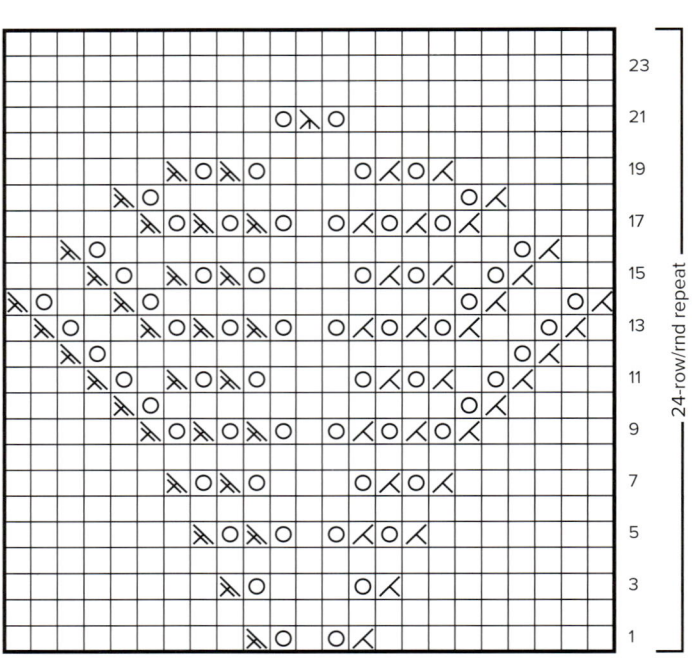

23-st panel / 24-row/rnd repeat

Milady's Fan (CONT'D)

TOP-DOWN FLAT

(panel of 23 sts worked on a background of St st; 24-row repeat)

ROW 1 (RS): K10, yo, sk2p, yo, k10.

ROW 2: Purl.

ROW 3: K7, [yo, ssk] twice, k1, [k2tog, yo] twice, k7.

ROW 4: P5, yo, p2tog, p9, ssp, yo, p5.

ROW 5: K6, [yo, ssk] twice, yo, sk2p, [yo, k2tog] twice, yo, k6.

ROW 6: P3, yo, p2tog, p13, ssp, yo, p3.

ROW 7: K4, yo, ssk, k1, [yo, ssk] twice, k1, [k2tog, yo] twice, k1, k2tog, yo, k4.

ROW 8: P1, yo, p2tog, p2, yo, p2tog, p9, ssp, yo, p2, ssp, yo, p1.

ROW 9: K2, yo, ssk, k2, [yo, ssk] twice, yo, sk2p, [yo, k2tog] twice, yo, k2, k2tog, yo, k2.

ROW 10: P3, yo, p2tog, p13, ssp, yo, p3.

ROW 11: Repeat Row 7.

ROWS 12 AND 13: Repeat Rows 4 and 5.

ROW 14: Purl.

ROW 15: Repeat Row 3.

ROW 16: Purl.

ROW 17: K8, yo, ssk, yo, sk2p, yo, k2tog, yo, k8.

ROW 18: Purl.

ROW 19: K9, yo, ssk, k1, k2tog, yo, k9.

ROW 20: Purl.

ROW 21: K10, yo, sk2p, yo, k10.

ROW 22: Purl.

ROW 23: Knit.

ROW 24: Purl.

Repeat Rows 1–24 for Milady's Fan Top-Down Flat.

TOP-DOWN IN THE ROUND

(panel of 23 sts worked on a background of St st; 24-rnd repeat)

RND 1: K10, yo, sk2p, yo, k10.

RND 2: Knit.

RND 3: K7, [yo, ssk] twice, k1, [k2tog, yo] twice, k7.

RND 4: K5, yo, ssk, k9, k2tog, yo, k5.

RND 5: K6, [yo, ssk] twice, yo, sk2p, [yo, k2tog] twice, yo, k6.

RND 6: K3, yo, ssk, k13, k2tog, yo, k3.

RND 7: K4, yo, ssk, k1, [yo, ssk] twice, k1, [k2tog, yo] twice, k1, k2tog, yo, k4.

RND 8: K1, yo, ssk, k2, yo, ssk, k9, k2tog, yo, k2, k2tog, yo, k1.

RND 9: K2, yo, ssk, k2, [yo, ssk] twice, yo, sk2p, [yo, k2tog] twice, yo, k2, k2tog, yo, k2.

RND 10: K3, yo, ssk, k13, k2tog, yo, k3.

RND 11: Repeat Rnd 7.

RND 12 AND 13: Repeat Rnds 4 and 5.

RND 14: Knit.

RND 15: Repeat Rnd 3.

RND 16: Knit.

RND 17: K8, yo, ssk, yo, sk2p, yo, k2tog, yo, k8.

RND 18: Knit.

RND 19: K9, yo, ssk, k1, k2tog, yo, k9.

RND 20: Knit.

RND 21: K10, yo, sk2p, yo, k10.

RNDS 22–24: Knit.

Repeat Rnds 1–24 for Milady's Fan Top-Down in the Round.

TOP-DOWN FLAT & IN THE ROUND

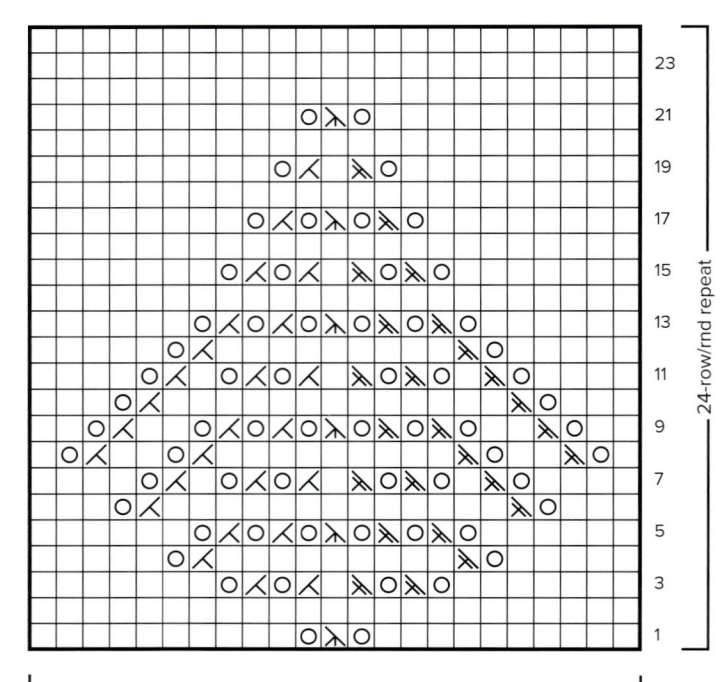

23-st panel

24-row/rnd repeat

Fish Scale Lace

FLAT

(panel of 17 sts worked on a background of St st; 8-row repeat)

ROW 1 (RS): K1, yo, k3, skp, p5, k2tog, k3, yo, k1.

ROW 2 AND ALL WS ROWS: Knit the knit sts and purl the purl sts as they face you; purl all yos.

ROW 3: K2, yo, k3, skp, p3, k2tog, k3, yo, k2.

ROW 5: K3, yo, k3, skp, p1, k2tog, k3, yo, k3.

ROW 7: K4, yo, k3, sk2p, k3, yo, k4.

ROW 8: Purl.

Repeat Rows 1–8 for Fish Scale Lace Flat.

IN THE ROUND

(panel of 17 sts worked on a background of St st; 8-rnd repeat)

RND: K1, yo, k3, skp, p5, k2tog, k3, yo, k1.

RND 2 AND ALL EVEN-NUMBERED RNDS: Knit the knit sts and purl the purl sts as they face you; knit all yos.

RND 3: K2, yo, k3, skp, p3, k2tog, k3, yo, k2.

RND 5: K3, yo, k3, skp, p1, k2tog, k3, yo, k3.

RND 7: K4, yo, k3, sk2p, k3, yo, k4.

RND 8: Knit.

Repeat Rnds 1–8 for Fish Scale Lace in the Round.

FLAT & IN THE ROUND

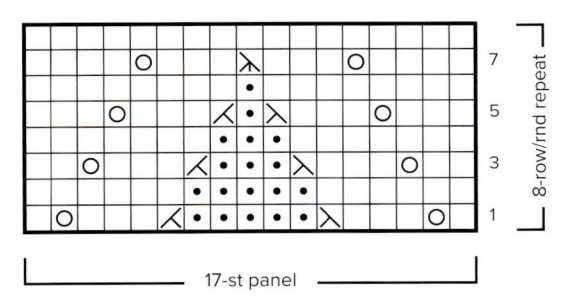

17-st panel

8-row/rnd repeat

Pagoda Lace

BOTTOM-UP FLAT

(panel of 23 sts; 10-row repeat)

ROW 1 (RS): K1, [yo, ssk] twice, k2, [yo, ssk] twice, k1, [k2tog, yo] twice, k2, [k2tog, yo] twice, k1.

ROW 2: P2, [yo, p2tog] twice, p11, [ssp, yo] twice, p2.

ROW 3: K3, [yo, ssk] twice, k1, yo, ssk, yo, sk2p, yo, k2tog, yo, k1, [k2tog, yo] twice, k3.

ROW 4: P4, [yo, p2tog] twice, p7, [ssp, yo] twice, p4.

ROW 5: K5, [yo, ssk] twice, k2, yo, ssk, k1, [k2tog, yo,] twice, k5.

ROW 6: Purl.

ROW 7: K6, [yo, ssk] twice, k3, [k2tog, yo] twice, k6.

ROW 8: Purl.

ROW 9: K7, [yo, ssk] twice, k1, [k2tog, yo] twice, k7.

ROW 10: Purl.

Repeat Rows 1–10 for Pagoda Lace Bottom-Up Flat.

BOTTOM-UP IN THE ROUND

(panel of 23 sts; 10-rnd repeat)

RND 1: K1, [yo, ssk] twice, k2, [yo, ssk] twice, k1, [k2tog, yo] twice, k2, [k2tog, yo] twice, k1.

RND 2: K2, [yo, ssk] twice, k11, [k2tog, yo] twice, k2.

RND 3: K3, [yo, ssk] twice, k1, yo, ssk, yo, sk2p, yo, k2tog, yo, k1, [k2tog, yo] twice, k3.

RND 4: K4, [yo, ssk] twice, k7, [k2tog, yo] twice, k4.

RND 5: K5, [yo, ssk] twice, k2, yo, ssk, k1, [k2tog, yo] twice, k5.

RND 6: Knit.

RND 7: K6, [yo, ssk] twice, k3, [k2tog, yo] twice, k6.

RND 8: Knit.

RND 9: K7, [yo, ssk] twice, k1, [k2tog, yo] twice, k7.

RND 10: Knit.

Repeat Rnds 1–10 for Pagoda Lace Bottom-Up in the Round.

BOTTOM-UP FLAT & IN THE ROUND

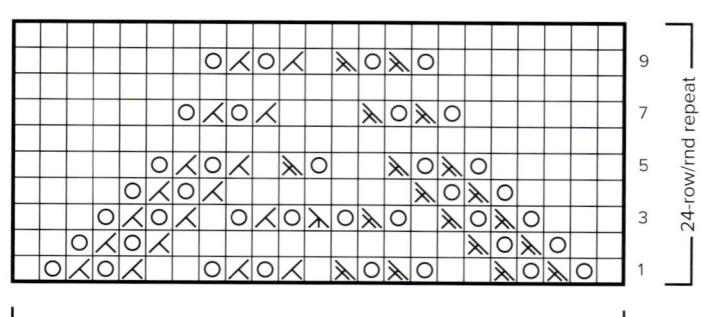

24-row/rnd repeat

23-st panel

TOP-DOWN FLAT

(panel of 23 sts; 10-row repeat)

ROW 1 (RS): K7, [k2tog, yo] twice, k1, [yo, ssk] twice, k7.

ROW 2: Purl.

ROW 3: K6, [k2tog, yo] twice, k3, [yo, ssk] twice, k6.

ROW 4: Purl.

ROW 5: K5, [k2tog, yo] twice, k2, yo, ssk, k1, [yo, ssk] twice, k5.

ROW 6: P4, [ssp, yo] twice, p7, [yo, p2tog] twice, p4.

ROW 7: K3, [k2tog, yo] twice, k1, yo, k2tog, yo, sk2p, yo, ssk, yo, k1, [yo, ssk] twice, k3.

ROW 8: P2, [ssp, yo] twice, p11, [yo, p2tog] twice, p2.

ROW 9: K1, [k2tog, yo] twice, k1, [k2tog, yo] twice, k3, [yo, ssk] twice, k1, [yo, ssk] twice, k1.

ROW 10: Purl.

Repeat Rows 1–10 for Pagoda Lace Top-Down Flat.

TOP-DOWN IN THE ROUND

(panel of 23 sts; 10-rnd repeat)

RND 1: K7, [k2tog, yo] twice, k1, [yo, ssk] twice, k7.

RND 2: Knit.

RND 3: K6, [k2tog, yo] twice, k3, [yo, ssk] twice, k6.

RND 4: Knit.

RND 5: K5, [k2tog, yo] twice, k2, yo, ssk, k1, [yo, ssk] twice, k5.

RND 6: K4, [k2tog, yo] twice, k7, [yo, ssk] twice, k4.

RND 7: K3, [k2tog, yo] twice, k1, yo, k2tog, yo, sk2p, yo, ssk, yo, k1, [yo, ssk] twice, k3.

RND 8: K2, [k2tog, yo] twice, k11, [yo, ssk] twice, k2.

RND 9: K1, [k2tog, yo] twice, k1, [k2tog, yo] twice, k3, [yo, ssk] twice, k1, [yo, ssk] twice, k1.

RND 10: Knit.

Repeat Rnds 1–10 for Pagoda Lace Top-Down in the Round.

TOP-DOWN FLAT & IN THE ROUND

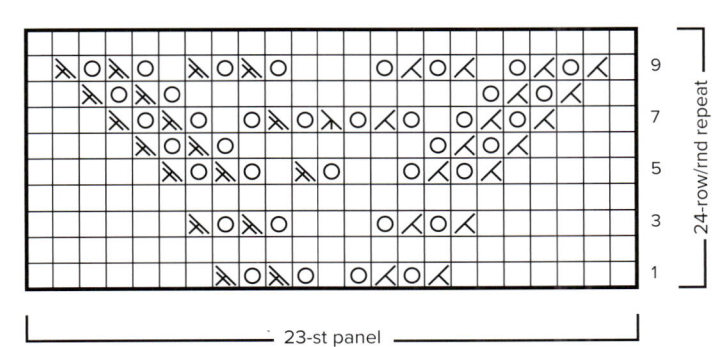

23-st panel

24-row/rnd repeat

Gothic Arches

FLAT

(multiple of 18 sts + 5; 32-row repeat)

ROW 1 (RS): K2, *k2, [ssk, yo] 3 times, k3, [yo, k2tog] 3 times, k1; repeat from * to last 3 sts, k3.

ROW 2 AND ALL WS ROWS: Purl.

ROWS 3 AND 5: Repeat Row 1.

ROW 7: K2, *k4, [yo, ssk] twice, yo, sk2p, [yo, k2tog] twice, yo, k3; repeat from * to last 3 sts, k3.

ROW 9: K2, *k5, [yo, ssk] twice, yo, sk2p, yo, k2tog, yo, k4; repeat from * to last 3 sts, k3.

ROW 11: K2, *k3, k2tog, yo, k1, yo, ssk, yo, sk2p, yo, k2tog, yo, k1, yo, ssk, k2; repeat from * to last 3 sts, k3.

ROW 13: K2, *k2, [k2tog, yo] twice, k1, yo, ssk, yo, sk2p, yo, k1, [yo, ssk] twice, k1; repeat from * to last 3 sts, k3.

ROW 15: K2, *k1, [k2tog, yo] 3 times, k1, yo, sk2p, yo, k1, [yo, ssk] 3 times; repeat from * to last 3 sts, k3.

ROWS 17, 19, AND 21: K2, *k2, [yo, k2tog] 3 times, k3, [ssk, yo] 3 times, k1; repeat from * to last 3 sts, k3.

ROW 23: K1, yo, *sk2p, [yo, k2tog] twice, yo, k7, [yo, ssk] twice, yo; repeat from * to last 4 sts, sk2p, yo, k1.

ROW 25: K2, *yo, sk2p, yo, k2tog, yo, k9, [yo, ssk] twice; repeat from * to last 3 sts, yo, ssk, k1.

ROW 27: K1, yo, *sk2p, yo, k2tog, yo, k1, yo, ssk, k5, k2tog, yo, k1, yo, ssk, yo; repeat from * to last 4 sts, sk2p, yo, k1.

ROW 29: K2, *yo, sk2p, yo, k1, [yo, ssk] twice, k3, [k2tog, yo] twice, k1, yo, ssk; repeat from * to last 3 sts, yo, ssk, k1.

ROW 31: K1, yo, *sk2p, yo, k1, [yo, ssk] 3 times, k1, [k2tog, yo] 3 times, k1, yo; repeat from * to last 4 sts, sk2p, yo, k1.

ROW 32: Purl.

Repeat Rows 1–32 for Gothic Arches Flat.

FLAT

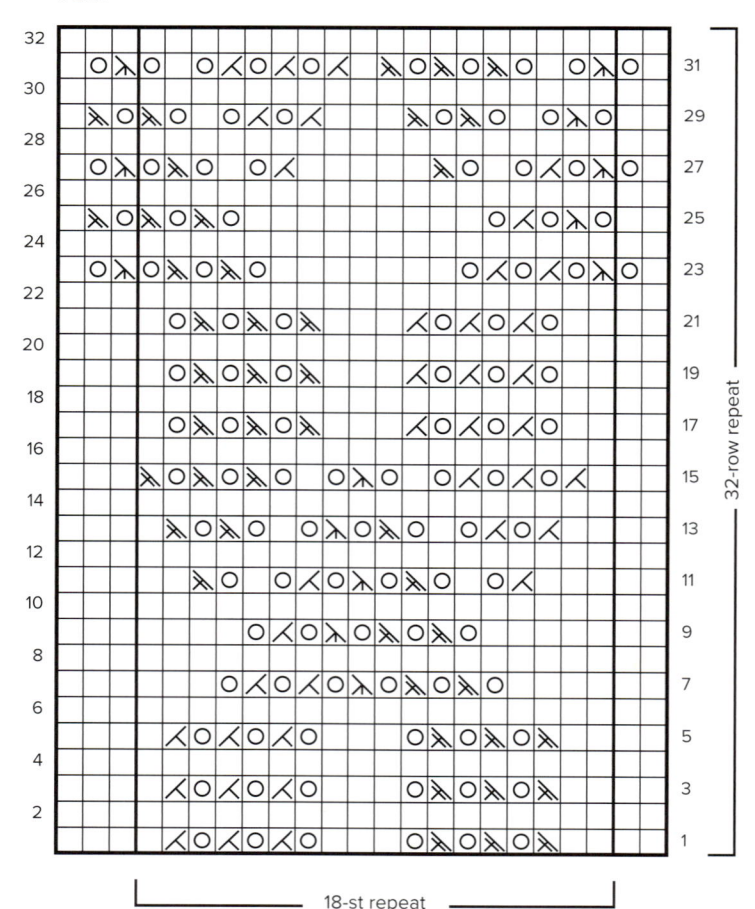

18-st repeat

32-row repeat

Gothic Arches (CONT'D)

IN THE ROUND

(multiple of 18 sts; 32-rnd repeat)

RND 1: *K2, [ssk, yo] 3 times, k3, [yo, k2tog] 3 times, k1; repeat from * to end.

RND 2: Knit.

RNDS 3–6: Repeat Rnds 1 and 2.

RND 7: *K4, [yo, ssk] twice, yo, sk2p, yo, [k2tog, yo] twice, k3; repeat from * to end.

RND 8: Knit.

RND 9: *K5, [yo, ssk] twice, yo, sk2p, yo, k2tog, yo, k4; repeat from * to end.

RND 10: Knit.

RND 11: *K3, k2tog, yo, k1, yo, ssk, yo, sk2p, yo, k2tog, yo, k1, yo, ssk, k2; repeat from * to end.

RND 12: Knit.

RND 13: *K2, [k2tog, yo] twice, k1, yo, ssk, yo, sk2p, yo, k1, [yo, ssk] twice, k1; repeat from * to end.

RND 14: Knit.

RND 15: *K1, [k2tog, yo] 3 times, k1, yo, sk2p, yo, k1, [yo, ssk] 3 times; repeat from * to end.

RND 16: Knit.

RND 17: *K2, [yo, k2tog] 3 times, k3, [ssk, yo] 3 times, k1; repeat from * to end.

RNDS 18–21: Repeat Rnds 16 and 17.

RND 22: Knit to last st, reposition beginning-of-rnd marker to before last st.

RND 23: *Sk2p, yo, [k2tog, yo] twice, k7, [yo, ssk] twice, yo; repeat from * to end.

RND 24: Knit.

RND 25: *Yo, sk2p, yo, k2tog, yo, k9, [yo, ssk] twice; repeat from * to end.

RND 26: Repeat Rnd 22.

RND 27: *Sk2p, yo, k2tog, yo, k1, yo, ssk, k5, k2tog, yo, k1, yo, ssk, yo; repeat from * to end.

RND 28: Knit.

RND 29: *Yo, sk2p, yo, k1, [yo, ssk] twice, k3, [k2tog, yo] twice, k1, yo, ssk; repeat from * to end.

RND 30: Repeat Rnd 22.

RND 31: *Sk2p, yo, k1, [yo, ssk] 3 times, k1, [k2tog, yo] 3 times, k1, yo; repeat from * to end.

RND 32: Knit.

Repeat Rnds 1–32 for Gothic Arches in the Round.

IN THE ROUND

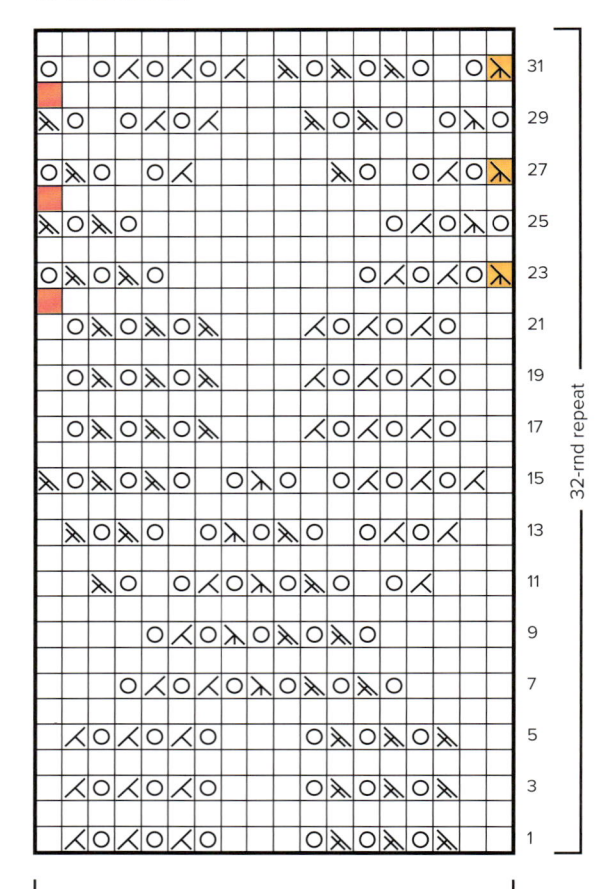

18-st repeat

32-rnd repeat

On Rnds 22, 26, and 30 only, end rnd 1 st before beginning-of-rnd marker; reposition beginning-of-rnd marker to before final st of rnd.

On first repeat of Rnds 23, 27, and 31 only, work sk2p on what was last st of Rnds 22, 26, and 30 and first 2 sts of Rnds 23, 27, and 31; beginning-of-rnd marker should be before this sk2p.

English Lace

FLAT

(multiple of 6 sts + 1; 8-row repeat)

ROW 1 (RS): *K1, yo, ssk, k1, k2tog, yo; repeat from * to last st, k1.

ROW 2 AND ALL WS ROWS: Purl.

ROW 3: *K1, yo, k1, sk2p, k1, yo; repeat from * to last st, k1.

ROW 5: *K1, k2tog, yo, k1, yo, ssk; repeat from * to last st, k1.

ROW 7: K2tog, *[k1, yo] twice, k1, sk2p; repeat from * to last 5 sts, [k1, yo] twice, k1, ssk.

ROW 8: Purl.

Repeat Rows 1–8 for English Lace Flat.

FLAT

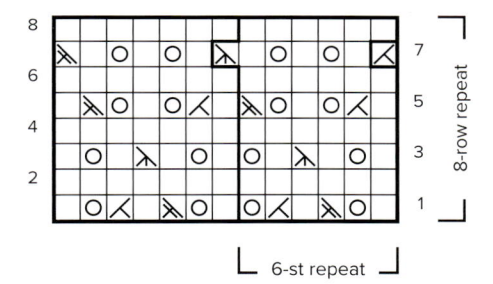

6-st repeat

IN THE ROUND

(multiple of 6 sts; 8-rnd repeat)

RND 1: *K1, yo, ssk, k1, k2tog, yo; repeat from * to end.

RND 2: Knit.

RND 3: *K1, yo, k1, sk2p, k1, yo; repeat from * to end.

RND 4: Knit.

RND 5: *K1, k2tog, yo, k1, yo, ssk; repeat from * to end.

RND 6: Knit to last st, reposition beginning-of-rnd marker before last st.

RND 7: *Sk2p, [k1, yo] twice, k1; repeat from * to end.

RND 8: Knit.

Repeat Rnds 1–8 for English Lace in the Round.

IN THE ROUND

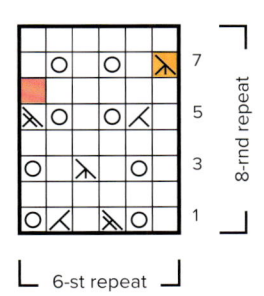

6-st repeat

On Rnd 6 only, end rnd 1 st before beginning-of-rnd marker; reposition beginning-of-rnd marker to before final st of rnd.

On first repeat of Rnd 7 only, work sk2p on what was last st of Rnd 6 and first 2 sts of Rnd 7; beginning-of-rnd marker should be before this sk2p.

Faggoting and Fancy Rib

FLAT

(multiple of 8 sts + 4; 8-row repeat)

ROW 1 (RS): Ssk, yo, *k2, yo, ssk, k2, ssk, yo; repeat from * to last 2 sts, k2.

ROW 2 AND ALL WS ROWS: P2tog, yo, *p6, p2tog, yo; repeat from * to last 2 sts, p2.

ROW 3: Ssk, yo, *k3, yo, ssk, k1, ssk, yo; repeat from * to last 2 sts, k2.

ROW 5: Ssk, yo, *k4, yo, [ssk] twice, yo; repeat from * to last 2 sts, k2.

ROW 7: Ssk, yo, *k5, yo, sk2p, yo; repeat from * to last 2 sts, k2.

ROW 8: Repeat Row 2.

Repeat Rows 1–8 for Faggoting and Fancy Rib Flat.

IN THE ROUND

(multiple of 8 sts; 8-rnd repeat)

RND 1: *Yo, ssk, k2, ssk, yo, k2; repeat from * to end.

RND 2 AND ALL EVEN-NUMBERED RNDS: *K6, yo, k2tog; repeat from * to end.

RND 3: *K1, yo, ssk, k1, ssk, yo, k2; repeat from * to end.

RND 5: *K2, yo, [ssk] twice, yo, k2; repeat from * to end.

RND 7: *K3, yo, sk2p, yo, k2; repeat from * to end.

RND 8: Repeat Rnd 2.

Repeat Rnds 1–8 for Faggoting and Fancy Rib in the Round.

FLAT

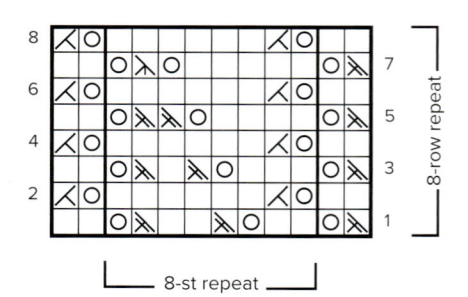

8-st repeat · 8-row repeat

IN THE ROUND

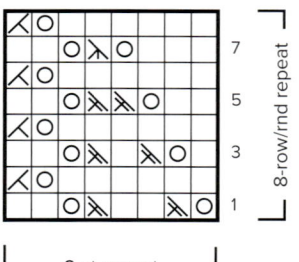

8-st repeat · 8-row/rnd repeat

Miniature Leaves

FLAT

(multiple of 6 sts + 5; 4-row repeat)

ROW 1 (RS): K1, *k3, yo, sk2p, yo; repeat from * to last 4 sts, k4.

ROW 2: Purl.

ROW 3: K1, *yo, sk2p, yo, k3; repeat from * to last 4 sts, yo, sk2p, yo, k1.

ROW 4: Purl.

Repeat Rows 1–4 for Miniature Leaves Flat.

FLAT

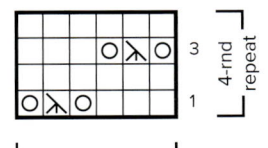

6-st repeat

IN THE ROUND

(multiple of 6 sts; 4-rnd repeat)

RND 1: *K3, yo, sk2p, yo; repeat from * to end.

RND 2: Knit.

RND 3: *Yo, sk2p, yo, k3; repeat from * to end.

RND 4: Knit.

Repeat Rnds 1–4 for Miniature Leaves in the Round.

IN THE ROUND

6-st repeat

Gate Pattern (TWO-SIDED)

FLAT

(multiple of 10 sts + 2; 16-row repeat)

ROW 1 (RS): K1, *yo, ssk, k3, p5; repeat from * to last st, k1.

ROW 2 AND ALL WS ROWS: Knit the knit sts and purl the purl sts as they face you; purl all yos.

ROW 3: K1, *k1, yo, ssk, k2, p5; repeat from * to last st, k1.

ROW 5: K1, *k2, yo, ssk, k1, p5; repeat from * to last st, k1.

ROW 7: K1, *k3, yo, ssk, p5; repeat from * to last st, k1.

ROW 9: K1, *p5, k3, k2tog, yo; repeat from * to last st, k1.

ROW 11: K1, *p5, k2, k2tog, yo, k1; repeat from * to last st, k1.

ROW 13: K1, *p5, k1, k2tog, yo, k2; repeat from * to last st, k1.

ROW 15: K1, *p5, k2tog, yo, k3; repeat from * to last st, k1.

ROW 16: Repeat Row 2.

Repeat Rows 1–16 for Gate Pattern Flat.

IN THE ROUND

(multiple of 10 sts; 16-rnd repeat)

RND 1: *Yo, ssk, k3, p5; repeat from * to end.

RND 2 AND ALL EVEN-NUMBERED RNDS: Knit the knit sts and purl the purl sts as they face you; knit all yos.

RND 3: *K1, yo, ssk, k2, p5; repeat from * to end.

RND 5: *K2, yo, ssk, k1, p5; repeat from * to end.

RND 7: *K3, yo, ssk, p5; repeat from * to end.

RND 9: *P5, k3, k2tog, yo; repeat from * to end.

RND 11: *P5, k2, k2tog, yo, k1; repeat from * to end.

RND 13: *P5, k1, k2tog, yo, k2; repeat from * to end.

RND 15: *P5, k2tog, yo, k3; repeat from * to end.

RND 16: Repeat Rnd 2.

Repeat Rnds 1–16 for Gate Pattern in the Round.

FLAT

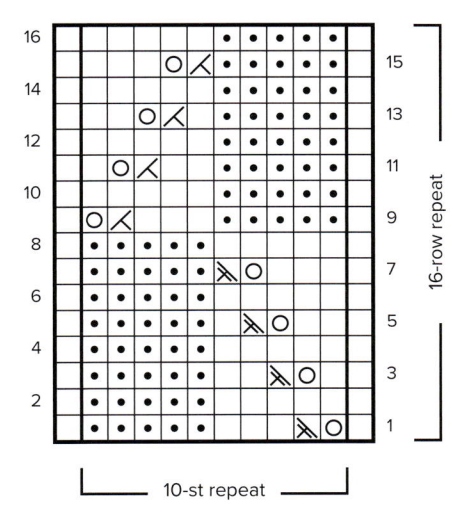

IN THE ROUND

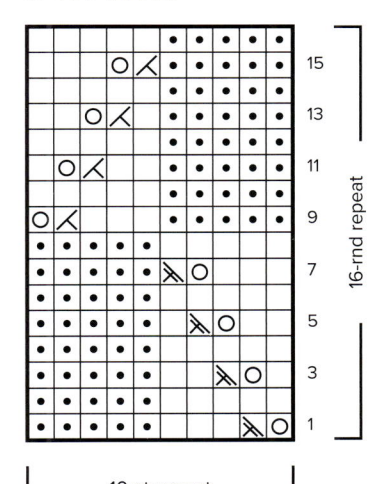

Cable Twist Lace

BOTTOM-UP FLAT

(panel of 15 sts worked on a background of St st; 18-row repeat)

ROW 1 (RS): K2, [yo, ssk] twice, k3, [k2tog, yo] twice, k2.

ROW 2 AND ALL WS ROWS: Purl.

ROW 3: K3, [yo, ssk] twice, k1, [k2tog, yo] twice, k3.

ROW 5: K4, yo, ssk, yo, sk2p, yo, k2tog, yo, k4.

ROW 7: K5, yo, ssk, yo, sk2p, yo, k5.

ROW 9: K6, [yo, ssk] twice, k5.

ROW 11: K4, k2tog, yo, k1, [yo, ssk] twice, k4.

ROW 13: K3, [k2tog, yo] twice, k1, [yo, ssk] twice, k3.

ROW 15: K2, [k2tog, yo] twice, k3, [yo, ssk] twice, k2.

ROW 17: K1, [k2tog, yo] twice, k5, [yo, ssk] twice, k1.

ROW 18: Repeat Row 2.

Repeat Rows 1–18 for Cable Twist Lace Bottom-Up Flat.

BOTTOM-UP FLAT & IN THE ROUND

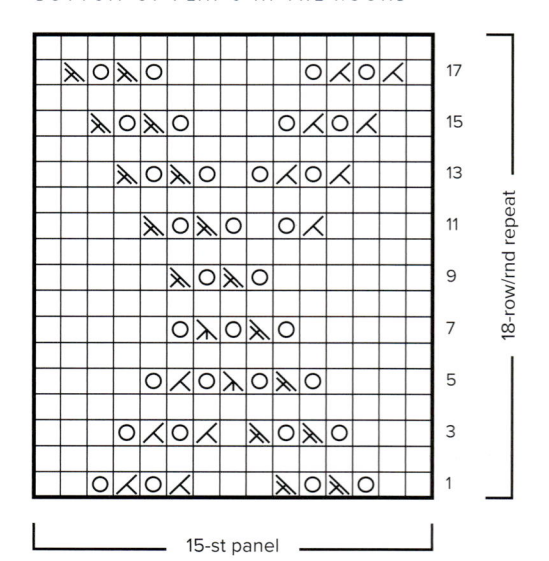

15-st panel

18-row/rnd repeat

BOTTOM-UP IN THE ROUND

(panel of 15 sts worked on a background of St st; 18-rnd repeat)

RND 1: K2, [yo, ssk] twice, k3, [k2tog, yo] twice, k2.

RND 2 AND ALL EVEN-NUMBERED RNDS: Knit.

RND 3: K3, [yo, ssk] twice, k1, [k2tog, yo] twice, k3.

RND 5: K4, yo, ssk, yo, sk2p, yo, k2tog, yo, k4.

RND 7: K5, yo, ssk, yo, sk2p, yo, k5.

RND 9: K6, [yo, ssk] twice, k5.

RND 11: K4, k2tog, yo, k1, [yo, ssk] twice, k4.

RND 13: K3, [k2tog, yo] twice, k1, [yo, ssk] twice, k3.

RND 15: K2, [k2tog, yo] twice, k3, [yo, ssk] twice, k2.

RND 17: K1, [k2tog, yo] twice, k5, [yo, ssk] twice, k1.

RND 18: Repeat Rnd 2.

Repeat Rnds 1–18 for Cable Twist Lace Bottom-Up in the Round.

TOP-DOWN FLAT

(panel of 15 sts worked on a background of St st; 18-row repeat)

ROW 1 (RS): K1, [ssk, yo] twice, k5, [yo, k2tog] twice, k1.

ROW 2 AND ALL WS ROWS: Purl.

ROW 3: K2, [ssk, yo] twice, k3, [yo, k2tog] twice, k2.

ROW 5: K3, [ssk, yo] twice, k1, [yo, k2tog] twice, k3.

ROW 7: K4, [ssk, yo] twice, k1, yo, k2tog, k4.

ROW 9: K5, [ssk, yo] twice, k6.

ROW 11: K5, yo, ssk, yo, sk2p, yo, k5.

ROW 13: K4, yo, k2tog, yo, ssk, yo, sk2p, yo, k4.

ROW 15: K3, [yo, k2tog] twice, k1, [ssk, yo] twice, k3.

ROW 17: K2, [yo, k2tog] twice, k3, [ssk, yo] twice, k2.

ROW 18: Repeat Row 2.

Repeat Rows 1–18 for Cable Twist Lace Top-Down Flat.

TOP-DOWN IN THE ROUND

(panel of 15 sts worked on a background of St st; 18-rnd repeat)

RND 1: K1, [ssk, yo] twice, k5, [yo, k2tog] twice, k1.

RND 2 AND ALL EVEN-NUMBERED RNDS: Knit.

RND 3: K2, [ssk, yo] twice, k3, [yo, k2tog] twice, k2.

RND 5: K3, [ssk, yo] twice, k1, [yo, k2tog] twice, k3.

RND 7: K4, [ssk, yo] twice, k1, yo, k2tog, k4.

RND 9: K5, [ssk, yo] twice, k6.

RND 11: K5, yo, ssk, yo, sk2p, yo, k5.

RND 13: K4, yo, k2tog, yo, ssk, yo, sk2p, yo, k4.

RND 15: K3, [yo, k2tog] twice, k1, [ssk, yo] twice, k3.

RND 17: K2, [yo, k2tog] twice, k3, [ssk, yo] twice, k2.

RND 18: Repeat Rnd 2.

Repeat 18 Rnds for Cable Twist Lace Top-Down in the Round.

TOP-DOWN FLAT & IN THE ROUND

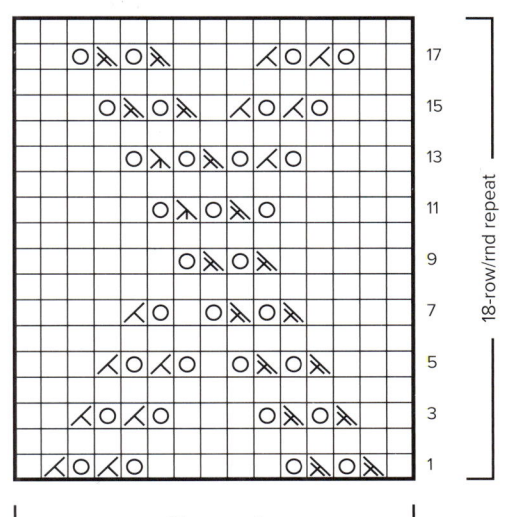

15-st panel

18-row/rnd repeat

Kimono Lace

FLAT

(multiple of 16 sts + 9; 32-row repeat)

ROW 1 (RS): *P1, [ssk, yo] 3 times, k1, p1, yo, k2, ssk, k3; repeat from * to last 9 sts, p1, [ssk, yo] 3 times, k1, p1.

ROW 2 AND ALL WS ROWS: Knit the knit sts and purl the purl sts as they face you; purl all yos.

ROW 3: *P1, [ssk, yo] 3 times, k1, p1, k1, yo, k2, ssk, k2; repeat from * to last 9 sts, p1, [ssk, yo] 3 times, k1, p1.

ROW 5: *P1, [ssk, yo] 3 times, k1, p1, k2, yo, k2, ssk, k1; repeat from * to last 9 sts, p1, [ssk, yo] 3 times, k1, p1.

ROW 7: *P1, [ssk, yo] 3 times, k1, p1, k3, yo, k2, ssk; repeat from * to last 9 sts, p1, [ssk, yo] 3 times, k1, p1.

ROWS 9-16: Repeat Rows 1–8.

ROW 17: *P1, k3, k2tog, k2, yo, p1, k1, [yo, k2tog] 3 times; repeat from * to last 9 sts, p1, k3, k2tog, k2, yo, p1.

FLAT

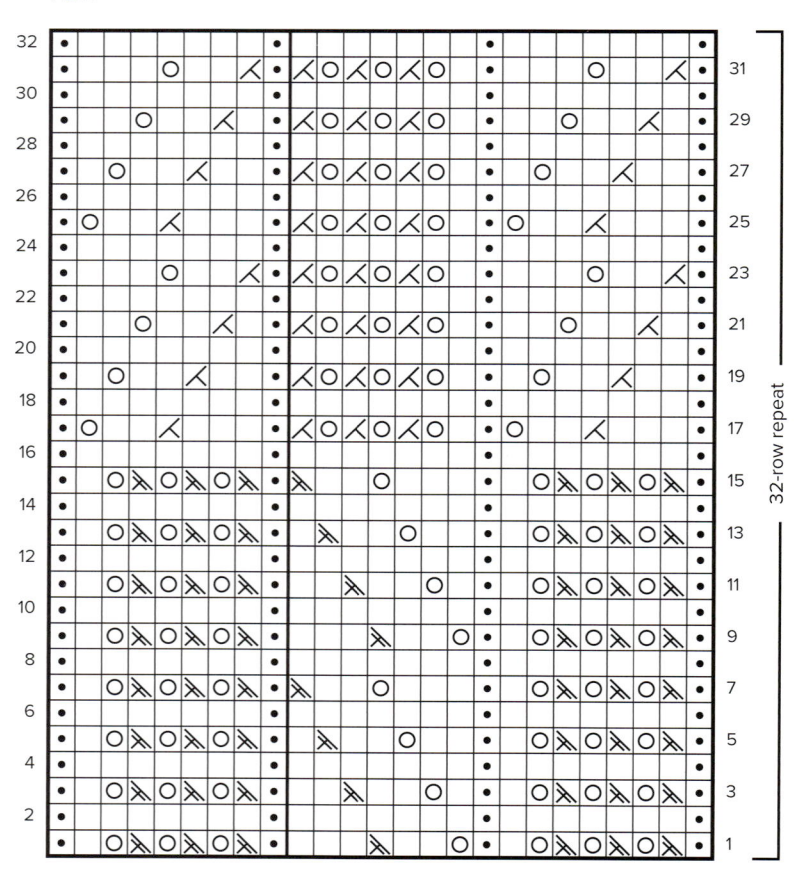

16-st repeat

32-row repeat

ROW 19: *P1, k2, k2tog, k2, yo, k1, p1, k1, [yo, k2tog] 3 times; repeat from * to last 9 sts, p1, k2, k2tog, k2, yo, k1, p1.

ROW 21: *P1, k1, k2tog, k2, yo, k2, p1, k1, [yo, k2tog] 3 times; repeat from * to last 9 sts, p1, k1, k2tog, k2, yo, k2, p1.

ROW 23: *P1, k2tog, k2, yo, k3, p1, k1, [yo, k2tog] 3 times; repeat from * to last 9 sts, p1, k2tog, k2, yo, k3, p1.

ROWS 25-32: Repeat Rows 17–24.

Repeat Rows 1–32 for Kimono Lace Flat.

IN THE ROUND

(multiple of 16 sts; 32-rnd repeat)

RND 1: *P1, [ssk, yo] 3 times, k1, p1, yo, k2, ssk, k3; repeat from * to end.

RND 2 AND ALL EVEN-NUMBERED RNDS: Knit the knit sts and purl the purl sts as they face you; knit all yos.

RND 3: *P1, [ssk, yo] 3 times, k1, p1, k1, yo, k2, ssk, k2; repeat from * to end.

RND 5: *P1, [ssk, yo] 3 times, k1, p1, k2, yo, k2, ssk, k1; repeat from * to end.

RND 7: *P1, [ssk, yo] 3 times, k1, p1, k3, yo, k2, ssk; repeat from * to end.

RND 9-16: Repeat Rnds 1–8.

RND 17: *P1, k3, k2tog, k2, yo, p1, k1, [yo, k2tog] 3 times; repeat from * to end.

RND 19: *P1, k2, k2tog, k2, yo, k1, p1, k1, [yo, k2tog] 3 times; repeat from * to end.

RND 21: *P1, k1, k2tog, k2, yo, k2, p1, k1, [yo, k2tog] 3 times; repeat from * to end.

RND 23: *P1, k2tog, k2, yo, k3, p1, k1, [yo, k2tog] 3 times; repeat from * to end.

RNDS 25-32: Repeat Rnds 17–24.

Repeat Rnds 1–32 for Kimono Lace in the Round.

IN THE ROUND

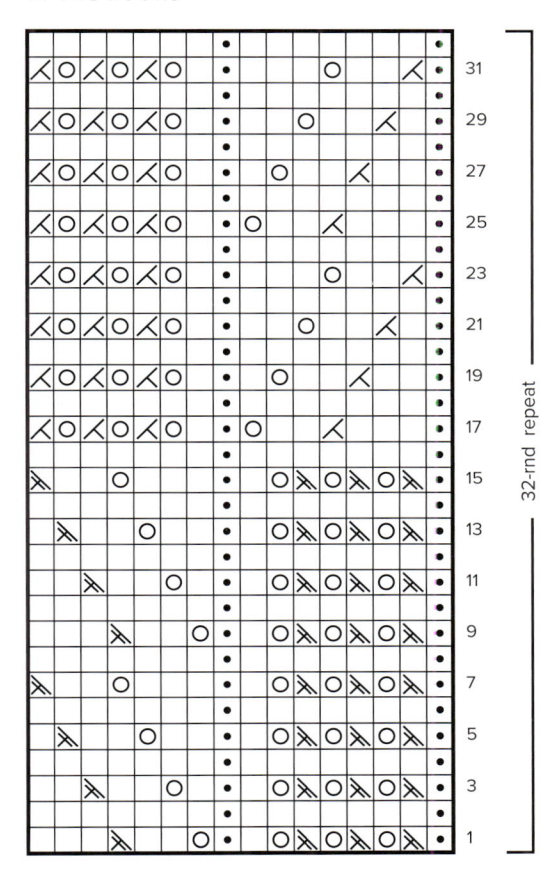

16-st repeat

32-rnd repeat

Wavy Lace

BOTTOM-UP FLAT

(panel of 6 sts worked on a background of Rev St st; 16-row repeat)

ROW 1 (RS): Knit.
ROW 2 AND ALL WS ROWS: Purl.
ROW 3: Yo, k2, ssk, k2.
ROW 5: K1, yo, k2, ssk, k1.
ROW 7: K2, yo, k2, ssk.
ROW 9: Knit.
ROW 11: K2, k2tog, k2, yo.
ROW 13: K1, k2tog, k2, yo, k1.
ROW 15: K2tog, k2, yo, k2.
ROW 16: Purl.
Repeat Rows 1–16 for Wavy Lace Bottom-Up Flat.

BOTTOM-UP IN THE ROUND

(panel of 6 sts worked on a background of Rev St st; 16-rnd repeat)

RND 1: Knit.
RND 2 AND ALL EVEN-NUMBERED RNDS: Knit.
RND 3: Yo, k2, ssk, k2.
RND 5: K1, yo, k2, ssk, k1.
RND 7: K2, yo, k2, ssk.
RND 9: Knit.
RND 11: K2, k2tog, k2, yo.
RND 13: K1, k2tog, k2, yo, k1.
RND 15: K2tog, k2, yo, k2.
RND 16: Knit.
Repeat Rnds 1–16 for Wavy Lace Bottom-Up in the Round.

TOP-DOWN FLAT

(panel of 6 sts worked on a background of Rev St st; 16-row repeat)

ROW 1 (RS): Knit.
ROW 2 AND ALL WS ROWS: Purl.
ROW 3: K2, yo, k2, k2tog.
ROW 5: K1, yo, k2, k2tog, k1.
ROW 7: Yo, k2, k2tog, k2.
ROW 9: Knit.
ROW 11: Ssk, k2, yo, k2.
ROW 13: K1, ssk, k2, yo, k1.
ROW 15: K2, ssk, k2, yo.
ROW 16: Purl.
Repeat Rows 1–16 for Wavy Lace Top-Down Flat.

TOP-DOWN IN THE ROUND

(panel of 6 sts worked on a background of Rev St st; 16-rnd repeat)

RND 1: Knit.
RND 2 AND ALL EVEN-NUMBERED RNDS: Knit.
RND 3: K2, yo, k2, k2tog.
RND 5: K1, yo, k2, k2tog, k1.
RND 7: Yo, k2, k2tog, k2.
RND 9: Knit.
RND 11: Ssk, k2, yo, k2.
RND 13: K1, ssk, k2, yo, k1.
RND 15: K2, ssk, k2, yo.
RND 16: Knit.
Repeat Rnds 1–16 for Wavy Lace Top-Down in the Round.

BOTTOM-UP FLAT & IN THE ROUND

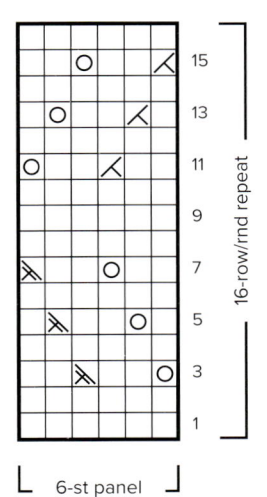

6-st panel

TOP-DOWN FLAT & IN THE ROUND

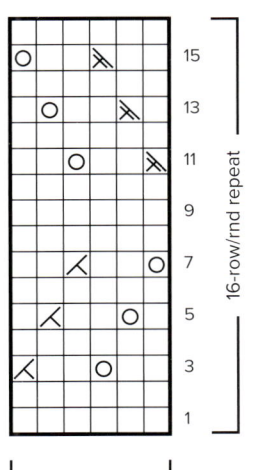

6-st panel

Ostrich Plumes

FLAT

(multiple of 16 sts + 1; 32-row repeat)

NOTE: Pattern begins with a WS row.

ROW 1 (WS): Purl.

ROW 2: Knit.

ROW 3: Purl.

ROW 4: [K1, yo] 3 times, *[ssk] twice, s2kp2, [k2tog] twice, [yo, k1] 5 times, yo; repeat from * to last 14 sts, [ssk] twice, s2kp2, [k2tog] twice, [yo, k1] 3 times.

ROWS 5–16: Repeat Rows 1–4.

ROWS 17–19: Repeat Rows 1–3.

ROW 20: [K2tog] 3 times, *[yo, k1] 5 times, yo, [ssk] twice, s2kp2, [k2tog] twice; repeat from * to last 11 sts, [yo, k1] 5 times, yo, [ssk] 3 times.

ROWS 21–32: Repeat Rows 17–20.

Repeat Rows 1–32 for Ostrich Plumes Flat.

FLAT

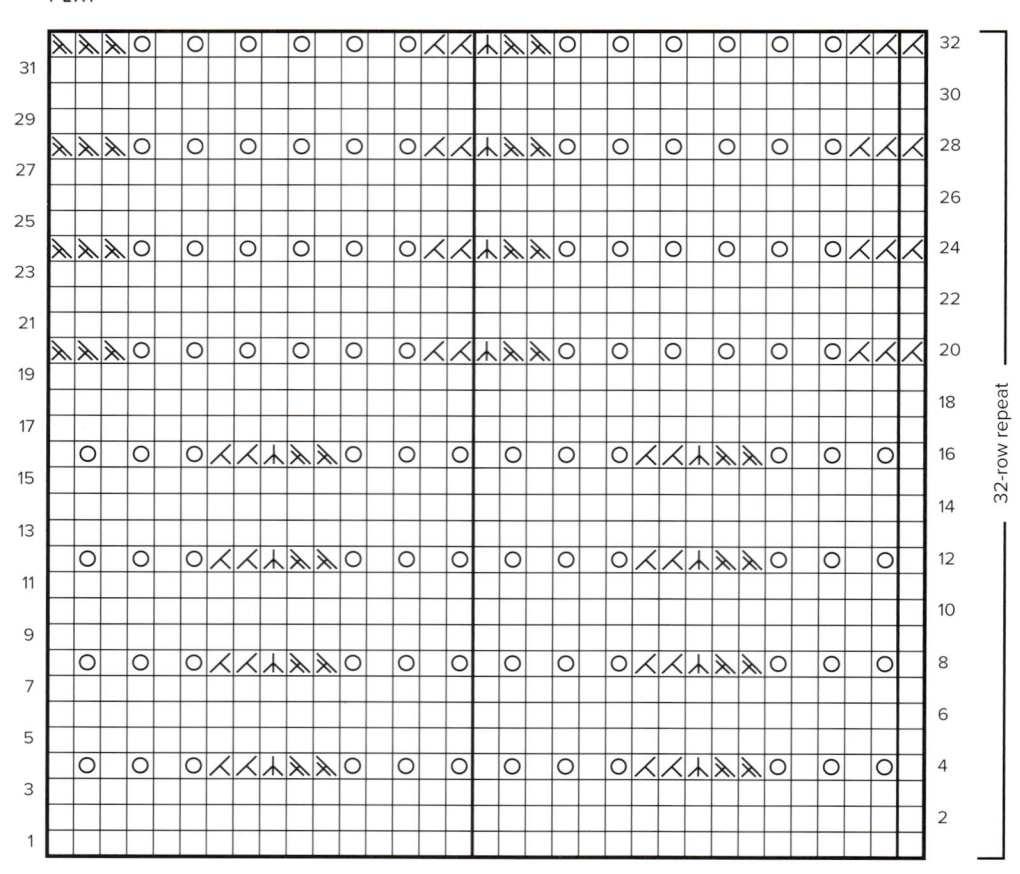

Note: Pattern begins with a WS row.

16-st repeat

IN THE ROUND

(multiple of 16 sts; 32-rnd repeat)

RNDS 1–3: Knit.

RND 4: [K1, yo] 3 times, *[ssk] twice, s2kp2, [k2tog] twice, [yo, k1] 5 times, yo; repeat from * to last 13 sts, [ssk] twice, s2kp2, [k2tog] twice, [yo, k1] twice, yo.

RNDS 5–16: Repeat Rnds 1–4.

RNDS 17 AND 18: Knit.

RND 19: Knit to last st, reposition beginning-of-rnd marker to before last st.

RNDS 20: *S2kp2, [k2tog] twice, [yo, k1] 5 times, yo, [ssk] twice; repeat from * to end.

RNDS 21 AND 22: Knit.

RNDS 23-30: Repeat Rnds 19–22.

RNDS 31 AND 32: Repeat Rnds 19 and 20.

Repeat Rnds 1–32 for Ostrich Plumes in the Round.

IN THE ROUND

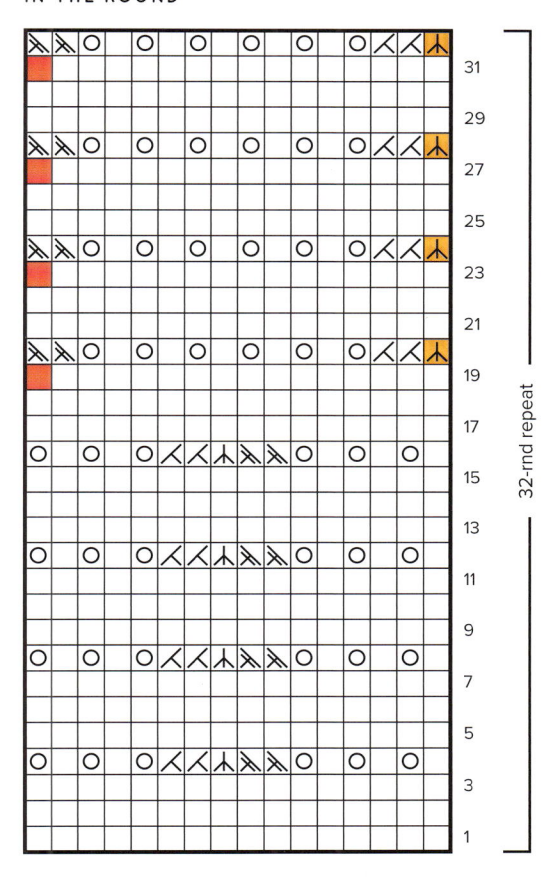

16-st repeat

32-rnd repeat

On Rnds 19, 23, 27, and 31, end rnd 1 st before beginning-of-rnd marker; reposition beginning-of-rnd marker to before final st of rnd.

On first repeat of Rnds 20, 24, 28, and 32 only, work s2kp2 on what was last st of Rnds 19, 23, 27, and 31, and first 2 sts of Rnds 20, 24, 28, and 32; beginning-of-rnd marker should be before this s2k2p2.

Pinecone Ladder

BOTTOM-UP FLAT

(panel of 7 sts worked on a background of Rev St st; 8-row repeat)

ROW 1 (RS): Knit.

ROW 2 AND ALL WS ROWS: Purl.

ROWS 3 AND 5: K1, yo, k2tog, k1, ssk, yo, k1.

ROW 7: K2, yo, s2kp2, yo, k2.

ROW 8: Purl.

Repeat Rows 1–8 for Pinecone Ladder Bottom-Up Flat.

BOTTOM-UP IN THE ROUND

(panel of 7 sts worked on a background of Rev St st; 8-rnd repeat)

RNDS 1 AND 2: Knit.

RND 3: K1, yo, k2tog, k1, ssk, yo, k1.

RNDS 4 AND 5: Repeat Rnds 2 and 3.

RND 6: Knit.

RND 7: K2, yo, s2kp2, yo, k2.

RND 8: Knit.

Repeat Rnds 1–8 for Pinecone Ladder Bottom-Up in the Round.

TOP-DOWN FLAT

(panel of 7 sts worked on a background of Rev St st; 8-row repeat)

ROW 1 (RS): Knit.

ROW 2 AND ALL WS ROWS: Purl.

ROW 3: K2, yo, s2kp2, yo, k2.

ROWS 5 AND 7: K1, yo, ssk, k1, k2tog, yo, k1.

ROW 8: Purl.

Repeat Rows 1–8 for Pinecone Ladder Top-Down Flat.

TOP-DOWN IN THE ROUND

(panel of 7 sts worked on a background of Rev St st; 8-rnd repeat)

RNDS 1 AND 2: Knit.

RND 3: K2, yo, s2kp2, yo, k2.

RND 4: Knit.

RND 5: K1, yo, ssk, k1, k2tog, yo, k1.

RND 6: Knit.

RNDS 7 AND 8: Repeat Rnds 5 and 6.

Repeat Rnds 1–8 for Pinecone Ladder Top-Down in the Round.

TOP-DOWN FLAT & IN THE ROUND

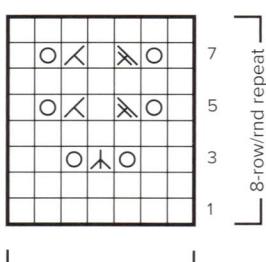

7-st panel · 8-row/rnd repeat

BOTTOM-UP FLAT & IN THE ROUND

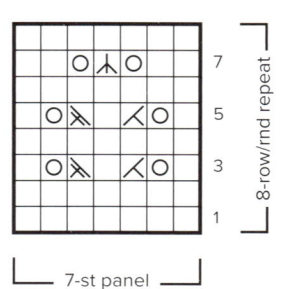

7-st panel · 8-row/rnd repeat

Floral Mesh Lace

FLAT

(multiple of 8 sts + 7; 12-row repeat)

ROW 1 (RS): *K5, yo, ssk, k1, k2tog, yo, k3; repeat from * to last 10 sts, yo, ssk, k1, k2tog, yo, k5.

ROW 2 AND ALL WS ROWS: Purl.

ROW 3: K3, *yo, s2kp2, yo, k3, yo, k2tog; repeat from * to last 4 sts, yo, ssk, k2.

ROW 5: K2, *yo, s2kp2, yo, k2tog, yo, k1, yo, ssk; repeat from * to last 5 sts, yo, s2kp2, yo, k2.

ROW 7: K4, *k2tog, yo, k3, yo, ssk, k1; repeat from * to last 3 sts, k3.

ROW 9: K5, *yo, k2tog, yo, s2kp2, yo, k3; repeat from * to last 10 sts, yo, k2tog, yo, s2kp2, yo, k5.

ROW 11: K1, k2tog, yo, *k1, yo, ssk, yo, s2kp2, yo, k2tog, yo; repeat from * to last 4 sts, k1, yo, ssk, k1.

ROW 12: Repeat Row 2.

Repeat Rows 1–12 rows for Floral Mesh Lace Flat.

FLAT

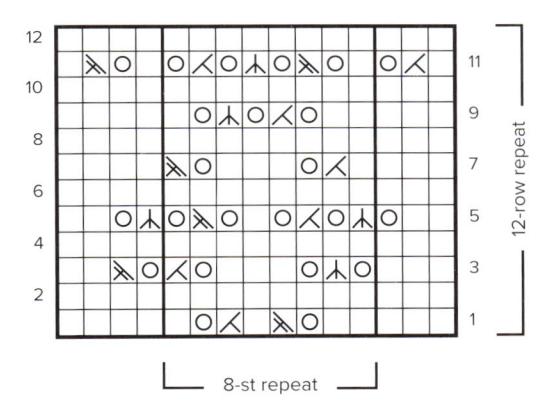

8-st repeat · 12-row repeat

IN THE ROUND

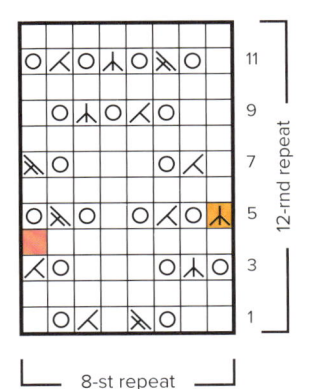

8-st repeat · 12-rnd repeat

On Rnd 4 only, end rnd 1 st before beginning-of-rnd marker; reposition beginning-of-rnd marker to before final st of rnd.

On first repeat of Rnd 5 only, work s2kp2 on what was last st of Rnd 4 and first 2 sts of Rnd 5; beginning-of-rnd marker should be before this s2kp2.

IN THE ROUND

(multiple of 8 sts; 12-rnd repeat)

RND 1: *K2, yo, ssk, k1, k2tog, yo, k1; repeat from * to end.

RND 2: Knit.

RND 3: *Yo, s2kp2, yo, k3, yo, k2tog; repeat from * to end.

RND 4: Knit to last st, reposition beginning-of-rnd marker to before last st.

RND 5: *S2kp2, yo, k2tog, yo, k1, yo, ssk, yo; repeat from * to end.

RND 6: Knit.

RND 7: *K1, k2tog, yo, k3, yo, ssk; repeat from * to end.

RND 8: Knit.

RND 9: *K2, yo, k2tog, yo, s2kp2, yo, k1; repeat from * to end.

RND 10: Knit.

RND 11: *K1, yo, ssk, yo, s2kp2, yo, k2tog, yo; repeat from * to end.

RND 12: Knit.

Repeat Rnds 1–12 for Floral Mesh Lace in the Round.

Yarn-Over Cable

FLAT

(panel of 3 sts worked on a background of Rev St st; 4-row repeat)

NOTE: You will decrease 1 st on Row 1; original st count is restored on Row 2.

ROW 1 (RS): Slip 1 purlwise, k2, psso.

ROW 2: P1, yo, p1.

ROW 3: Knit.

ROW 4: Purl.

Repeat Rows 1–4 for Yarn-Over Cables Flat.

IN THE ROUND

(panel of 3 sts worked on a background of Rev St st; 4-rnd repeat)

NOTE: You will decrease 1 st on Rnd 1; original st count is restored on Rnd 2.

RND 1: Slip 1 purlwise, k2, psso.

RND 2: K1, yo, k1.

RNDS 3 AND 4: Knit.

Repeat Rnds 1–4 for Yarn-Over Cables in the Round.

Japanese Foliage

FLAT

(multiple of 9 sts + 1; 12-row repeat)

ROW 1 (RS): *[K1, yo] 3 times, [k2tog] 3 times; repeat from * to last st, k1.

ROW 2 AND ALL WS ROWS: Purl.

ROWS 3 AND 5: Repeat Row 1.

ROWS 7, 9, AND 11: *K1, [ssk] 3 times, [yo, k1] twice, yo; repeat from * to last st, k1.

ROW 12: Purl.

Repeat Rows 1–12 for Japanese Foliage Flat.

FLAT

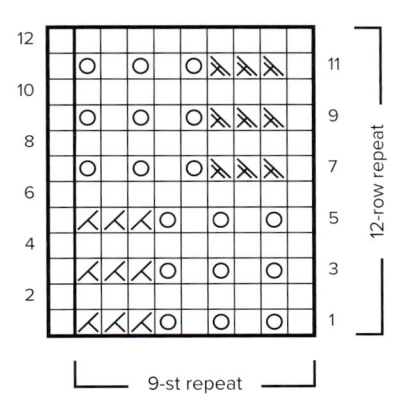

9-st repeat · 12-row repeat

IN THE ROUND

(multiple of 9 sts; 12-rnd repeat)

RND 1: *[K1, yo] 3 times, [k2tog] 3 times; repeat from * to end.

RND 2 AND ALL EVEN-NUMBERED RNDS: Knit.

RNDS 3 AND 5: Repeat Rnd 1.

RNDS 7, 9, AND 11: *K1, [ssk] 3 times, [yo, k1] twice, yo; repeat from * to end.

RND 12: Knit.

Repeat Rnds 1–12 for Japanese Foliage in the Round.

IN THE ROUND

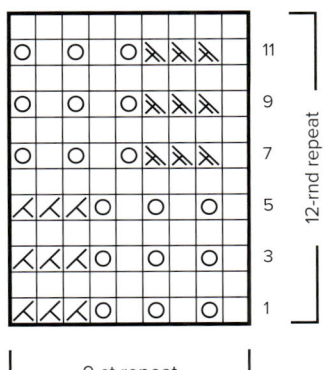

9-st repeat · 12-rnd repeat

Vertical Openwork Stripes

FLAT

(multiple of 7 sts; 4-row repeat)

ROW 1 (RS): *K1, yo, skp, k1, k2tog, yo, k1; repeat from * to end.

ROW 2: Purl.

ROW 3: Knit.

ROW 4: Purl.

Repeat Rows 1–4 for Vertical Openwork Stripes Flat.

IN THE ROUND

(multiple of 7 sts; 4-rnd repeat)

RND 1: *K1, yo, skp, k1, k2tog, yo, k1; repeat from * to end.

RNDS 2–4: Knit.

Repeat Rnds 1–4 for Vertical Openwork Stripes in the Round.

FLAT & IN THE ROUND

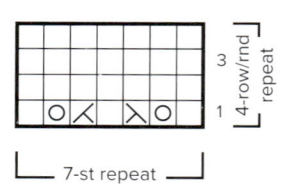

Traveling Ribbed Eyelets

FLAT

(multiple of 7 sts + 2; 16-row repeat)

ROW 1 (RS): *P2, k5; repeat from * to last 2 sts, p2.

ROW 2 AND ALL WS ROWS: Knit the knit sts and purl the purl sts as they face you; purl all yos.

ROWS 3, 5, AND 7: *P2, yo, ssk, k1, k2tog, yo; repeat from * to last 2 sts, p2.

ROW 9: Repeat Row 1.

ROWS 11, 13, AND 15: *P2, k2tog, yo, k1, yo, ssk; repeat from * to last 2 sts, p2.

ROW 16: Repeat Row 2.

Repeat Rows 1–16 for Traveling Ribbed Eyelet Flat.

IN THE ROUND

(multiple of 7 sts; 16-rnd repeat)

RND 1: *P2, k5; repeat from * to end.

RND 2 AND ALL EVEN-NUMBERED RNDS: Repeat Rnd 1.

RNDS 3, 5, AND 7: *P2, yo, ssk, k1, k2tog, yo; repeat from * to end.

RND 9: Repeat Rnd 1.

RNDS 11, 13, AND 15: *P2, k2tog, yo, k1, yo, ssk; repeat from * to end.

RND 16: Repeat Rnd 1.

Repeat Rnds 1–16 for Traveling Ribbed Eyelet in the Round.

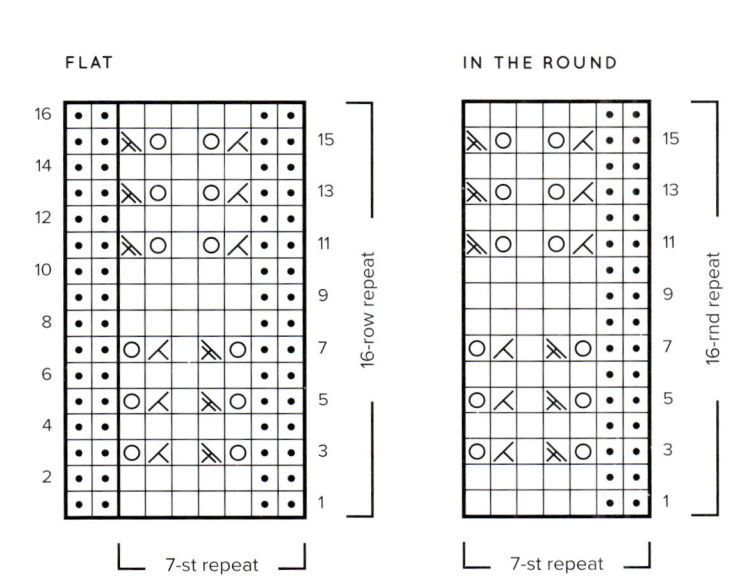

FLAT

IN THE ROUND

Shetland Eyelets

FLAT

(multiple of 9 sts; 8-row repeat)

ROW 1 (RS): *K2, k2tog, yo, k1, yo, ssk, k2; repeat from * to end.

ROW 2 AND ALL WS ROWS: Purl.

ROW 3: *K1, k2tog, yo, k3, yo, ssk, k1; repeat from * to end.

ROW 5: *K1, yo, ssk, yo, s2kp2, yo, k2tog, yo, k1; repeat from * to end.

ROW 7: *K3, yo, s2kp2, yo, k3; repeat from * to end.

ROW 8: Purl.

Repeat Rows 1–8 for Shetland Eyelets Flat.

IN THE ROUND

(multiple of 9 sts; 8-rnd repeat)

RND 1: *K2, k2tog, yo, k1, yo, ssk, k2; repeat from * to end.

RND 2 AND ALL EVEN-NUMBERED RNDS: Knit.

RND 3: *K1, k2tog, yo, k3, yo, ssk, k1; repeat from * to end.

RND 5: *K1, yo, ssk, yo, s2kp2, yo, k2tog, yo, k1; repeat from * to end.

RND 7: *K3, yo, s2kp2, yo, k3; repeat from * to end.

RND 8: Repeat Rnd 2.

Repeat Rnds 1–8 for Shetland Eyelets in the Round.

FLAT & IN THE ROUND

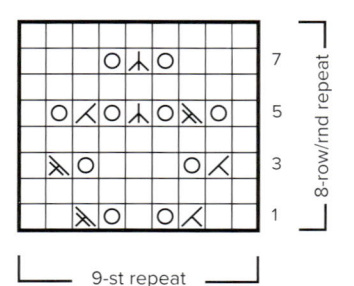

Herringbone Lace

FLAT

(multiple of 6 sts + 2; 12-row repeat)

ROW 1 (RS): *Ssk, k2, yo, k2; repeat from * to last 2 sts, k2.

ROW 2 AND ALL WS ROWS: Purl.

ROWS 3 AND 5: Repeat Row 1.

ROWS 7, 9, AND 11: K1, *k2, yo, k2, k2tog; repeat from * to last st, k1.

ROW 12: Purl.

Repeat Rows 1–12 for Herringbone Lace Flat.

FLAT

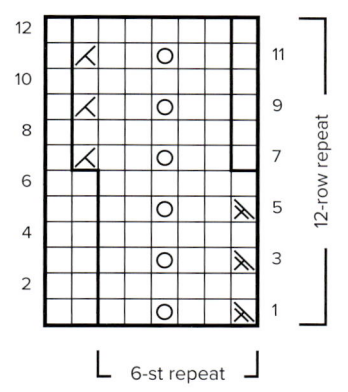

6-st repeat

IN THE ROUND

(multiple of 6 sts; 12-rnd repeat)

RND 1: *Ssk, k2, yo, k2; repeat from * to end.

RND 2: Knit.

RNDS 3 AND 4: Repeat Rnds 1 and 2.

RND 5: Repeat Rnd 1.

RND 6: Knit to last st, remove beginning-of-rnd marker, k1, place replace marker.

RND 7: *K2, yo, k2, k2tog; repeat from * to end.

RND 8: Knit.

RNDS 9 AND 10: Repeat Rnds 7 and 8.

RND 11: Repeat Rnd 7.

RND 12: Knit to last st, reposition beginning-of-rnd marker to before last st.

Repeat Rnds 1–12 for Herringbone Lace in the Round.

IN THE ROUND

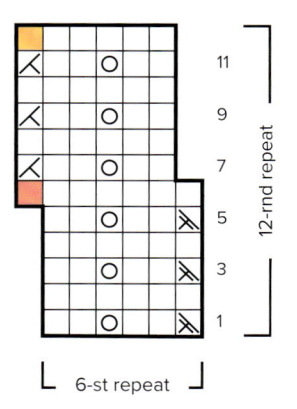

6-st repeat

At end of Rnd 6 only, remove beginning-of-rnd marker, knit first st of Rnd 7, replace marker. On all preceding repeats, omit this st.

At end of Rnd 12 only, reposition beginning-of-rnd marker to before final st. On all preceding repeats, knit this st.

Blossom Cami

Knit in one piece—in the round and from the bottom up—this lace camisole is the perfect multiseason layering piece. It starts out with a classic stitch pattern, Feather and Fan (page 166), and transitions into Floral Mesh Lace (page 201). The top portion is worked last after separating the in-the-round Body into a Front and a Back. Want to swap out the stitch patterns for some of your own choosing? Just look for your size and the corresponding cast-on numbers. Adjust the numbers to fit the required multiples, cast on, and knit (but don't forget to keep notes for yourself as you go)!

SIZES
Small (Medium, Large, 1X-Large, 2X-Large, 3X-Large)

FINISHED MEASUREMENTS
32 (35¼, 42, 45½, 48¾, 54)" [81.5 (89.5, 106.5, 115.5, 124, 137) cm]

YARN
Blue Sky Alpacas Royal (100% alpaca; 288 yards / 100 grams): 2 (2, 3, 3, 3, 3) hanks #711 Vermillion

NEEDLES
One 29" (74 cm) long circular needle size US 4 (3.5 mm)

One pair of double-pointed needles (dpn) size US 3 (3.25 mm)

Change needle size if necessary to obtain correct gauge.

NOTIONS
Stitch marker; stitch holder or waste yarn

GAUGE
19 sts and 27 rows = 4" (10 cm) in Floral Mesh Lace, using larger needle, washed and blocked

STITCH PATTERNS

Feather and Fan
(multiple of 17 sts; 4-rnd repeat)
RND 1: Knit.
RND 2: *[K2tog] 3 times, [yo, k1] 5 times, yo, [ssk] 3 times; repeat from * to end.
RND 3: Purl.
RND 4: Knit.
Repeat Rnds 1–4 for Feather and Fan.

Floral Mesh Lace
(multiple of 8 sts; 12-rnd repeat)
RND 1: *K2, yo, ssk, k1, k2tog, yo, k1; repeat from * to end.
RND 2: Knit.
RND 3: *Yo, s2kp2, yo, k3, yo, k2tog; repeat from * to end.
RND 4: Knit to last st, reposition beginning-of-rnd marker to before last st.
RND 5: *S2kp2, yo, k2tog, yo, k1, yo, ssk, yo; repeat from * to end.
RND 6: Knit.
RND 7: *K1, k2tog, yo, k3, yo, ssk; repeat from * to end.
RND 8: Knit.
RND 9: *K2, yo, k2tog, yo, s2kp2, yo, k1; repeat from * to end.
RND 10: Knit.
RND 11: *K1, yo, ssk, yo, s2kp2, yo, k2tog, yo; repeat from * to end.
RND 12: Knit.
Repeat Rnds 1–12 for Floral Mesh Lace.

FEATHER & FAN

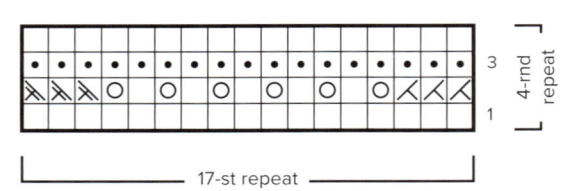

17-st repeat · 4-rnd repeat

FLORAL MESH LACE

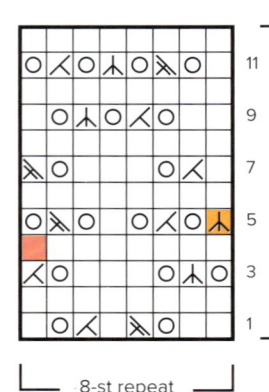

8-st repeat · 12-rnd repeat

On Rnd 4 only, end rnd 1 st before beginning-of-rnd marker; reposition beginning-of-rnd marker to before final st of rnd.

On first repeat of Rnd 5 only, work s2kp2 on what was last st of Rnd 4 and first 2 sts of Rnd 5; beginning-of-rnd marker should be before this s2kp2.

Garter Stitch

(any number of sts; 2-rnd repeat)

RND 1: Knit.

RND 2: Purl.

Repeat Rnds 1 and 2 for Garter Stitch.

CAMI

Using larger needles, CO 153 (170, 204, 221, 238, 255) sts. Join for working in the rnd, being careful not to twist sts; pm for beginning of rnd. Begin Feather and Fan; work Rnds 1–4 seven (7, 7, 8, 8, 8) times.

NEXT RND: Knit, decrease 1 (2, 4, 5, 6, 0) st(s) or increase 0 (0, 0, 0, 0, 1) st(s) evenly—152 (168, 200, 216, 232, 256) sts. Knit 1 rnd.

EYELET RND: *K2tog, yo; repeat from * to end. Knit 2 rnds, purl 1 rnd.

NEXT RND: Change to Floral Mesh Lace; work even until 6 vertical repeats of pattern have been completed. Purl 1 rnd, knit 2 rnds.

EYELET RND: *K2tog, yo; repeat from * to end. Knit 2 rnds, purl 1 rnd.

NEXT RND: Change to Garter st; work even for 8 (8, 8, 12, 12, 12) rnds.

Shape Armholes

NEXT RND: BO 10 (12, 14, 16, 16, 16) sts, k55 (59, 71, 75, 83, 95) and place last 56 (60, 72, 76, 84, 96) sts on holder for Front, BO next 20 (24, 28, 32, 32, 32) sts, knit to last 10 (12, 14, 16, 16, 16) sts, BO to end—56 (60, 72, 76, 84, 96) sts remain for Back. Cut yarn.

BACK

With WS facing, rejoin yarn to Back sts. Knit 1 row.

Shape Back

DECREASE ROW (RS): Slip 1, k1, [ssk] twice, knit to last 6 sts, [k2tog] twice, k2—52 (56, 68, 72, 80, 92) sts remain.

NEXT ROW: Slip 1, knit to end. Repeat last 2 rows once—48 (52, 64, 68, 76, 88) sts remain. BO all sts knitwise.

FRONT

Transfer Front sts to larger needle. With WS facing, rejoin yarn. Knit 1 row.

Shape Front

DECREASE ROW (RS): Slip 1, k1, [ssk] twice, knit to last 6 sts, [k2tog] twice, k2—52 (56, 68, 72, 80, 92) sts remain.

NEXT ROW: Slip 1, knit to end. Repeat last 2 rows twice—44 (48, 60, 64, 72, 84) sts remain. Knit 2 rows, slipping first st of each row. BO all sts knitwise.

FINISHING

Block piece to measurements.

Straps

Using dpns, CO 3 sts; do not turn. *Slide sts back to right-hand end of needle; k3, pulling yarn across back of work; repeat from * until piece measures 15" (38 cm), or to desired length. BO all sts. Sew 1 end to top corner of Front. Pin opposite end to top corner of Back. Try piece on and adjust length of Straps if necessary, then sew to Back.

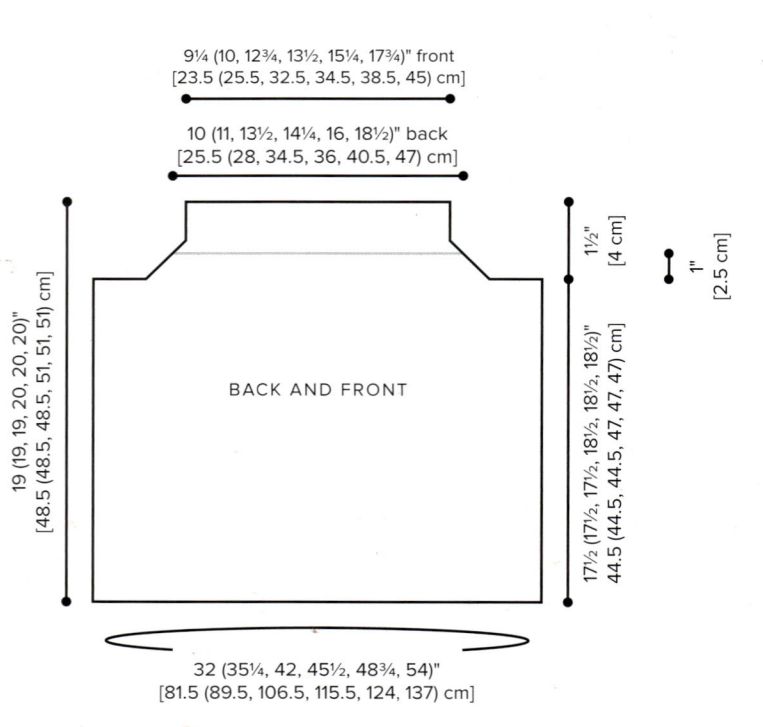

9¼ (10, 12¾, 13½, 15¼, 17¾)" front
[23.5 (25.5, 32.5, 34.5, 38.5, 45) cm]

10 (11, 13½, 14¼, 16, 18½)" back
[25.5 (28, 34.5, 36, 40.5, 47) cm]

1½"
[4 cm]

1"
[2.5 cm]

19 (19, 19, 20, 20, 20)"
[48.5 (48.5, 48.5, 51, 51, 51) cm]

17½ (17½, 17½, 18½, 18½, 18½)"
44.5 (44.5, 44.5, 47, 47, 47) cm]

BACK AND FRONT

32 (35¼, 42, 45½, 48¾, 54)"
[81.5 (89.5, 106.5, 115.5, 124, 137) cm]

CHAPTER 6
MOSAICS

IN THE REALM OF KNITTING, mosaic knitting is a relatively new thing. I'm not completely sure of its origin, but in her first book *A Treasury of Knitting Patterns* (Charles Scribner's Sons; 1968), Barbara G. Walker simply referred to it as "slip-stitch color knitting" and included the patterns in a chapter called "Color-Change Patterns" that featured all manner of colorwork, including Fair Isle. Later, with the publication of *Mosaic Knitting* (Charles Scribner's Sons, 1976), also by Walker, the term "mosaic" as we all know it hit the scene.

Mosaic knitting is a color-knitting technique that requires that you work with only one color at a time (as opposed to Fair Isle, or stranded color knitting, which requires that you carry more than one color). As a result, mosaic knitting is far easier to wrangle than stranded knitting. An interesting and mesmerizing aspect of mosaics is that, even though they were originally designed to depict something specific pictorially, you can sometimes see other images that change into faces or animals, much like the phenomenon *pareidolia*, where people find recognizable images in clouds or on toast. Mosaics lend themselves well to cuffs and hems, hat brims, or even home décor projects like pillow tops, because even though you're using two colors, you only use one color at a time; therefore, you won't be adding extra weight to your fabric, and the drape won't change significantly from the main body of your project. If you've never knit a mosaic before, check out the overview on page 18. xx

STITCHES

HERRINGBONE 1
GEOMETRIC CURLICUES
FOUR-POINT STARS
TOADS
ARTICHOKE
HERRINGBONE 2
CHEVRON BANDS
STAGHEADS
HANGING FRUIT
WAVES
INTERLOCKING FISH
FLOCK OF BIRDS
EGYPTIAN HANDS

OLD OAKS
SIMULATED BASKET-
　WEAVE
LONG ZIGZAG
CHAINS
T-SQUARES
TONGUE AND GROOVE
　STRIPES
SYNCOPATION

PROJECT

MOSAIC AND
　TEXTURE COWL

Herringbone 1

FLAT

(multiple of 8 sts + 3; 16-row repeat)

Using L, CO or work 1 row.

ROW 1 (RS): Using D, k1, *k3, slip 1, k4; repeat from * to last 2 sts, k2.

ROW 2 AND ALL WS ROWS: Using current color, knit or purl the purl sts and slip the slipped sts as they face you.

ROW 3: Using L, k1, *k2, [slip 1, k1] 3 times; repeat from * to last 2 sts, k2.

ROW 5: Using D, k1, *k5, slip 1, k2; repeat from * to last 2 sts, k2.

ROW 7: Using L, k1, *slip 1, k3, [slip 1, k1] twice; repeat from * to last 2 sts, slip 1, k1.

ROW 9: Using D, k1, *k7, slip 1; repeat from * to last 2 sts, k2.

ROW 11: Using L, k1, *slip 1, k1, slip 1, k3, slip 1, k1; repeat from * to last 2 sts, slip 1, k1.

ROW 13: Using D, k1, *k1, slip 1, k6; repeat from * to last 2 sts, k2.

ROW 15: Using L, k1, *[slip 1, k1] twice, slip 1, k3; repeat from * to last 2 sts, slip 1, k1.

ROW 16: Repeat Row 2.

Repeat Rows 1–16 for Herringbone Flat.

IN THE ROUND

(multiple of 8 sts; 16-rnd repeat)

Using L, CO or work 1 rnd.

RND 1: Using D, *k3, slip 1, k4; repeat from * to end.

RND 2 AND ALL EVEN-NUMBERED RNDS: Using current color, knit or purl the knit sts and slip the slipped sts as they face you.

RND 3: Using L, *k2, [slip 1, k1] 3 times; repeat from * to end.

RND 5: Using D, *k5, slip 1, k2; repeat from * to end.

RND 7: Using L, *slip 1, k3, [slip 1, k1] twice; repeat from * to end.

RND 9: Using D, *k7, slip 1; repeat from * to end.

RND 11: Using L, *slip 1, k1, slip 1, k3, slip 1, k1; repeat from * to end.

RND 13: Using D, *k1, slip 1, k6; repeat from * to end.

RND 15: Using L, *[slip 1, k1] twice, slip 1, k3; repeat from * to end.

RND 16: Repeat Rnd 2.

Repeat Rnds 1–16 for Herringbone in the Round.

FLAT

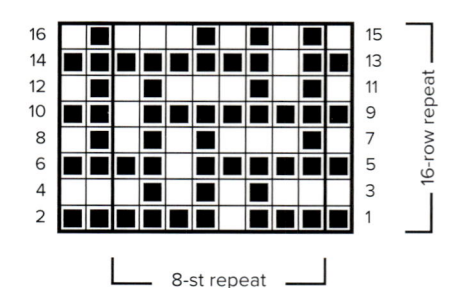

8-st repeat — 16-row repeat

IN THE ROUND

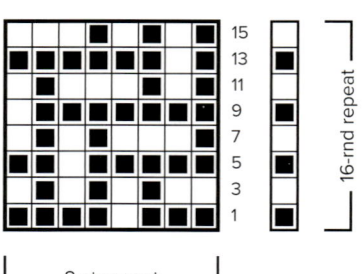

8-st repeat — 16-rnd repeat

NOTE: Swatch is shown in St st. Purl all non-slipped sts on Row 2 when working flat; knit all non-slipped sts on Rnd 2 when working in the round.

Geometric Curlicues

NOTE: Swatch is shown in St st. Purl all non-slipped sts on Row 2 when working flat; knit all non-slipped sts on Rnd 2 when working in the round.

FLAT

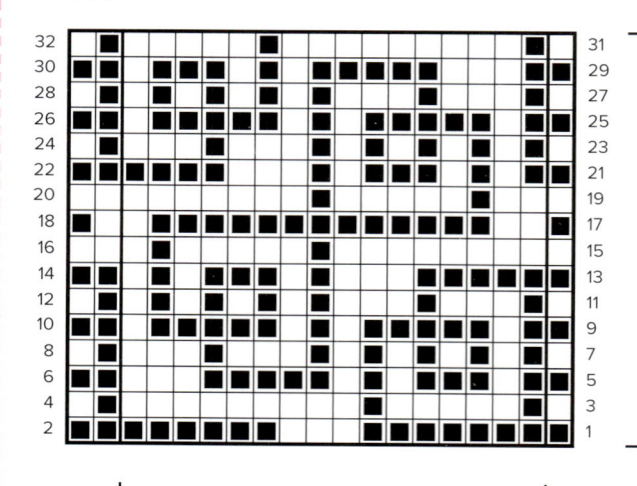

16-st repeat

32-row repeat

(multiple of 16 sts + 3; 32-row repeat)

Using L, CO or work 1 row.

ROW 1 (RS): Using D, k1, *k7, slip 3, k6; repeat from * to last 2 sts, k2.

ROW 2 AND ALL WS ROWS: Using current color, knit or purl the purl sts and slip the slipped sts as they face you.

ROW 3: Using L, k1, *slip 1, k5, slip 1, k9; repeat from * to last 2 sts, slip 1, k1.

ROW 5: Using D, k1, *k1, slip 1, k3, slip 1, k1, slip 1, k5, slip 3; repeat from * to last 2 sts, k2.

ROW 7: Using L, k1, *[slip 1, k1] 4 times, [slip 1, k3] twice; repeat from * to last 2 sts, slip 1, k1.

ROW 9: Using D, k1, *k1, slip 1, k5, slip 1; repeat from * to last 2 sts, k2.

ROW 11: Using L, k1, *[slip 1, k3] twice, [slip 1, k1] 4 times; repeat from * to last 2 sts, slip 1, k1.

ROW 13: Using D, k1, *k5, slip 3, k1, slip 1, k3, slip 1, k1, slip 1; repeat from * to last 2 sts, k2.

ROW 15: Using L, k1, *k8, slip 1, k5, slip 1, k1; repeat from * to last 2 sts, k2.

ROW 17: Using D, k1, *slip 2, k13, slip 1; repeat from * to last 2 sts, slip 1, k1.

ROW 19: Using L, k1, *k2, slip 1, k5, slip 1, k7; repeat from * to last 2 sts, k2.

ROW 21: Using D, k1, *[k1, slip 1] twice, k3, slip 1, k1, slip 3, k4; repeat from * to last 2 sts, k2.

ROW 23: Using L, k1, *[slip 1, k1] 4 times, [slip 1, k3] twice; repeat from * to last 2 sts, slip 1, k1.

ROW 25: Repeat Row 9.

ROW 27: Repeat Row 11.

ROW 29: Using D, k1, *k1, slip 3, k5, slip 1, k1, slip 1, k3, slip 1; repeat from * to last 2 sts, k2.

ROW 31: Using L, k1, *slip 1, k9, slip 1, k5; repeat from * to last 2 sts, slip 1, k1.

ROW 32: Repeat Row 2.

Repeat Rows 1–32 for Geometric Curlicues Flat.

IN THE ROUND

(multiple of 16 sts; 32-rnd repeat)

Using L, CO or work 1 rnd.

RND 1: Using D, *k7, slip 3, k6; repeat from * to end.

RND 2 AND ALL EVEN-NUMBERED RNDS: Using current color, knit or purl the knit sts and slip the slipped sts as they face you.

RND 3: Using L, *slip 1, k5, slip 1, k9; repeat from * to end.

RND 5: Using D, *k1, slip 1, k3, slip 1, k1, slip 1, k5, slip 3; repeat from * to end.

RND 7: Using L, *[slip 1, k1] 4 times, [slip 1, k3] twice; repeat from * to end.

RND 9: Using D, *k1, slip 1, k5, slip 1; repeat from * to end.

RND 11: Using L, *[slip 1, k3] twice, [slip 1, k1] 4 times; repeat from * to end.

RND 13: Using D, *k5, slip 3, k1, slip 1, k3, slip 1, k1, slip 1; repeat from * to end.

RND 15: Using L, *k8, slip 1, k5, slip 1, k1; repeat from * to end.

RND 17: Using D, *slip 2, k13, slip 1; repeat from * to end.

RND 19: Using L, *k2, slip 1, k5, slip 1, k7; repeat from * to end.

RND 21: Using D, *[k1, slip 1] twice, k3, slip 1, k1, slip 3, k4; repeat from * to end.

RND 23: Using L, *[slip 1, k1] 4 times, [slip 1, k3] twice; repeat from * to end.

RND 25: Repeat Rnd 9.

RND 27: Repeat Rnd 11.

RND 29: Using D, *k1, slip 3, k5, slip 1, k1, slip 1, k3, slip 1; repeat from * to end.

RND 31: Using L, *slip 1, k9, slip 1, k5; repeat from * to end.

RND 32: Repeat Rnd 2.

Repeat Rnds 1–32 for Geometric Curlicues in the Round.

IN THE ROUND

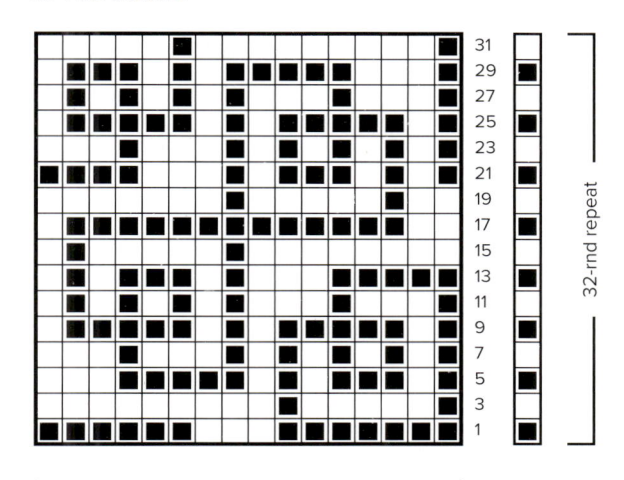

16-st repeat

32-rnd repeat

Four-Point Stars

FLAT

(multiple of 12 sts + 3; 24-row repeat)

Using L, CO or work 1 row.

ROW 1 (RS): Using D, k1, *k5, slip 3, k4; repeat from * to last 2 sts, k2.

ROW 2 AND ALL WS ROWS: Using current color, knit or purl the purl sts and slip the slipped sts as they face you.

ROW 3: Using L, k1, *slip 1, k1, slip 1, k5, slip 1, k3; repeat from * to last 2 sts, slip 1, k1.

ROW 5: Using D, k1, *k1, slip 1, k5, slip 1, k1, slip 1, k2; repeat from * to last 2 sts, k2.

ROW 7: Using L, k1, *slip 1, k5, [slip 1, k1] 3 times; repeat from * to last 2 sts, slip 1, k1.

ROW 9: Using D, k1, *k5, slip 1, k3, slip 1, k1, slip 1; repeat from * to last 2 sts, k2.

ROW 11: Using L, k1, *k4, slip 1, k1, slip 1, k3, slip 1, k1; repeat from * to last 2 sts, k2.

ROW 13: Using D, k1, *slip 2, k9, slip 1; repeat from * to last 2 sts, slip 1, k1.

ROW 15: Using L, k1, *k2, slip 1, k3, slip 1, k1, slip 1, k3; repeat from * to last 2 sts, k2.

ROW 17: Using D, k1, *[k1, slip 1] twice, k3, slip 1, k4; repeat from * to last 2 sts, k2.

ROW 19: Using L, k1, *[slip 1, k1] 3 times, slip 1, k5; repeat from * to last 2 sts, slip 1, k1.

ROW 21: Using D, k1, *k3, slip 1, k1, slip 1, k5, slip 1; repeat from * to last 2 sts, k2.

ROW 23: Using L, k1, *slip 1, k3, slip 1, k5, slip 1, k1; repeat from * to last 2 sts, slip 1, k1.

ROW 24: Repeat Row 2.

Repeat Rows 1–24 for Four-Point Stars Flat.

IN THE ROUND

(multiple of 12 sts; 24-rnd repeat)

Using L, CO or work 1 rnd.

RND 1: Using D, *k5, slip 3, k4; repeat from * to end.

RND 2 AND ALL EVEN-NUMBERED RNDS: Using current color, knit or purl the knit sts and slip the slipped sts as they face you.

RND 3: Using L, *slip 1, k1, slip 1, k5, slip 1, k3; repeat from * to end.

RND 5: Using D, *k1, slip 1, k5, slip 1, k1, slip 1, k2; repeat from * to end.

RND 7: Using L, *slip 1, k5, [slip 1, k1] 3 times; repeat from * to end.

RND 9: Using D, *k5, slip 1, k3, slip 1, k1, slip 1; repeat from * to end.

RND 11: Using L, *k4, slip 1, k1, slip 1, k3, slip 1, k1; repeat from * to end.

RND 13: Using D, *slip 2, k9, slip 1; repeat from * to end.

RND 15: Using L, *k2, slip 1, k3, slip 1, k1, slip 1, k3; repeat from * to end.

RND 17: Using D, [k1, slip 1] twice, k3, slip 1, k4; repeat from * to end.

RND 19: Using L, *[slip 1, k1] 3 times, slip 1, k5; repeat from * to end.

RND 21: Using D, *k3, slip 1, k1, slip 1, k5, slip 1; repeat from * to end.

RND 23: Using L, *slip 1, k3, slip 1, k5, slip 1, k1; repeat from * to end.

RND 24: Repeat Rnd 2.

Repeat Rnds 1–24 for Four-Point Stars in the Round.

FLAT

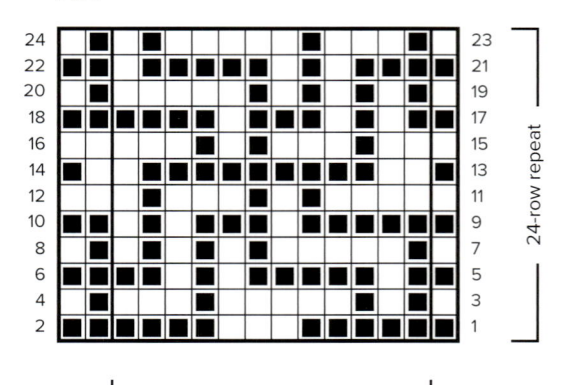

24-row repeat

12-st repeat

IN THE ROUND

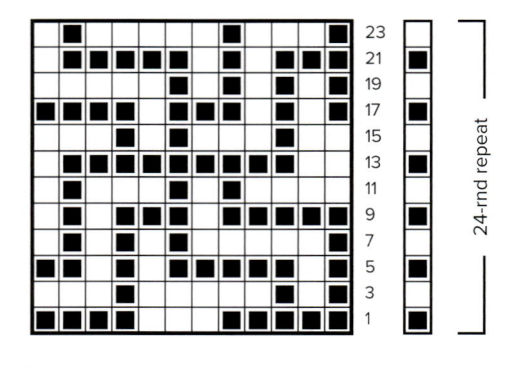

24-rnd repeat

12-st repeat

NOTE: Swatch is shown in St st. Purl all non-slipped sts on Row 2 when working flat; knit all non-slipped sts on Rnd 2 when working in the round.

Toads

FLAT

(multiple of 10 sts + 3; 20-row repeat)

Using L, CO or work 1 row.

ROW 1 (RS): Using D, k1, *slip 3, k3, slip 1, k3; repeat from * to last 2 sts, slip 1, k1.

ROW 2 AND ALL WS ROWS: Using current color, knit or purl the purl sts and slip the slipped sts as they face you.

ROW 3: Using L, k1, *k3, slip 1, k5, slip 1; repeat from * to last 2 sts, k2.

ROW 5: Using D, k1, *k4, slip 1, k3, slip 1, k1; repeat from * to last 2 sts, k2.

ROW 7: Using L, k1, *k1, slip 1, k3, slip 3, k2; repeat from * to last 2 sts, k2.

ROW 9: Using D, k1, *k2, slip 1, k5, slip 1, k1; repeat from * to last 2 sts, k2.

ROW 11: Using L, k1, *k3, slip 3, k3, slip 1; repeat from * to last 2 sts, k2.

ROW 13: Using D, k1, *k2, [slip 1, k3] twice; repeat from * to last 2 sts, k2.

ROW 15: Using L, k1, *k1, slip 1, k5, slip 1, k2; repeat from * to last 2 sts, k2.

ROW 17: Using D, k1, *[slip 1, k3] twice, slip 2; repeat from * to last 2 sts, slip 1, k1.

ROW 19: Using L, k1, *[k3, slip 1] twice, k2; repeat from * to last 2 sts, k2.

ROW 20: Repeat Row 2.

Repeat Rows 1–20 for Toads Flat.

IN THE ROUND

(multiple of 10 sts; 20-rnd repeat)

Using L, CO or work 1 rnd.

RND 1: Using D, *slip 3, k3, slip 1, k3; repeat from * to end.

RND 2 AND ALL EVEN-NUMBERED RNDS: Using current color, knit or purl the knit sts and slip the slipped sts as they face you.

RND 3: Using L, *k3, slip 1, k5, slip 1; repeat from * to end.

RND 5: Using D, *k4, slip 1, k3, slip 1, k1; repeat from * to end.

RND 7: Using L, *k1, slip 1, k3, slip 3, k2; repeat from * to end.

RND 9: Using D, *k2, slip 1, k5, slip 1, k1; repeat from * to end.

RND 11: Using L, *k3, slip 3, k3, slip 1; repeat from * to end.

RND 13: Using D, *k2, [slip 1, k3] twice; repeat from * to end.

RND 15: Using L, *k1, slip 1, k5, slip 1, k2; repeat from * to end.

RND 17: Using D, *[slip 1, k3] twice, slip 2; repeat from * to end.

RND 19: Using L, *[k3, slip 1] twice, k2; repeat from * to end.

RND 20: Repeat Rnd 2.

Repeat Rnds 1–20 for Toads in the Round.

FLAT

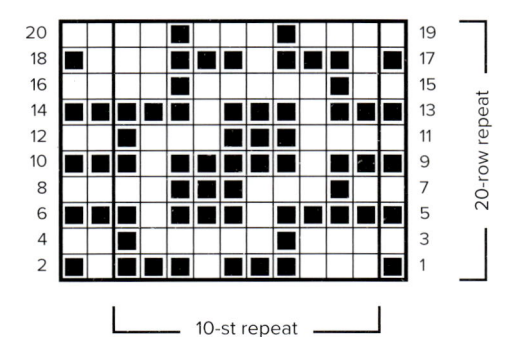

IN THE ROUND

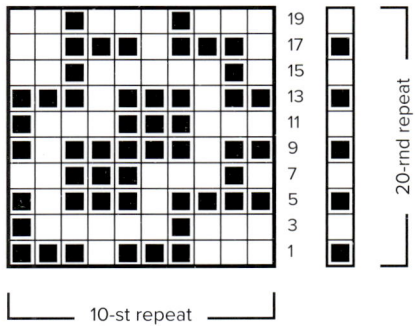

NOTE: Swatch is shown in St st. Purl all non-slipped sts on Row 2 when working flat; knit all non-slipped sts on Rnd 2 when working in the round.

Artichoke

FLAT

(multiple of 10 sts + 3; 20-row repeat)

Using L, CO or work 1 row.

ROW 1 (RS): Using D, k1, *slip 1, k1, slip 1, k3, [slip 1, k1] twice; repeat from * to last 2 sts, slip 1, k1.

ROW 2 AND ALL WS ROWS: Using current color, knit or purl the purl sts and slip the slipped sts as they face you.

ROW 3: Using L, k1, *k3, slip 1, k1, slip 1, k4; repeat from * to last 2 sts, k2.

ROW 5: Using D, k1, *slip 1, k7, slip 1, k1; repeat from * to last 2 sts, slip 1, k1.

ROW 7: Using L, k1, *[k1, slip 1] 4 times, k2; repeat from * to last 2 sts, k2.

ROW 9: Using D, k1, *slip 1, k9; repeat from * to last 2 sts, slip 1, k1.

ROW 11: Using L, k1, *k3, [slip 1, k1] 3 times, slip 1; repeat from * to last 2 sts, k2.

ROW 13: Using D, k1, *slip 1, k1, slip 1, k7; repeat from * to last 2 sts, slip 1, k1.

ROW 15: Using L, k1, *k5, slip 1, k1, slip 1, k2; repeat from * to last 2 sts, k2.

ROW 17: Using D, k1, *[slip 1, k1] twice, slip 1, k3, slip 1, k1; repeat from * to last 2 sts, slip 1, k1.

ROW 19: Using L, k1, *k5, slip 1, k4; repeat from * to last 2 sts, k2.

ROW 20: Repeat Row 2.

Repeat Rows 1–19 for Artichoke Flat.

IN THE ROUND

(multiple of 10 sts; 20-rnd repeat)

Using L, CO or work 1 rnd.

RND 1: Using D, *slip 1, k1, slip 1, k3, [slip 1, k1] twice; repeat from * to end.

RND 2 AND ALL EVEN-NUMBERED RNDS: Using current color, knit or purl the knit sts and slip the slipped sts as they face you.

RND 3: Using L, *k3, slip 1, k1, slip 1, k4; repeat from * to end.

RND 5: Using D, slip 1, k7, slip 1, k1; repeat from to end.

RND 7: Using L, *[k1, slip 1] 4 times, k2; repeat from * to end.

RND 9: Using D, *slip 1, k9; repeat from * to end.

RND 11: Using L, *k3, [slip 1, k1] 3 times, slip 1; repeat from * to end.

RND 13: Using D, *slip 1, k1, slip 1, k7; repeat from * to end.

RND 15: Using L, *k5, slip 1, k1, slip 1, k2; repeat from * to end.

RND 17: Using D, *[slip 1, k1] twice, slip 1, k3, slip 1, k1; repeat from * to end.

RND 19: Using L, *k5, slip 1, k4; repeat from * to end.

RND 20: Repeat Rnd 2.

Repeat Rnds 1–20 for Artichoke in the Round.

FLAT

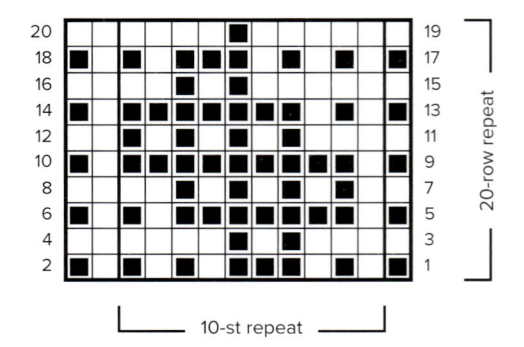

IN THE ROUND

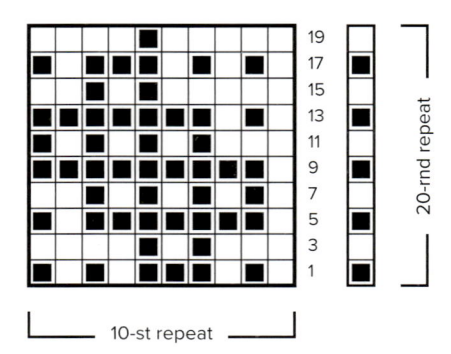

NOTE: Swatch is shown in St st. Purl all non-slipped sts on Row 2 when working flat; knit all non-slipped sts on Rnd 2 when working in the round.

Herringbone 2

FLAT

(multiple of 8 sts + 3; 16-row repeat)

Using L, CO or work 1 row.

ROW 1 (RS): Using D, k1, *k2, slip 1, k3, slip 2; repeat from * to last 2 sts, k2.

ROW 2 AND ALL WS ROWS: Using current color, knit or purl the purl sts and slip the slipped sts as they face you.

ROW 3: Using L, k1, *[k1, slip 1] 3 times, k2; repeat from * to last 2 sts, k2.

ROW 5: Using D, k1, *slip 1, k3, slip 1, k2, slip 1; repeat from * to last 2 sts, slip 1, k1.

ROW 7: Using L, k1, *k2, slip 1, k3, slip 1, k1; repeat from * to last 2 sts, k2.

ROW 9: Using D, k1, *slip 1, k2, slip 2, k3; repeat from * to last 2 sts, slip 1, k1.

ROW 11: Using L, k1, *k1, slip 1, k3, slip 1, k1, slip 1; repeat from * to last 2 sts, k2.

ROW 13: Using D, k1, *k2, slip 2, k2, slip 1, k1; repeat from * to last 2 sts, k2.

ROW 15: Using L, k1, *[slip 1, k3] twice; repeat from * to last 2 sts, slip 1, k1.

ROW 16: Repeat Row 2.

Repeat Rows 1–15 for Herringbone 2 Flat.

IN THE ROUND

(multiple of 8 sts; 16-rnd repeat)

Using L, CO or work 1 rnd.

RND 1: Using D, *k2, slip 1, k3, slip 2; repeat from * to end.

RND 2 AND ALL EVEN-NUMBERED RNDS: Using current color, knit or purl the knit sts and slip the slipped sts as they face you.

RND 3: Using L, *[k1, slip 1] 3 times, k2; repeat from * to end.

RND 5: Using D, *slip 1, k3, slip 1, k2, slip 1; repeat from * to end.

RND 7: Using L, *k2, slip 1, k3, slip 1, k1; repeat from * to end.

RND 9: Using D, *slip 1, k2, slip 2, k3; repeat from * to end.

RND 11: Using L, *k1, slip 1, k3, slip 1, k1, slip 1; repeat from * to end.

RND 13: Using D, *k2, slip 2, k2, slip 1, k1; repeat from * to end.

RND 15: Using L, *[slip 1, k3] twice; repeat from * to end.

RND 16: Repeat Rnd 2.

Repeat Rnds 1–16 for Herringbone 2 in the Round.

FLAT

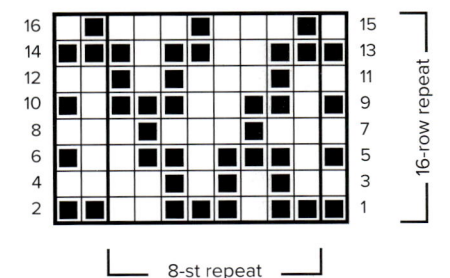

8-st repeat

16-row repeat

IN THE ROUND

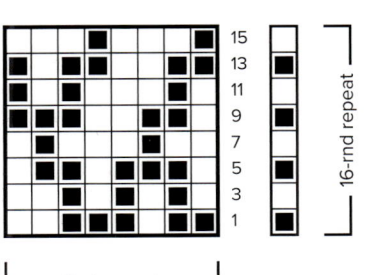

8-st repeat

16-rnd repeat

NOTE: Swatch is shown in St st. Purl all non-slipped sts on Row 2 when working flat; knit all non-slipped sts on Rnd 2 when working in the round.

Chevron Bands

NOTE: Swatch is shown in Garter st. Knit all non-slipped sts on Row 2 when working flat; purl all non-slipped sts on Rnd 2 when working in the round.

FLAT

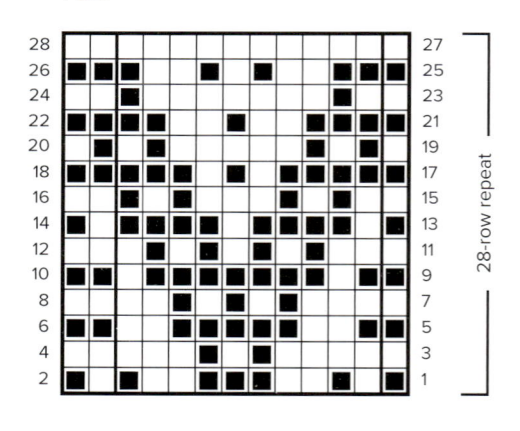

10-st repeat

FLAT

(multiple of 10 sts + 3; 28-row repeat)

Using L, CO or work 1 row.

ROW 1 (RS): Using D, k1, *slip 1, k1, slip 2, k3, slip 2, k1; repeat from * to last 2 sts, slip 1, k1.

ROW 2 AND ALL WS ROWS: Using current color, knit or purl the purl sts and slip the slipped sts as they face you.

ROW 3: Using L, k1, *k4, slip 1, k1, slip 1, k3; repeat from * to last 2 sts, k2.

ROW 5: Using D, k1, *k1, slip 2, k5, slip 2; repeat from * to last 2 st, k2.

ROW 7: Using L, k1, *k3, [slip 1, k1] twice, slip 1, k2; repeat from * to last 2 sts, k2.

ROW 9: Using D, k1, *k1, slip 1, k7, slip 1; repeat from * to last 2 sts, k2.

ROW 11: Using L, k1, *k2, [slip 1, k1] 4 times; repeat from * last 2 sts, k2.

ROW 13: Using D, k1, *slip 1, k4; repeat from * to last 2 sts, slip 1, k1.

ROW 15: Using L, k1, *[k1, slip 1] twice, k3, slip 1, k1, slip 1; repeat from * to last 2 sts, k2.

ROW 17: Using D, k1, *k4, slip 1, k1, slip 1, k3; repeat from * to last 2 sts, k2.

ROW 19: Using L, k1, *slip 1, k1, slip 1, k5, slip 1, k1; repeat from * to last 2 sts, slip 1, k1.

ROW 21: Using D, k1, *k3, slip 2, k1, slip 2, k2; repeat from * to last 2 sts, k2.

ROW 23: Using L, k1, *k1, slip 1, k7, slip 1; repeat from * to last 2 sts, k2.

ROW 25: Using D, k1, *k2, slip 2, k1, slip 1, k1, slip 2, k1; repeat from * to last 2 sts, k2.

ROW 27: Using L, knit.

ROW 28: Repeat Row 2.

Repeat Rows 1–28 for Chevron Bands Flat.

IN THE ROUND

(multiple of 10 sts; 28-rnd repeat)

Using L, CO or work 1 rnd.

RND 1: Using D, *slip 1, k1, slip 2, k3, slip 2, k1; repeat from * to end.

RND 2 AND ALL EVEN-NUMBERED RNDS: Using current color, knit or purl the knit sts and slip the slipped sts as they face you.

RND 3: Using L, *k4, slip 1, k1, slip 1, k3; repeat from * to end.

RND 5: Using D, *k1, slip 2, k5, slip 2; repeat from * to end.

RND 7: Using L, *k3, [slip 1, k1] twice, slip 1, k2; repeat from * to end.

RND 9: Using D, *k1, slip 1, k7, slip 1; repeat from * to end.

RND 11: Using L, *k2, [slip 1, k1] 4 times; repeat from * to end.

RND 13: Using D, *slip 1, k4; repeat from * to end.

RND 15: Using L, *[k1, slip 1] twice, k3, slip 1, k1, slip 1; repeat from * to end.

RND 17: Using D, *k4, slip 1, k1, slip 1, k3; repeat from * to end.

RND 19: Using L, *slip 1, k1, slip 1, k5, slip 1, k1; repeat from * to end.

RND 21: Using D, *k3, slip 2, k1, slip 2, k2; repeat from * to end.

RND 23: Using L, *k1, slip 1, k7, slip 1; repeat from * to end.

RND 25: Using D, *k2, slip 2, k1, slip 1, k1, slip 2, k1; repeat from * to end.

RND 27: Using L, knit.

RND 28: Repeat Rnd 2.

Repeat Rnds 1–28 for Chevron Bands in the Round.

IN THE ROUND

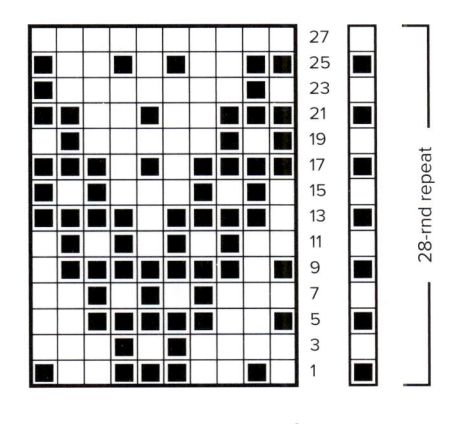

10-st repeat

28-rnd repeat

Stagheads

NOTE: Swatch is shown in Garter st. Knit all non-slipped sts on Row 2 when working flat; purl all non-slipped sts on Rnd 2 when working in the round.

FLAT

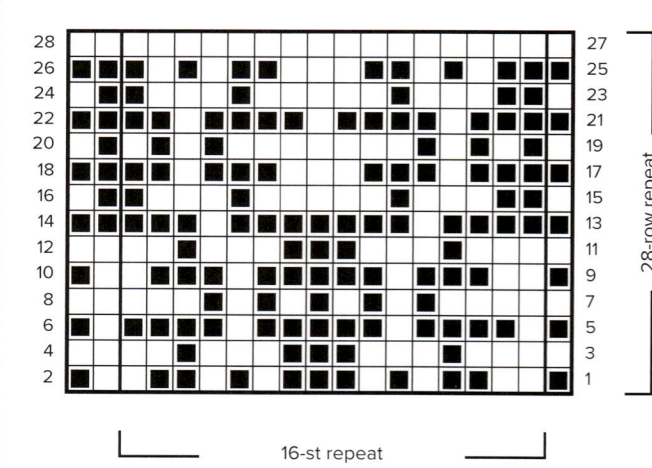

16-st repeat

28-row repeat

FLAT

(multiple of 16 sts + 3; 28-row repeat)

Using L, CO or work 1 row.

ROW 1 (RS): Using D, k1, *slip 2, k2, slip 1, k1, slip 1, k3, slip 1, k1, slip 1, k2, slip 1; repeat from * to last 2 sts, slip 1, k1.

ROW 2 AND ALL WS ROWS: Using current color, knit or purl the purl sts and slip the slipped sts as they face you.

ROW 3: Using L, k1, *k3, slip 1, k3, slip 3, k3, slip 1, k2; repeat from * to last 2 sts, k2.

ROW 5: Using D, k1, *slip 1, k4, slip 1, k5, slip 1, k4; repeat from * to last 2 sts, slip 1, k1.

ROW 7: Using L, k1, *k4, [slip 1, k1] 4 times, slip 1, k3; repeat from * to last 2 sts, k2.

ROW 9: Using D, k1, *slip 2, k3, slip 1, k5, slip 1, k3, slip 1; repeat from * to last 2 sts, slip 1, k1.

ROW 11: Repeat Row 3.

ROW 13: Using D, k1, *k4, slip 1, k7, slip 1, k3; repeat from * to last 2 sts, k2.

ROW 15: Using L, repeat Row 9.

ROW 17: Using D, repeat Row 3.

ROW 19: Using L, k1, *[slip 1, k1] twice, slip 1, k7, [slip 1, k1] twice; repeat from * to last 2 sts, slip 1, k1.

ROW 21: Using D, k1, *k3, [slip 1, k4] twice, slip 1, k2; repeat from * to last 2 sts, k2.

ROW 23: Using L, repeat Row 9.

ROW 25: Using D, k1, *k2, slip 1, k1, slip 1, k2, slip 3, k2, [slip 1, k1] twice; repeat from * to last 2 sts, k2.

ROW 27: Using L, knit.

ROW 28: Repeat Row 2.

Repeat Rows 1–28 for Stagheads Flat.

IN THE ROUND

(multiple of 16 sts; 28-rnd repeat)

Using L, CO or work 1 rnd.

RND 1: Using D, *slip 2, k2, slip 1, k1, slip 1, k3, slip 1, k1, slip 1, k2, slip 1; repeat from * to end.

RND 2 AND ALL EVEN-NUMBERED RNDS: Using current color, knit or purl the knit sts and slip the slipped sts as they face you.

RND 3: Using L, *k3, slip 1, k3, slip 3, k3, slip 1, k2; repeat from * to end.

RND 5: Using D, *slip 1, k4, slip 1, k5, slip 1, k4; repeat from * to end.

RND 7: Using L, *k4, [slip 1, k1] 4 times, slip 1, k3; repeat from * to end.

RND 9: Using D, *slip 2, k3, slip 1, k5, slip 1, k3, slip 1; repeat from * to end.

RND 11: Repeat Rnd 3.

RND 13: Using D, *k4, slip 1, k7, slip 1, k3; repeat from * to end.

RND 15: Using L, repeat Rnd 9.

RND 17: Using D, repeat Rnd 3.

RND 19: Using L, *[slip 1, k1] twice, slip 1, k7, [slip 1, k1] twice; repeat from * to end.

RND 21: Using D, *k3, [slip 1, k4] twice, slip 1, k2; repeat from * to end.

RND 23: Using L, repeat Rnd 9.

RND 25: Using D, *k2, slip 1, k1, slip 1, k2, slip 3, k2, [slip 1, k1] twice; repeat from * to end.

RND 27: Using L, knit.

RND 28: Repeat Rnd 2.

Repeat Rnds 1–28 for Stagheads in the Round.

IN THE ROUND

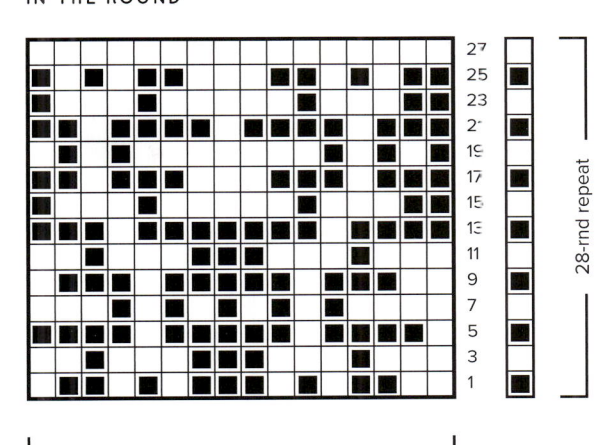

16-st repeat

28-rnd repeat

Hanging Fruit

NOTE: Swatch is shown in Garter st. Knit all non-slipped sts on Row 2 when working flat; purl all non-slipped sts on Rnd 2 when working in the round.

BOTTOM-UP FLAT

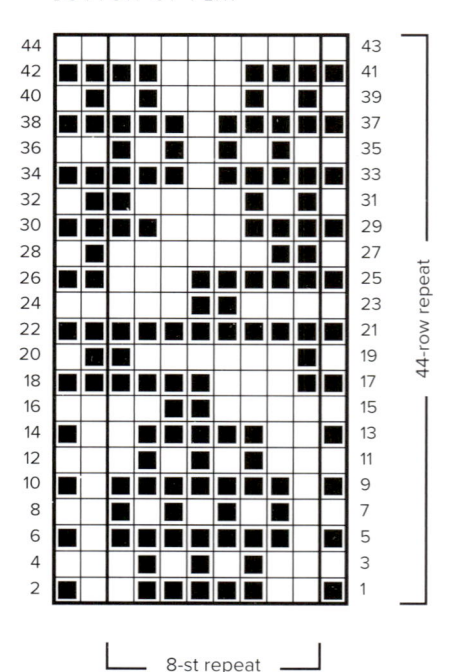

8-st repeat

44-row repeat

BOTTOM-UP FLAT

(multiple of 8 sts + 3; 44-row repeat)

Using L, CO or work 1 row.

ROW 1 (RS): Using D, k1, *slip 2, k5, slip 1; repeat from * to last 2 sts, slip 1, k1.

ROW 2 AND ALL WS ROWS: Using current color, knit or purl the purl sts and slip the slipped sts as they face you.

ROW 3: Using L, k1, *k2, [slip 1, k1] 3 times; repeat from * to last 2 sts, k2.

ROW 5: Using D, k1, *slip 1, k7; repeat from * to last 2 sts, slip 1, k1.

ROW 7: Using L, k1, *[k1, slip 1] 4 times; repeat from * to last 2 sts, k2.

ROW 9: Repeat Row 5.

ROW 11: Repeat Row 3.

ROW 13: Repeat Row 1.

ROW 15: Using L, k1, *k4, slip 2, k2; repeat from * to last 2 sts, k2.

ROW 17: Using D, k1, *k1, slip 3, k4; repeat from * to last 2 sts, k2.

ROW 19: Using L, k1, *slip 1, k6, slip 1; repeat from * to last 2 sts, slip 1, k1.

ROW 21: Using D, knit.

ROW 23: Using L, k1, *k3, slip 2, k3; repeat from * to last 2 sts, k2.

ROW 25: Using D, k1, *k5, slip 3; repeat from * to last 2 sts, k2.

ROW 27: Using L, k1, *slip 2, k6; repeat from * to last 2 sts, slip 1, k1.

ROW 29: Using D, k1, *k3, slip 3, k2; repeat from * to last 2 sts, k2.

ROW 31: Using L, k1, *slip 1, k1, slip 1, k4, slip 1; repeat from * to last 2 sts, slip 1, k1.

ROW 33: Using D, k1, *k4, slip 1, k3; repeat from * to last 2 sts, k2.

ROW 35: Repeat Row 7.

ROW 37: Repeat Row 33.

ROW 39: Using L, k1, *slip 1, k1, slip 1, k3, slip 1, k1; repeat from * to last 2 sts, slip 1, k1.

ROW 41: Using D, k1, *k3, slip 3, k2; repeat from * to last 2 sts, k2.

ROW 43: Using L, knit.

ROW 44: Repeat Row 2.

Repeat Rows 1–44 for Hanging Fruit Bottom-Up Flat.

BOTTOM-UP IN THE ROUND

(multiple of 8 sts; 44-rnd repeat)

Using L, CO or work 1 rnd.

RND 1: Using D, *slip 2, k5, slip 1; repeat from * to end.

RND 2 AND ALL EVEN-NUMBERED RNDS: Using current color, knit or purl the knit sts and slip the slipped sts as they face you.

RND 3: Using L, *k2, [slip 1, k1] 3 times; repeat from * to end.

RND 5: Using D, *slip 1, k7; repeat from * to end.

RND 7: Using L, *[k1, slip 1] 4 times; repeat from * to end.

RND 9: Repeat Rnd 5.

RND 11: Repeat Row 3.

RND 13: Repeat Rnd 1.

RND 15: Using L, *k4, slip 2, k2; repeat from * to end.

RND 17: Using D, *k1, slip 3, k4; repeat from * to end.

RND 19: Using L, *slip 1, k6, slip 1; repeat from * to end.

RND 21: Using D, knit.

RND 23: Using L, *k3, slip 2, k3; repeat from * to end.

RND 25: Using D, *k5, slip 3; repeat from * to end.

RND 27: Using L, *slip 2, k6; repeat from * to end.

RND 29: Using D, *k3, slip 3, k2; repeat from * to end.

RND 31: Using L, *slip 1, k1, slip 1, k4, slip 1; repeat from * to end.

RND 33: Using D, *k4, slip 1, k3; repeat from * to end.

RND 35: Repeat Rnd 7.

RND 37: Repeat Rnd 33.

RND 39: Using L, *slip 1, k1, slip 1, k3, slip 1, k1; repeat from * to end.

RND 41: Using D, *k3, slip 3, k2; repeat from * to end.

RND 43: Using L, knit.

RND 44: Repeat Rnd 2.

Repeat Rnds 1–44 for Hanging Fruit Bottom-Up in the Round.

BOTTOM-UP IN THE ROUND

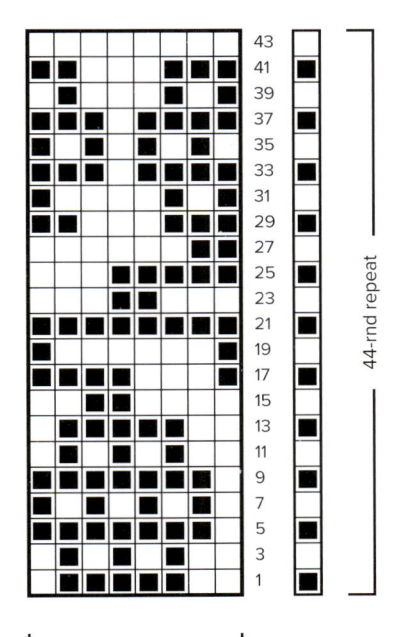

8-st repeat

44-rnd repeat

Hanging Fruit (CONT'D)

TOP-DOWN FLAT

(multiple of 8 sts + 3; 44-row repeat)

Using L, CO or work 1 row.

ROW 1 (RS): Using D, k2, *k2, slip 3, k3; repeat from * to last st, k1.

ROW 2 AND ALL WS ROWS: Using current color, knit or purl the purl sts and slip the slipped sts as they face you.

ROW 3: Using L, k1, slip 1, *k1, slip 1, k3, slip 1, k1, slip 1; repeat from * to last st, k1.

ROW 5: Using D, k2, *k3, slip 1, k4; repeat from * to last st, k1.

ROW 7: Using L, k2, *sl 1, k1; repeat from * to last st, k1.

ROW 9: Repeat Row 5.

ROW 11: Using L, k1, slip 1, *slip 1, k4, slip 1, k1, slip 1; repeat from * to last st, k1.

ROW 13: Repeat Row 1.

ROW 15: Using L, k1, slip 1, *k6, slip 2; repeat from * to last st, k1.

ROW 17: Using D, k2, *slip 3, k5; repeat from * to last st, k1.

ROW 19: Using L, k2, *k3, slip 2, k3; repeat from * to last st, k1.

ROW 21: Using D, knit.

ROW 23: Using L, k1, slip 1, *slip 1, k6, slip 1; repeat from * to last st, k1.

ROW 25: Using D, k2, *k4, slip 3, k1; repeat from * to last st, k1.

ROW 27: Using L, k2, *k2, slip 2, k4; repeat from * to last st, k1.

ROW 29: Using D, k1, slip 1, *slip 1, k5, slip 2; repeat from * to last st, k1.

ROW 31: Using L, k2, *[k1, slip 1] 3 times, k2; repeat from * to last st, k1.

ROW 33: Using D, k1, slip 1, *k7, slip 1; repeat from * to last st, k1.

ROW 35: Repeat Row 7.

ROW 37: Repeat Row 33.

ROW 39: Repeat Row 31.

ROW 41: Repeat Row 29.

ROW 43: Using L, knit.

ROW 44: Repeat Row 2.

Repeat Rows 1–44 for Hanging Fruit Top-Down Flat.

TOP-DOWN FLAT

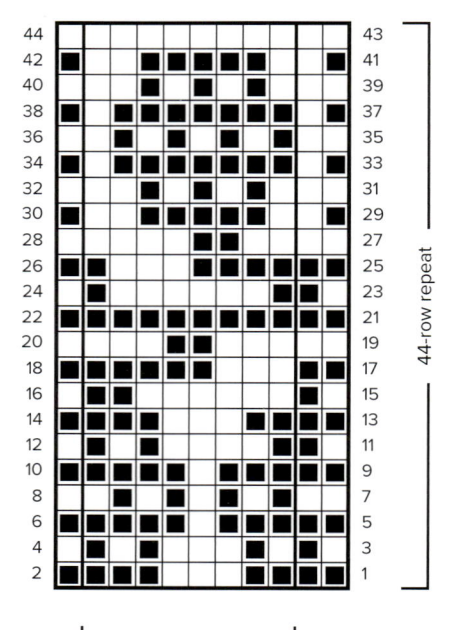

8-st repeat

44-row repeat

TOP-DOWN IN THE ROUND

(multiple of 8 sts; 44-rnd repeat)

Using L, CO or work 1 rnd.

RND 1: Using D, *k2, slip 3, k3; repeat from * to end.

RND 2 AND ALL EVEN-NUMBERED RNDS: Using current color, knit or purl the knit sts and slip the slipped sts as they face you.

RND 3: Using L, *k1, slip 1, k3, slip 1, k1, slip 1; repeat from * to end.

RND 5: Using D, *k3, slip 1, k4; repeat from * to end.

RND 7: Using L, *slip 1, k1; repeat from * to end.

RND 9: Repeat Rnd 5.

RND 11: Using L, *slip 1, k4, slip 1, k1, slip 1; repeat from * to end.

RND 13: Repeat Rnd 1.

RND 15: Using L, *k6, slip 2; repeat from * to end.

RND 17: Using D, *slip 3, k5; repeat from * to end.

RND 19: Using L, *k3, slip 2, k3; repeat from * to end.

RND 21: Using D, knit.

RND 23: Using L, *slip 1, k6, slip 1; repeat from * to end.

RND 25: Using D, *k4, slip 3, k1; repeat from * to end.

RND 27: Using L, *k2, slip 2, k4; repeat from * to end.

RND 29: Using D, *slip 1, k5, slip 2; repeat from * to end.

RND 31: Using L, *[k1, slip 1] 3 times, k2; repeat from * to end.

RND 33: Using D, *k7, slip 1; repeat from * to end.

RND 35: Repeat Rnd 7.

RND 37: Repeat Rnd 33.

RND 39: Repeat Rnd 31.

RND 41: Repeat Rnd 29.

RND 43: Using L, knit.

RND 44: Repeat Rnd 2.

Repeat Rnds 1–44 for Hanging Fruit Top-Down in the Round.

TOP-DOWN IN THE ROUND

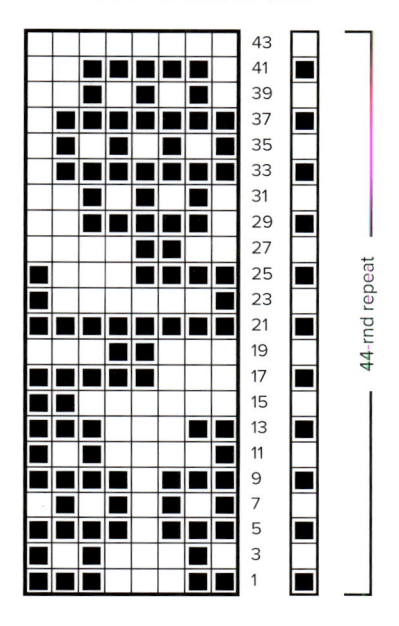

8-st repeat

44-rnd repeat

Waves

BOTTOM-UP FLAT

(multiple of 5 sts + 2; 32-row repeat)

Using L, CO or work 1 row.

ROW 1 (RS): Using D, k1, *k4, slip 1; repeat from * to last st, k1.

ROW 2 AND ALL WS ROWS: Using current color, knit or purl the purl sts and slip the slipped sts as they face you.

ROW 3: Using L, k1, *slip 1, k4; repeat from * last st, k1.

ROW 5: Using D, k2, *slip 1, k4; repeat from * to end.

ROW 7: Using L, k3, *slip 1, k4; repeat from * to last 4 sts, slip 1, k3.

ROW 9: Using D, *k4, slip 1; repeat from * to last 2 sts, k2.

ROW 11: Using L, repeat Row 1.

ROW 13: Using D, repeat Row 3.

ROW 15: Using L, repeat Row 5.

ROW 17: Using D, repeat Row 7.

ROW 19: Repeat Row 15.

ROW 21: Repeat Row 13.

ROW 23: Repeat Row 11.

ROW 25: Repeat Row 9.

ROW 27: Repeat Row 7.

ROW 29: Repeat Row 5.

ROW 31: Repeat Row 3.

ROW 32: Repeat Row 2.

Repeat Rows 1–32 for Waves Bottom-Up Flat.

BOTTOM-UP IN THE ROUND

(multiple of 5 sts; 32-rnd repeat)

Using L, CO or work 1 rnd.

RND 1: Using D, *k4, slip 1; repeat from * to end.

RND 2 AND ALL EVEN-NUMBERED RNDS: Using current color, knit or purl the knit sts and slip the slipped sts as they face you.

RND 3: Using L, *slip 1, k4; repeat from * to end.

RND 5: Using D, k1, *slip 1, k4; repeat from * to last 4 sts, slip 1, k3.

RND 7: Using L, k2, *slip 1, k4; repeat from * to last 3 sts, slip 1, k2.

RND 9: Using D, k3, *slip 1, k4; repeat from * to last 2 sts, slip 1, k1.

RND 11: Using L, repeat Rnd 1.

RND 13: Using D, repeat Rnd 3.

RND 15: Using L, repeat Rnd 5.

RND 17: Using D, repeat Rnd 7.

RND 19: Repeat Rnd 15.

RND 21: Repeat Rnd 13.

RND 23: Repeat Rnd 11.

RND 25: Repeat Rnd 9.

RND 27: Repeat Rnd 7.

RND 29: Repeat Rnd 5.

RND 31: Repeat Rnd 3.

RND 32: Repeat Rnd 2.

Repeat Rnds 1–32 for Waves Bottom-Up in the Round.

BOTTOM-UP FLAT

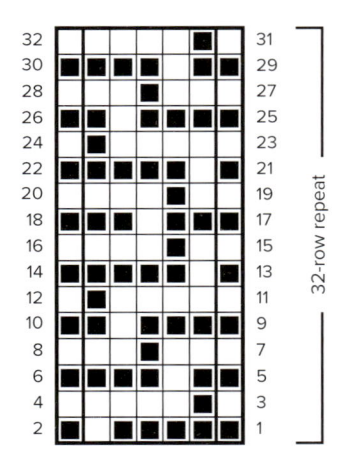

5-st repeat

BOTTOM-UP IN THE ROUND

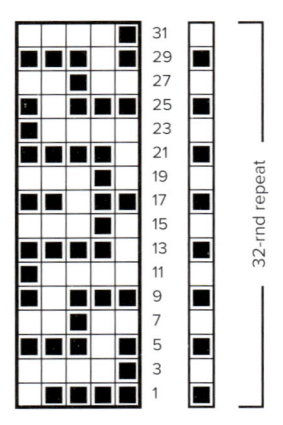

5-st repeat

NOTE: Swatch is shown in Garter st. Knit all non-slipped sts on Row 2 when working flat; purl all non-slipped sts on Rnd 2 when working in the round.

Waves (CONT'D)

TOP-DOWN FLAT

(multiple of 5 sts + 2; 32-row repeat)

Using L, CO or work 1 row.

ROW 1 (RS): Using D, k1, *k3, slip 1, k1; repeat from * to last st, k1.

ROW 2 AND ALL WS ROWS: Using current color, knit or purl the purl sts and slip the slipped sts as they face you.

ROW 3: Using L, k1, *k2, slip 1, k2; repeat from * to last st, k1.

ROW 5: Using D, k1, *k1, slip 1, k3; repeat from * to last st, k1.

ROW 7: Using L, k1, *slip 1, k4; repeat from * to last st, k1.

ROW 9: Using D, k1, *k4, slip 1; repeat from * to last st, k1.

ROW 11: Using L, k1, *k3, slip 1, k1; repeat from * to last st, k1.

ROW 13: Using D, repeat Row 3.

ROW 15: Repeat Row 11.

ROW 17: Repeat Row 9.

ROW 19: Repeat Row 7.

ROW 21: Repeat Row 5.

ROW 23: Repeat Row 3.

ROW 25: Repeat Row 1.

ROW 27: Using L, repeat Row 9.

ROW 29: Using D, repeat Row 7.

ROW 31: Repeat Row 27.

ROW 32: Repeat Row 2.

Repeat Rows 1–32 for Waves Top-Down Flat.

TOP-DOWN IN THE ROUND

(multiple of 5 sts; 32-rnd repeat)

Using L, CO or work 1 rnd.

RND 1: Using D, *k3, slip 1, k1; repeat from * to end.

RND 2 AND ALL EVEN-NUMBERED RNDS: Using current color, knit or purl the knit sts and slip the slipped sts as they face you.

RND 3: Using L, *k2, slip 1, k2; repeat from * to end.

RND 5: Using D, *k1, slip 1, k3; repeat from * to end.

RND 7: Using L, *slip 1, k4; repeat from * to end.

RND 9: Using D, *k4, slip 1; repeat from * to end.

RND 11: Using L, *k3, slip 1, k1; repeat from * to end.

RND 13: Using D, repeat Rnd 3.

RND 15: Repeat Rnd 11.

RND 17: Repeat Rnd 9.

RND 19: Repeat Rnd 7.

RND 21: Repeat Rnd 5.

RND 23: Repeat Rnd 3.

RND 25: Repeat Rnd 1.

RND 27: Using L, repeat Rnd 9.

RND 29: Using D, repeat Rnd 7.

RND 31: Repeat Rnd 27.

RND 32: Repeat Rnd 2.

Repeat Rnds 1–32 for Waves Top-Down in the Round.

TOP-DOWN FLAT

TOP-DOWN IN THE ROUND

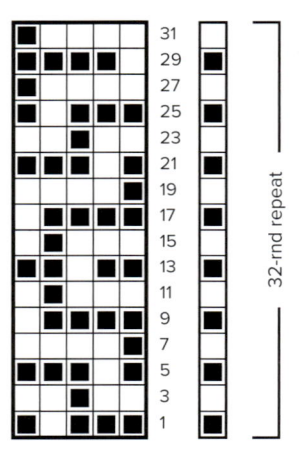

5-st repeat

5-st repeat

Interlocking Fish

FLAT

(multiple of 12 sts + 3; 12-row repeat)

Using L, CO or work 1 row.

ROW 1 (RS): Using D, k1, *k5, slip 1, k3, slip 3; repeat from * to last 2 sts, k2.

ROW 2 AND ALL WS ROWS: Using current color, knit or purl the purl sts and slip the slipped sts as they face you.

ROW 3: Using L, k1, *slip 1, k3, slip 1, k1, slip 1, k5; repeat from * to last 2 sts, slip 1, k1.

ROW 5: Using D, k1, *[k1, slip 1] twice, k3, slip 1, k1, slip 1, k2; repeat from * to last 2 sts, k2.

ROW 7: Using L, k1, *slip 1, k5, slip 1, k3, slip 1, k1; repeat from * to last 2 sts, slip 1, k1.

ROW 9: Using D, k1, *k3, slip 3, k5, slip 1; repeat from * to last 2 sts, k2.

ROW 11: Using L, k1, *k2, slip 1, k5, slip 1, k3; repeat from * to last 2 sts, k2.

ROW 12: Repeat Row 2.

Repeat Rows 1–12 for Interlocking Fish Flat.

NOTE: Swatch is shown in Garter st. Knit all non-slipped sts on Row 2 when working flat; purl all non-slipped sts on Rnd 2 when working in the round.

IN THE ROUND

(multiple of 12 sts; 12-rnd repeat)

Using L, CO or work 1 rnd.

RND 1: Using D, *k5, slip 1, k3, slip 3; repeat from * to end.

RND 2 AND ALL EVEN-NUMBERED RNDS: Using current color, knit or purl the knit sts and slip the slipped sts as they face you.

RND 3: Using L, *slip 1, k3, slip 1, k1, slip 1, k5; repeat from * to end.

RND 5: Using D, *[k1, slip 1] twice, k3, slip 1, k1, slip 1, k2; repeat from * to end.

RND 7: Using L, *slip 1, k5, slip 1, k3, slip 1, k1; repeat from * to end.

RND 9: Using D, k3, slip 3, k5, slip 1; repeat from to end.

RND 11: Using L, *k2, slip 1, k5, slip 1, k3; repeat from * to end.

RND 12: Repeat Rnd 2.

Repeat Rnds 1–12 for Interlocking Fish in the Round.

FLAT

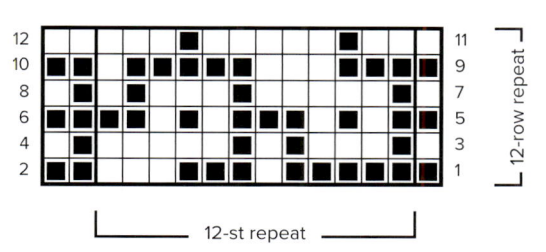

IN THE ROUND

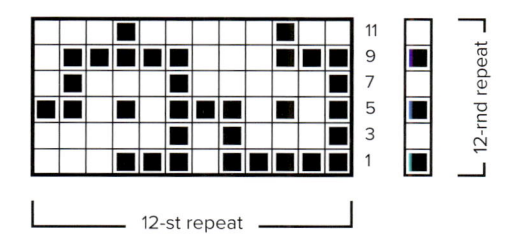

Flock of Birds

NOTE: Swatch is shown in Garter st. Knit all non-slipped sts on Row 2 when working flat; purl all non-slipped sts on Rnd 2 when working in the round.

BOTTOM-UP FLAT

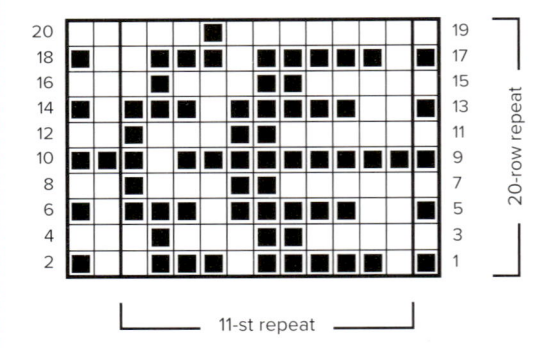

11-st repeat

20-row repeat

BOTTOM-UP IN THE ROUND

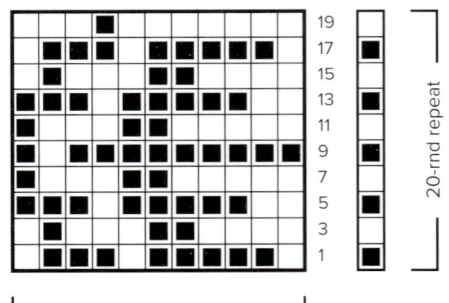

11-st repeat

20-rnd repeat

BOTTOM-UP FLAT

(multiple of 11 sts + 3; 20-row repeat)

Using L, CO or work 1 row.

ROW 1 (RS): Using D, k1, *slip 1, k5, slip 1, k3, slip 1; repeat from * to last 2 sts, slip 1, k1.

ROW 2 AND ALL WS ROWS: Using current color, knit or purl the purl sts and slip the slipped sts as they face you.

ROW 3: Using L, k1, *k4, slip 2, k3, slip 1, k1; repeat from * to last 2 sts, k2.

ROW 5: Using D, k1, *slip 2, k5, slip 1, k3; repeat from * to last 2 sts, slip 1, k1.

ROW 7: Using L, k1, *k5, slip 2, k3, slip 1; repeat from * to last 2 sts, k2.

ROW 9: Using D, k1, *k9, slip 1, k1; repeat from * to last 2 sts, k2.

ROW 11: Repeat Row 7.

ROW 13: Repeat Row 5.

ROW 15: Repeat Row 3.

ROW 17: Repeat Row 1.

ROW 19: Using L, k1, *k7, slip 1, k3; repeat from * to last 2 sts, k2.

ROW 20: Repeat Row 2.

Repeat Rows 1–20 for Flock of Birds Bottom-Up Flat.

BOTTOM-UP IN THE ROUND

(multiple of 11 sts; 20-rnd repeat)

Using L, CO or work 1 rnd.

RND 1: Using D, *slip 1, k5, slip 1, k3, slip 1; repeat from * to end.

RND 2 AND ALL EVEN-NUMBERED RNDS: Using current color, knit or purl the knit sts and slip the slipped sts as they face you.

RND 3: Using L, *k4, slip 2, k3, slip 1, k1; repeat from * to end.

RND 5: Using D, *slip 2, k5, slip 1, k3; repeat from * to end.

RND 7: Using L, *k5, slip 2, k3, slip 1; repeat from * to end.

RND 9: Using D, *k9, slip 1, k1; repeat from * to end.

RND 11: Repeat Rnd 7.

RND 13: Repeat Rnd 5.

RND 15: Repeat Rnd 3.

RND 17: Repeat Rnd 1.

RND 19: Using L, *k7, slip 1, k3; repeat from * to end.

RND 20: Repeat Rnd 2.

Repeat Rnds 1–20 for Flock of Birds Bottom-Up in the Round.

TOP-DOWN FLAT

(multiple of 11 sts + 3; 20-row repeat)

Using L, CO or work 1 row.

ROW 1 (RS): Using D, k1, slip 1, *slip 1, k3, slip 1, k5, slip 1; repeat from * to last st, k1.

ROW 2 AND ALL WS ROWS: Using current color, knit or purl the purl sts and slip the slipped sts as they face you.

ROW 3: Using L, k2, *k1, slip 1, k3, slip 2, k4; repeat from * to last st, k1.

ROW 5: Using D, k1, slip 1, *k3, slip 1, k5, slip 2; repeat from * to last st, k1.

ROW 7: Using L, k2, *slip 1, k3, slip 2, k5; repeat from * to last st, k1.

ROW 9: Using D, k2, *k1, slip 1, k9; repeat from * to last st, k1.

ROW 11: Repeat Row 7.

ROW 13: Repeat Row 5.

ROW 15: Repeat Row 3.

ROW 17: Repeat Row 1.

ROW 19: Using L, k2, *k3, slip 1, k7; repeat from * to last st, k1.

ROW 20: Repeat Row 2.

Repeat Rows 1–20 for Flock of Birds Top-Down Flat.

TOP-DOWN IN THE ROUND

(multiple of 11 sts; 20-rnd repeat)

Using L, CO or work 1 rnd.

RND 1: Using D, *slip 1, k3, slip 1, k5, slip 1; repeat from * to end.

RND 2 AND ALL EVEN-NUMBERED RNDS: Using current color, knit or purl the knit sts and slip the slipped sts as they face you.

RND 3: Using L, *k1, slip 1, k3, slip 2, k4; repeat from * to end.

RND 5: Using D, *k3, slip 1, k5, slip 2; repeat from * to end.

RND 7: Using L, *slip 1, k3, slip 2, k5; repeat from * to end.

RND 9: Using D, *k1, slip 1, k9; repeat from * to end.

RND 11: Repeat Rnd 7.

RND 13: Repeat Rnd 5

RND 15: Repeat Rnd 3.

RND 17: Repeat Rnd 1.

RND 19: Using L, *k3, slip 1, k7; repeat from * to end.

RND 20: Repeat Rnd 2.

Repeat Rnds 1–20 for Flock of Birds Top-Down in the Round.

TOP-DOWN FLAT

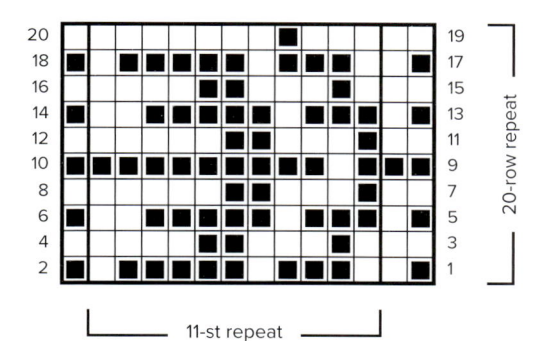

20-row repeat

11-st repeat

TOP-DOWN IN THE ROUND

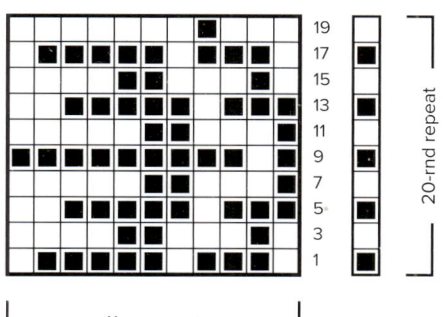

20-rnd repeat

11-st repeat

Egyptian Hands

NOTE: Swatch is shown in Garter st. Knit all non-slipped sts on Row 2 when working flat; purl all non-slipped sts on Rnd 2 when working in the round.

BOTTOM-UP FLAT

(multiple of 8 sts + 3; 16-row repeat)

Using L, CO or work 1 row.

ROW 1 (RS): Using D, k1, *slip 1, k3; repeat from * to last 2 sts, slip 1, k1.

ROW 2 AND ALL WS ROWS: Using current color, knit or purl the purl sts and slip the slipped sts as they face you.

ROW 3: Using L, k1, *k1, slip 3, k4; repeat from * to last 2 sts, k2.

ROW 5: Using D, k1, *k4, slip 3, k1; repeat from * to last 2 sts, k2.

ROW 7: Using L, k1, *k3, slip 1; repeat from * to last 2 sts, k2.

ROW 9: Repeat Row 1.

ROW 11: Using L, k1, *k5, slip 3; repeat from * to last 2 sts, k2.

ROW 13: Using D, k1, *slip 3, k5; repeat from * to last 2 sts, slip 1, k1.

ROW 15: Repeat Row 7.

ROW 16: Repeat Row 2.

Repeat Rows 1–16 for Egyptian Hands Bottom-Up Flat.

BOTTOM-UP IN THE ROUND

(multiple of 8 sts; 16-rnd repeat)

Using L, CO or work 1 rnd.

RND 1: Using D, *slip 1, k3; repeat from * to end.

RND 2 AND ALL EVEN-NUMBERED RNDS: Using current color, knit or purl the knit sts and slip the slipped sts as they face you.

RND 3: Using L, *k1, slip 3, k4; repeat from * to end.

RND 5: Using D, *k4, slip 3, k1; repeat from * to end.

RND 7: Using L, *k3, slip 1; repeat from * to end.

RND 9: Repeat Rnd 1.

RND 11: Using L, *k5, slip 3; repeat from * to end.

RND 13: Using D, *slip 3, k5; repeat from * to end.

RND 15: Repeat Rnd 7.

RND 16: Repeat Rnd 2.

Repeat Rnds 1–16 for Egyptian Hands Bottom-Up in the Round.

BOTTOM-UP FLAT

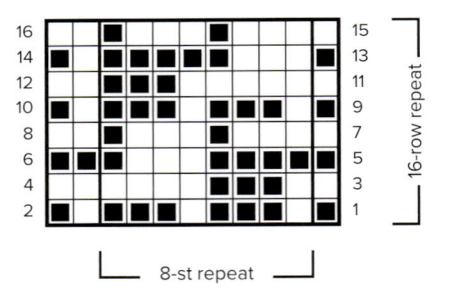

8-st repeat · 16-row repeat

BOTTOM-UP IN THE ROUND

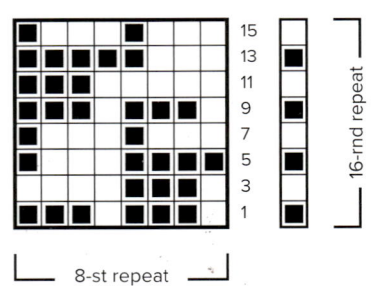

8-st repeat · 16-rnd repeat

TOP-DOWN FLAT

(multiple of 8 sts + 3; 16-row repeat)

Using L, CO or work 1 row.

ROW 1 (RS): Using D, k1, slip 1, *k5, slip 3; repeat from * to last st, k1.

ROW 2 AND ALL WS ROWS: Using current color, knit or purl the purl sts and slip the slipped sts as they face you.

ROW 3: Using L, k2, *slip 3, k5; repeat from * to last st, k1.

ROW 5: Using D, k1, slip 1, *k3, slip 1; repeat from * to last st, k1.

ROW 7: Using L, k2, *slip 1, k3; repeat from * to last st, k1.

ROW 9: Using D, k2, *k1, slip 3, k4; repeat from * to last st, k1.

ROW 11: Using L, k2, *k4, slip 3, k1; repeat from * to last st, k1.

ROW 13: Repeat Row 5.

ROW 15: Repeat Row 7.

ROW 16: Repeat Row 2.

Repeat Rows 1–16 for Egyptian Hands Top-Down Flat.

TOP-DOWN IN THE ROUND

(multiple of 8 sts; 16-rnd repeat)

Using L, CO or work 1 rnd.

RND 1: Using D, *k5, slip 3; repeat from * to end.

RND 2 AND ALL EVEN-NUMBERED RNDS: Using current color, knit or purl the knit sts and slip the slipped sts as they face you.

RND 3: Using L, *slip 3, k5; repeat from * to end.

RND 5: Using D, *k3, slip 1; repeat from * to end.

RND 7: Using L, *slip 1, k3; repeat from * to end.

RND 9: Using D, *k1, slip 3, k4; repeat from * to end.

RND 11: Using L, *k4, slip 3, k1; repeat from * to end.

RND 13: Repeat Rnd 5.

RND 15: Repeat Rnd 7.

RND 16: Repeat Rnd 2.

Repeat Rnds 1–16 for Egyptian Hands Top-Down in the Round.

TOP-DOWN FLAT

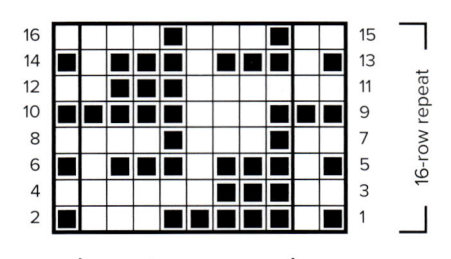

8-st repeat

16-row repeat

TOP-DOWN IN THE ROUND

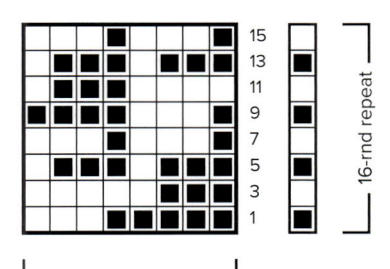

8-st repeat

16-rnd repeat

Old Oaks

BOTTOM-UP FLAT

(multiple of 18 sts + 3; 12-row repeat)

Using L, CO or work 1 row.

ROW 1 (RS): Using D, k1, *slip 1, k3, slip 1, k1, slip 1, k9, slip 2; repeat from * to last 2 sts, slip 1, k1.

ROW 2 AND ALL WS ROWS: Using current color, knit or purl the purl sts and slip the slipped sts as they face you.

ROW 3: Using L, k1, *[k1, slip 1] twice, k5, slip 3, k6; repeat from * to last 2 sts, k2.

ROW 5: Using D, k1, *slip 1, k5, [slip 1, k1, slip 1, k3] twice; repeat from * to last 2 sts, slip 1, k1.

ROW 7: Using L, k1, *k3, slip 1, k1, slip 1, k3, slip 1, k5, slip 1, k1, slip 1; repeat from * to last 2 sts, k2.

ROW 9: Using D, k1, *slip 3, k7, slip 1, k1, slip 1, k5; repeat from * to last 2 sts, slip 1, k1.

ROW 11: Using L, k1, *k7, slip 3, k3, slip 1, k1, slip 1, k2; repeat from * to last 2 sts, k2.

ROW 12: Repeat Row 2.

Repeat Rows 1–12 for Old Oaks Bottom-Up Flat.

BOTTOM-UP IN THE ROUND

(multiple of 18 sts; 12-rnd repeat)

Using L, CO or work 1 rnd.

RND 1: Using D, *slip 1, k3, slip 1, k1, slip 1, k9, slip 2; repeat from * to end.

RND 2 AND ALL EVEN-NUMBERED RNDS: Using current color, knit or purl the knit sts and slip the slipped sts as they face you.

RND 3: Using L, *[k1, slip 1] twice, k5, slip 3, k6; repeat from * to end.

RND 5: Using D, *slip 1, k5, [slip 1, k1, slip 1, k3] twice; repeat from * to end.

RND 7: Using L, *k3, slip 1, k1, slip 1, k3, slip 1, k5, slip 1, k1, slip 1; repeat from * to end.

RND 9: Using D, *slip 3, k7, slip 1, k1, slip 1, k5; repeat from * to end.

RND 11: Using L, *k7, slip 3, k3, slip 1, k1, slip 1, k2; repeat from * to end.

RND 12: Repeat Rnd 2.

Repeat Rnds 1–12 for Old Oaks Bottom-Up in the Round.

BOTTOM-UP FLAT

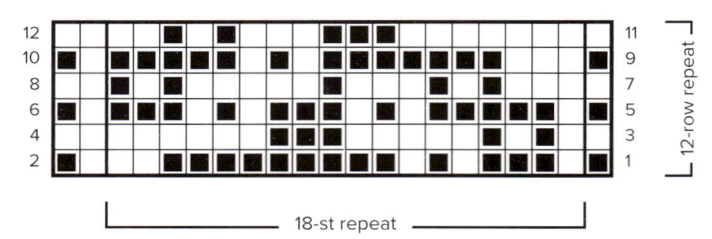

BOTTOM-UP IN THE ROUND

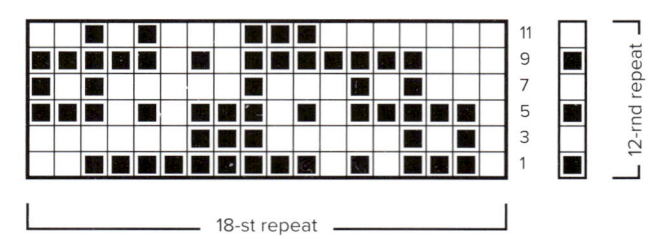

NOTE: Swatch is shown in Garter st. Knit all non-slipped sts on Row 2 when working flat; purl all non-slipped sts on Rnd 2 when working in the round.

Old Oaks (CONT'D)

TOP-DOWN FLAT

(multiple of 18 sts + 3; 12-row repeat)

Using L, CO or work 1 row.

ROW 1 (RS): Using D, k1, slip 1, *k5, slip 1, k1, slip 1, k7, slip 3; repeat from * to last st, k1.

ROW 2 AND ALL WS ROWS: Using current color, knit or purl the purl sts and slip the slipped sts as they face you.

ROW 3: Using L, k2, *slip 1, k1, slip 1, k5, slip 1, k3, slip 1, k1, slip 1, k3; repeat from * to last st, k1.

ROW 5: Using D, k1, slip 1, *[k3, slip 1, k1, slip 1] twice, k5, slip 1; repeat from * to last st, k1.

ROW 7: Using L, k2, *k6, slip 3, k5, [slip 1, k1] twice; repeat from * to last st, k1.

ROW 9: Using D, k1, slip 1, *slip 2, k9, slip 1, k1, slip 1, k3, slip 1; repeat from * to last st, k1.

ROW 11: Using L, k2, *k2, slip 1, k1, slip 1, k3, slip 3, k7; repeat from * to last st, k1.

ROW 12: Repeat Row 2.

Repeat Rows 1–12 for Old Oaks Top-Down Flat.

TOP-DOWN IN THE ROUND

(multiple of 18 sts; 12-rnd repeat)

Using L, CO or work 1 rnd.

RND 1: Using D, *k5, slip 1, k1, slip 1, k7, slip 3; repeat from * to end.

RND 2 AND ALL EVEN-NUMBERED RNDS: Using current color, knit or purl the knit sts and slip the slipped sts as they face you.

RND 3: Using L, *slip 1, k1, slip 1, k5, slip 1, k3, slip 1, k1, slip 1, k3; repeat from * to end.

RND 5: Using D, *[k3, slip 1, k1, slip 1] twice, k5, slip 1; repeat from * to end.

RND 7: Using L, *k6, slip 3, k5, [slip 1, k1] twice; repeat from * to end.

RND 9: Using D, *slip 2, k9, slip 1, k1, slip 1, k3, slip 1; repeat from * to end.

RND 11: Using L,*k2, slip 1, k1, slip 1, k3, slip 3, k7; repeat from * to end.

RND 12: Repeat Rnd 2.

Repeat Rnds 1–12 for Old Oaks Top-Down in the Round.

TOP-DOWN FLAT

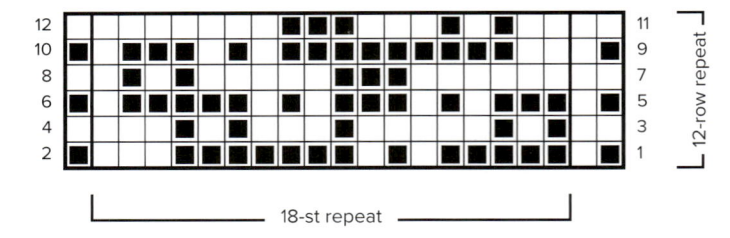

18-st repeat

TOP-DOWN IN THE ROUND

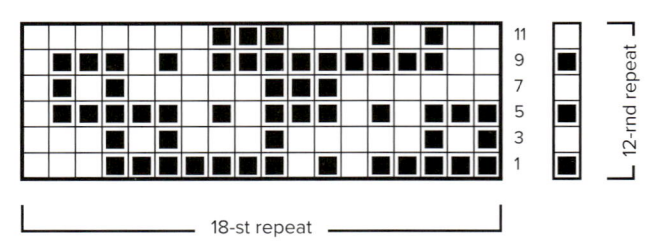

18-st repeat

Simulated Basketweave

FLAT

(multiple of 10 sts + 5; 16-row repeat)

Using L, CO or work 1 row.

ROW 1 (RS): Using D, k1, *k3, slip 2, k5; repeat from * to last 4 sts, k4.

ROW 2 AND ALL WS ROWS: Using current color, knit or purl the purl sts and slip the slipped sts as they face you.

ROW 3: Using L, k1, *[slip 1, k1, slip 1, k2] twice; repeat from * to last 4 sts, [slip 1, k1] twice.

ROW 5: Using D, k1, *k8, slip 2; repeat from * to last 4 sts, k4.

ROW 7: Using L, k1, *slip 1, k6, slip 1, k2; repeat from * to last 4 sts, slip 1, k3.

ROW 9: Repeat Row 5.

ROW 11: Repeat Row 3.

ROW 13: Repeat Row 1.

ROW 15: Using L, k1, *[k2, slip 1] twice, k4; repeat from * to last 4 sts, k2, slip 1, k1.

ROW 16: Repeat Row 2.

Repeat Rows 1–16 for Simulated Basketweave Flat.

NOTE: Swatch is shown in St st. Purl all non-slipped sts on Row 2 when working flat; knit all non-slipped sts on Rnd 2 when working in the round.

IN THE ROUND

(multiple of 10 sts; 16-rnd repeat)

Using L, CO or work 1 rnd.

RND 1: Using D, *k3, slip 2, k5; repeat from * to end.

RND 2 AND ALL EVEN-NUMBERED RNDS: Using current color, knit or purl the knit sts and slip the slipped sts as they face you.

RND 3: Using L, *slip 1, k1, slip 1, k2; repeat from * to end.

RND 5: Using D, *k8, slip 2; repeat from * to end.

RND 7: Using L, *slip 1, k6, slip 1, k2; repeat from * to end.

RND 9: Repeat Rnd 5.

RND 11: Repeat Rnd 3.

RND 13: Repeat Rnd 1.

RND 15: Using L, *[k2, slip 1] twice, k4; repeat from * to end.

RND 16: Repeat Rnd 2.

Repeat Rnds 1–16 for Simulated Basketweave in the Round.

FLAT

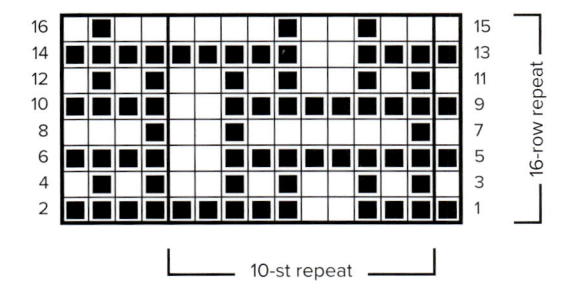

10-st repeat · 16-row repeat

IN THE ROUND

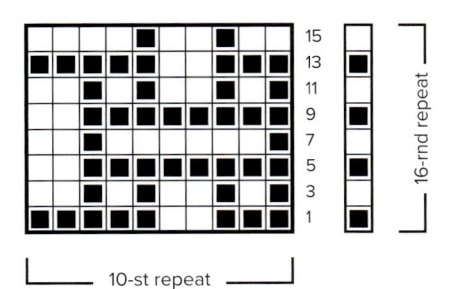

10-st repeat · 16-rnd repeat

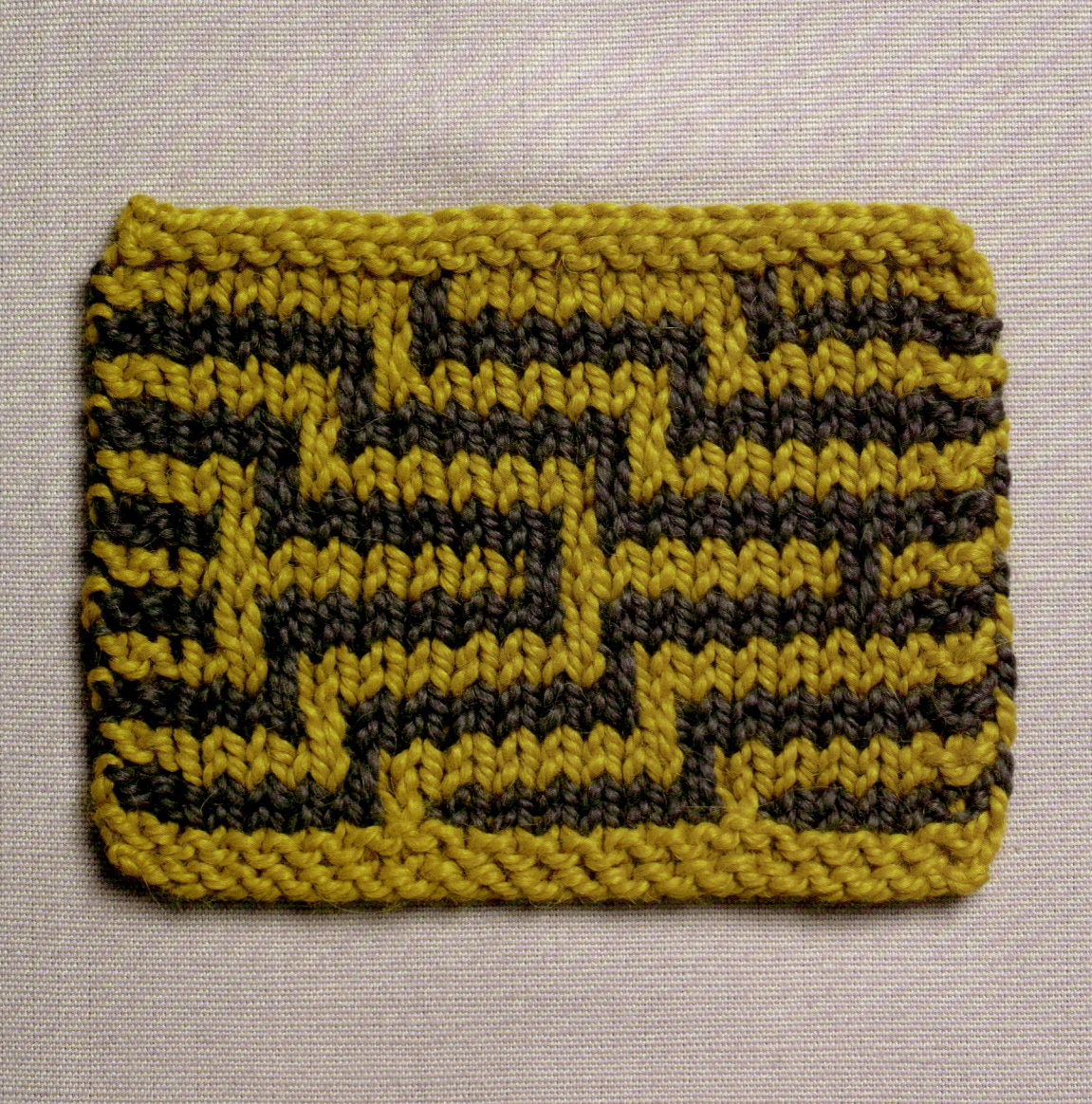

Long Zigzag

BOTTOM-UP FLAT

(multiple of 8 sts + 2; 24-row repeat)

Using L, CO or work 1 row.

ROW 1 (RS): Using D, k1, *k3, slip 1, k4; repeat from * to last st, k1.

ROW 2 AND ALL WS ROWS: Using current color, knit or purl the purl sts and slip the slipped sts as they face you.

ROW 3: Using L, k1, *k4, slip 1, k3; repeat from * to last st, k1.

ROW 5: Using D, k1, *k5, slip 1, k2; repeat from * to last st, k1.

ROW 7: Using L, k1, *k6, slip 1, k1; repeat from * to last st, k1.

ROW 9: Using D, k1, *k7, slip 1; repeat from * to last st, k1.

ROW 11: Using L, k1, *slip 1, k7; repeat from * to last st, k1.

ROW 13: Repeat Row 9.

ROW 15: Repeat Row 7.

ROW 17: Repeat Row 5.

ROW 19: Repeat Row 3.

ROW 21: Repeat Row 1.

ROW 23: Using L, k1, *k2, slip 1, k5; repeat from * to last st, k1.

ROW 24: Repeat Row 2.

Repeat Rows 1–24 for Long Zigzag Bottom-Up Flat.

BOTTOM-UP IN THE ROUND

(multiple of 8 sts; 24-rnd repeat)

Using L, CO or work 1 rnd.

RND 1: Using D, *k3, slip 1, k4; repeat from * to end.

RND 2 AND ALL EVEN-NUMBERED RNDS: Using current color, knit or purl the knit sts and slip the slipped sts as they face you.

RND 3: Using L, *k4, slip 1, k3; repeat from * to end.

RND 5: Using D, *k5, slip 1, k2; repeat from * to end.

RND 7: Using L, *k6, slip 1, k1; repeat from * to end.

RND 9: Using D, *k7, slip 1; repeat from * to end.

RND 11: Using L, *slip 1, k7; repeat from * to end.

RND 13: Repeat Rnd 9.

RND 15: Repeat Rnd 7.

RND 17: Repeat Rnd 5.

RND 19: Repeat Rnd 3.

RND 21: Repeat Rnd 1.

RND 23: Using L, *k2, slip 1, k5; repeat from * to end.

RND 24: Repeat Rnd 2.

Repeat Rnds 1–24 for Long Zigzag Bottom-Up in the Round.

BOTTOM-UP FLAT

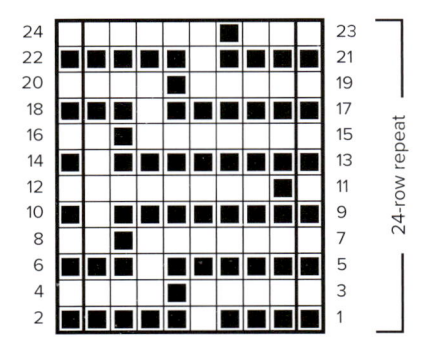

8-st repeat · 24-row repeat

BOTTOM-UP IN THE ROUND

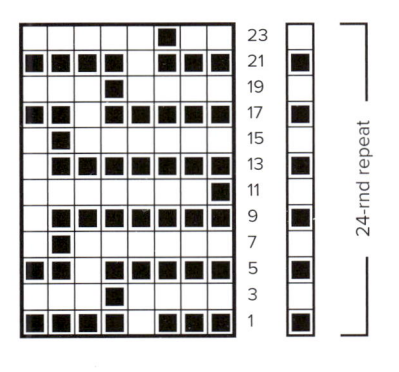

8-st repeat · 24-rnd repeat

NOTE: Swatch is shown in St st. Purl all non-slipped sts on Row 2 when working flat; knit all non-slipped sts on Rnd 2 when working in the round.

Long Zigzag (CONT'D)

TOP-DOWN FLAT

(multiple of 8 sts + 2; 24-row repeat)

Using L, CO or work 1 row.

ROW 1 (RS): Using D, k1, *k4, slip 1, k3; repeat from * to last st, k1.

ROW 2 AND ALL WS ROWS: Using current color, knit or purl the purl sts and slip the slipped sts as they face you.

Row 3; Using L, k1, *k3, slip 1, k4; repeat from * to last st, k1.

ROW 5: Using D, k1, *k2, slip 1, k5; repeat from * to last st, k1.

ROW 7: Using L, k1, *k1, slip 1, k6; repeat from * to last st, k1.

ROW 9: Using D, k1, *slip 1, k7; repeat from * to last st, k1.

ROW 11: Using L, k1, *k7, slip 1; repeat from * to last st, k1.

ROW 13: Repeat Row 9.

ROW 15: Repeat Row 7.

ROW 17: Repeat Row 5.

ROW 19: Repeat Row 3.

ROW 21: Repeat Row 1.

ROW 23: Using L, k1, *k5, slip 1, k2; repeat from * to last st, k1.

ROW 24: Repeat Row 2.

Repeat Rows 1–24 for Long Zigzag Top-Down Flat.

TOP-DOWN IN THE ROUND

(multiple of 8 sts; 24-rnd repeat)

Using L, CO or work 1 rnd.

RND 1: Using D, *k4, slip 1, k3; repeat from * to end.

RND 2 AND ALL EVEN-NUMBERED RNDS: Using current color, knit or purl the knit sts and slip the slipped sts as they face you.

RND 3: Using L, *k3, slip 1, k4; repeat from * to end.

RND 5: Using D, *k2, slip 1, k5; repeat from * to end.

RND 7: Using L, *k1, slip 1, k6; repeat from * to end.

RND 9: Using D, *slip 1, k7; repeat from * to end.

RND 11: Using L, *k7, slip 1; repeat from * to end.

RND 13: Repeat Rnd 9.

RND 15: Repeat Rnd 7.

RND 17: Repeat Rnd 5.

RND 19: Repeat Rnd 3.

RND 21: Repeat Rnd 1.

RND 23: Using L, *k5, slip 1, k2; repeat from * to end.

RND 24: Repeat Rnd 2.

Repeat Rnds 1–24 for Long Zigzag Top-Down in the Round.

TOP-DOWN FLAT

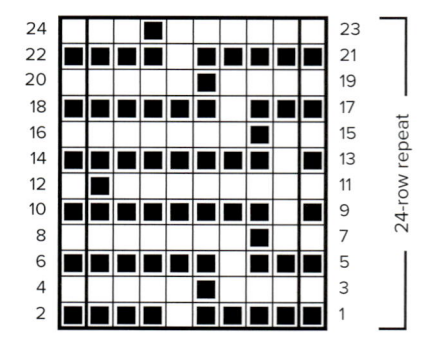

8-st repeat

TOP-DOWN IN THE ROUND

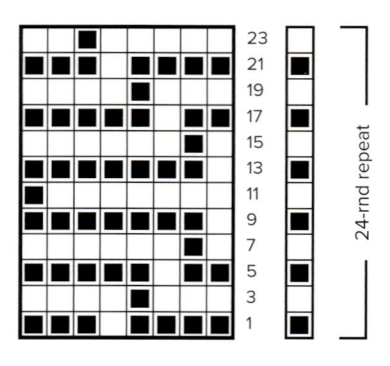

8-st repeat

Chains

FLAT

(multiple of 10 sts + 3; 12-row repeat)

Using L, CO or work 1 row.

ROW 1 (RS): Using D, k1, *[k3, slip 1] twice, k2; repeat from * to last 2 sts, k2.

ROW 2 AND ALL WS ROWS: Using current color, knit or purl the purl sts and slip the slipped sts as they face you.

ROW 3: Using L, k1, *k2, slip 1, k5, slip 1, k1; repeat from * to last 2 sts, k2.

ROW 5: Using D, k1, *slip 2, k7, slip 1; repeat from * last 2 sts, slip 1, k1.

ROW 7: Repeat Row 3.

ROW 9: Repeat Row 1.

ROW 11: Using L, k1, *k4, slip 3, k3; repeat from * to last 2 sts, k2.

ROW 12: Repeat Row 2.

Repeat Rows 1–12 for Chains Flat.

IN THE ROUND

(multiple of 10 sts; 12-rnd repeat)

Using L, CO or work 1 rnd.

RND 1: Using D, *[k3, slip 1] twice, k2; repeat from * to end.

RND 2 AND ALL EVEN-NUMBERED RNDS: Using current color, knit or purl the knit sts and slip the slipped sts as they face you.

RND 3: Using L, *k2, slip 1, k5, slip 1, k1; repeat from * to end.

RND 5: Using D, *slip 2, k7, slip 1; repeat from * to end.

RND 7: Repeat Rnd 3.

RND 9: Repeat Rnd 1.

RND 11: Using L, *k4, slip 3, k3; repeat from * to end.

RND 12: Repeat Rnd 2.

Repeat Rnds 1–12 for Chains in the Round.

NOTE: Swatch is shown in St st. Purl all non-slipped sts on Row 2 when working flat; knit all non-slipped sts on Rnd 2 when working in the round.

FLAT

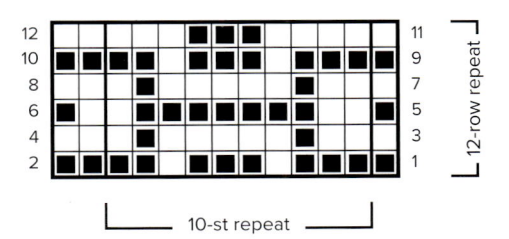

10-st repeat

12-row repeat

IN THE ROUND

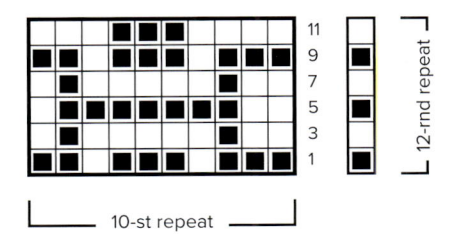

10-st repeat

12-rnd repeat

T-Squares

NOTE: Swatch is shown in Garter st. Knit all non-slipped sts on Row 2 when working flat; purl all non-slipped sts on Rnd 2 when working in the round.

BOTTOM-UP IN THE ROUND

(multiple of 10 sts; 8-rnd repeat)

Using L, CO or work 1 rnd.

RND 1: Using D, *k3, slip 1, k2, slip 1, k3; repeat from * to end.

RND 2 AND ALL EVEN-NUMBERED RNDS: Using current color, knit or purl the knit sts and slip the slipped sts as they face you.

RND 3: Using L, *k4, slip 2, k4; repeat from * to end.

RND 5: Using D, *k1, slip 1, k6, slip 1, k1; repeat from * to end.

RND 7: Using L, *slip 1, k8, slip 1; repeat from * to end.

RND 8: Repeat Rnd 2.

Repeat Rnds 1–8 for T-Squares Bottom-Up in the Round.

BOTTOM-UP FLAT

(multiple of 10 sts + 2; 8-row repeat)

Using L, CO or work 1 row.

ROW 1 (RS): Using D, k1, *k3, slip 1, k2, slip 1, k3; repeat from * to last st, k1.

ROW 2 AND ALL WS ROWS: Using current color, knit or purl the purl sts and slip the slipped sts as they face you.

ROW 3: Using L, k1, *k4, slip 2, k4; repeat from * to last st, k1.

ROW 5: Using D, k1, *k1, slip 1, k6, slip 1, k1; repeat from * to last st, k1.

ROW 7: Using L, k1, *slip 1, k8, slip 1; repeat from * to last st, k1.

ROW 8: Repeat Row 2.

Repeat Rows 1–8 for T-Squares Bottom-Up Flat.

BOTTOM-UP FLAT

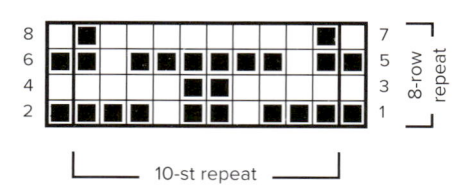

10-st repeat

BOTTOM-UP IN THE ROUND

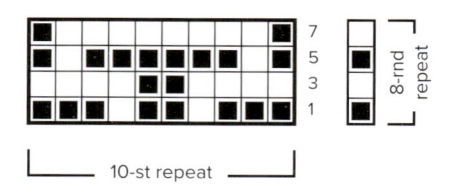

10-st repeat

TOP-DOWN FLAT

(multiple of 10 sts + 2; 8-row repeat)

Using L, CO or work 1 row.

ROW 1 (RS): Using D, k1, *k1, slip 1, k6, slip 1, k1; repeat from * to last st, k1.

ROW 2 AND ALL WS ROWS: Using current color, knit or purl the purl sts and slip the slipped sts as they face you.

ROW 3: Using L, k1, *k4, slip 2, k4; repeat from * to last st, k1.

ROW 5: Using D, k1, *k3, slip 1, k2, slip 1, k3; repeat from * to last st, k1.

ROW 7: Using L, k1, *slip 1, k8, slip 1; repeat from * to last st, k1.

ROW 8: Repeat Row 2.

Repeat Rows 1–8 for T-Squares Top-Down Flat.

TOP-DOWN IN THE ROUND

(multiple of 10 sts; 8-rnd repeat)

Using L, CO or work 1 rnd.

RND 1: Using D, *k1, slip 1, k6, slip 1, k1; repeat from * to end.

RND 2 AND ALL EVEN-NUMBERED RNDS: Using current color, knit or purl the knit sts and slip the slipped sts as they face you.

RND 3: Using L, *k4, slip 2, k4; repeat from * to end.

RND 5: Using D, *k3, slip 1, k2, slip 1, k3; repeat from * to end.

RND 7: Using L, *slip 1, k8, slip 1; repeat from * to end.

RND 8: Repeat Rnd 2.

Repeat Rnds 1–8 for T-Squares Top-Down in the Round.

TOP-DOWN FLAT

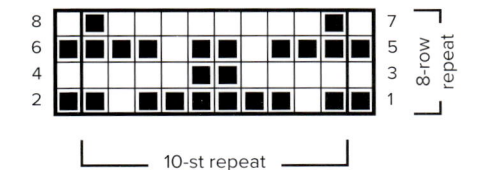

TOP-DOWN IN THE ROUND

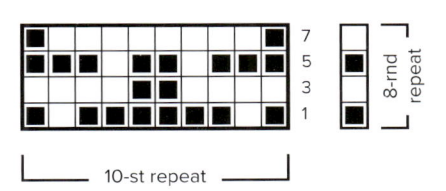

Tongue and Groove Stripes

NOTE: Swatch is shown in St st. Purl all non-slipped sts on Row 2 when working flat; knit all non-slipped sts on Rnd 2 when working in the round.

BOTTOM-UP FLAT

(multiple of 6 sts + 2; 12-row repeat)

Using L, CO or work 1 row.

ROW 1 (RS): Using D, k1, *k3, slip 1, k1, slip 1; repeat from * to last st, k1.

ROW 2 AND ALL WS ROWS: Using current color, knit or purl the purl sts and slip the slipped sts as they face you.

ROW 3: Using L, k1, *slip 1, k1, slip 1, k3; repeat from * to last st, k1.

ROW 5: Using D, k1, *k1, slip 1, k3, slip 1; repeat from * to last st, k1.

ROW 7: Using L, k1, *k2, [slip 1, k1] twice; repeat from * to last st, k1.

ROW 9: Using D, k1, *[k1, slip 1] twice, k2; repeat from * last st, k1.

ROW 11: Using L, k1, *slip 1, k3, slip 1, k1; repeat from * to last st, k1.

ROW 12: Repeat Row 2.

Repeat rows 1–12 for Tongue and Groove Stripes Bottom-Up Flat.

BOTTOM-UP IN THE ROUND

(multiple of 6 sts; 12-rnd repeat)

Using L, CO or work 1 rnd.

RND 1: Using D, *k3, slip 1, k1, slip 1; repeat from * to end.

RND 2 AND ALL EVEN-NUMBERED RNDS: Using current color, knit or purl the knit sts and slip the slipped sts as they face you.

RND 3: Using L, *slip 1, k1, slip 1, k3; repeat from * to end.

RND 5: Using D, *k1, slip 1, k3, slip 1; repeat from * to end.

RND 7: Using L, *k2, [slip 1, k1] twice; repeat from * to end.

RND 9: Using D, *[k1, slip 1] twice, k2; repeat from * to end.

RND 11: Using L, *slip 1, k3, slip 1, k1; repeat from * to end.

RND 12: Repeat Rnd 2.

Repeat Rnds 1–12 for Tongue and Groove Stripes Bottom-Up in the Round.

BOTTOM-UP FLAT

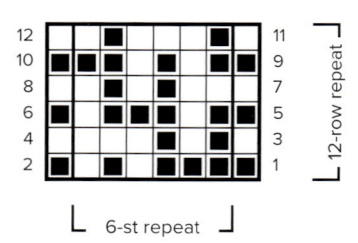

6-st repeat · 12-row repeat

BOTTOM-UP IN THE ROUND

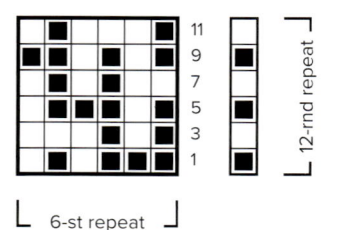

6-st repeat · 12-rnd repeat

TOP-DOWN FLAT

(multiple of 6 sts + 2; 12-row repeat)

Using L, CO or work 1 row.

ROW 1 (RS): Using D, k1, *k2, [slip 1, k1] twice; repeat from * to last st, k1.

ROW 2 AND ALL WS ROWS: Using current color, knit or purl the purl sts and slip the slipped sts as they face you.

ROW 3: Using L, k1, *[k1, slip 1] twice, k2; repeat from * to last st, k1.

ROW 5: Using D, k1, *slip 1, k3, slip 1, k1; repeat from * to last st, k1.

ROW 7: Using L, k1, *k3, slip 1, k1, slip 1; repeat from * to last st, k1.

ROW 9: Using D, k1, *slip 1, k1, slip 1, k3; repeat from * to last st, k1.

ROW 11: Using L, k1, *k1, slip 1, k3, slip 1; repeat from * to last st, k1.

ROW 12: Repeat Row 2.

Repeat Rows 1–12 for Tongue and Groove Stripes Top-Down Flat.

TOP-DOWN IN THE ROUND

(multiple of 6 sts; 12-rnd repeat)

Using L, CO or work 1 rnd.

RND 1: Using D, *k2, [slip 1, k1] twice; repeat from * to end.

RND 2 AND ALL EVEN-NUMBERED RNDS: Using current color, knit or purl the knit sts and slip the slipped sts as they face you.

RND 3: Using L, *[k1, slip 1] twice, k2; repeat from * to end.

RND 5: Using D, *slip 1, k3, slip 1, k1; repeat from * to end.

RND 7: Using L, *k3, slip 1, k1, slip 1; repeat from * to end.

RND 9: Using D, *slip 1, k1, slip 1, k3; repeat from * to end.

RND 11: Using L, *k1, slip 1, k3, slip 1; repeat from * to end.

RND 12: Repeat Rnd 2.

Repeat Rnds 1–12 for Tongue and Groove Stripes Top-Down in the Round.

TOP-DOWN FLAT

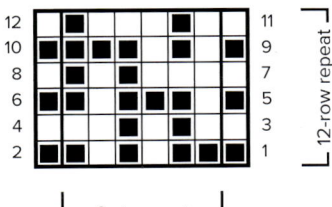

6-st repeat

TOP-DOWN IN THE ROUND

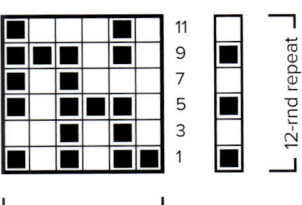

6-st repeat

Syncopation

NOTE: Swatch is shown in Garter st. Knit all non-slipped sts on Row 2 when working flat; purl all non-slipped sts on Rnd 2 when working in the round.

FLAT

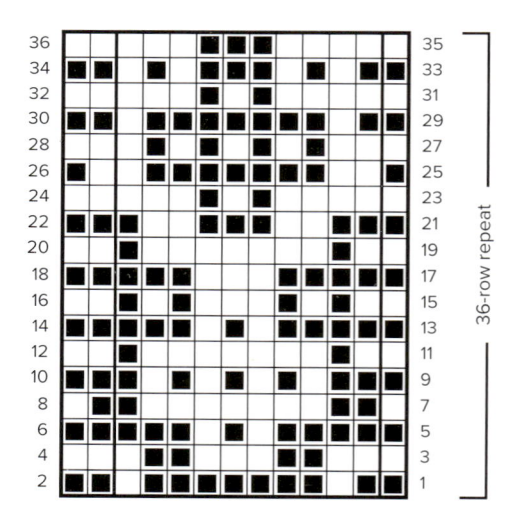

10-st repeat

FLAT

(multiple of 10 sts + 3; 36-row repeat)

Using L, CO or work 1 row.

ROW 1 (RS): Using D, k1, *k1, slip 1, k7, slip 1; repeat from * to last 2 sts, k2.

ROW 2 AND ALL WS ROWS: Using current color, knit or purl the purl sts and slip the slipped sts as they face you.

ROW 3: Using L, k1, *k2, slip 2, k3, slip 2, k1; repeat from * to last 2 sts, k2.

ROW 5: Using D, k1, *k4, slip 1, k1, slip 1, k3; repeat from * to last 2 sts, k2.

ROW 7: Using L, k1, *slip 2, k7, slip 1; repeat from * to last 2 sts, slip 1, k1.

ROW 9: Using D, k1, *slip 2, [slip 1, k1] 4 times; repeat from * to last 2 sts, k2.

ROW 11: Using L, repeat Row 1.

ROW 13: Using D, repeat Row 5.

ROW 15: Using L, k1, *[k1, slip 1] twice, k3, slip 1, k1, slip 1; repeat from * to last 2 sts, k2.

ROW 17: Using D, k1, *k4, slip 3, k3; repeat from * to last 2 sts, k2.

ROW 19: Using L, repeat Row 1.

ROW 21: Using D, repeat Row 3.

ROW 23: Using L, repeat Row 5.

ROW 25: Using D, repeat Row 7.

ROW 27: Using L, repeat Row 9.

ROW 29: Repeat Row 1.

ROW 31: Using L, repeat Row 5.

ROW 33: Using D, repeat Row 15.

ROW 35: Using L, repeat Row 17.

ROW 36: Repeat Row 2.

Repeat Rows 1–36 for Syncopation Flat.

IN THE ROUND

(multiple of 10 sts; 36-rnd repeat)

Using L, CO or work 1 rnd.

RND 1: Using D, *k1, slip 1, k7, slip 1; repeat from * to end.

RND 2 AND ALL EVEN-NUMBERED RNDS: Using current color, knit or purl the knit sts and slip the slipped sts as they face you.

RND 3: Using L, *k2, slip 2, k3, slip 2, k1; repeat from * to end.

RND 5: Using D, *k4, slip 1, k1, slip 1, k3; repeat from * to end.

RND 7: Using L, *slip 2, k7, slip 1; repeat from * to end.

RND 9: Using D, *slip 2, [slip 1, k1] 4 times; repeat from * to end.

RND 11: Using L, repeat Rnd 1.

RND 13: Repeat Rnd 5.

RND 15: Using L, *[k1, slip 1] twice, k3, slip 1, k1, slip 1; repeat from * to end.

RND 17: Using D, *k4, slip 3, k3; repeat from * to end.

RND 19: Using L, repeat Rnd 1.

RND 21: Using D, repeat Row 3.

RND 23: Using L, repeat Rnd 5.

RND 25: Using D, repeat Rnd 7.

RND 27: Using L, repeat Rnd 9.

RND 29: Repeat Row 1.

RND 31: Using L, repeat Rnd 5.

RND 33: Using D, repeat Rnd 15.

RND 35: Using L, repeat Rnd 17.

RND 36: Repeat Rnd 2.

Repeat Rnds 1–36 for Syncopation in the Round.

IN THE ROUND

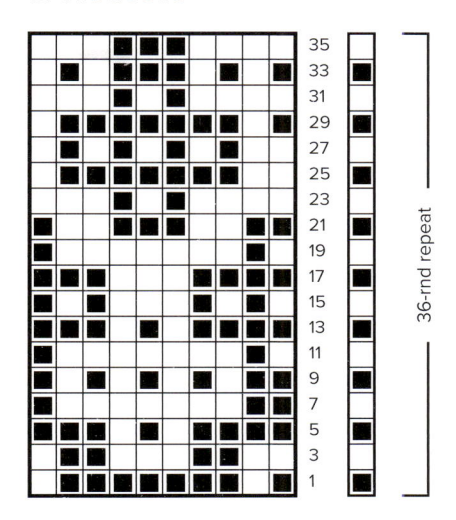

10-st repeat

36-rnd repeat

Mosaic and Texture Cowl

This versatile cowl is a fun way to experiment with the textures and colors found in the mosaic stitch patterns covered in this chapter. What is particularly exciting about this project is that you can select practically any stitch pattern from this book to create something completely unique! When choosing stitches to combine for your cowl, make sure to find stitch patterns that are within about 4 or 5 stitches from each other to keep the final piece from rippling or looking wavy along the edges.

FINISHED MEASUREMENTS
Approximately 60" (152.5 cm) circumference x 11" (28 cm) wide

YARN
Blue Sky Alpacas Extra (55% baby alpaca / 45% fine merino; 218 yards / 150 grams): 2 hanks #3521 Lake Ice; 1 hank each #3520 Shale and #3523 Black Swan

NEEDLES
One pair straight needles size US 9 (5.5 mm)

One spare straight or circular needle size US 9 (5.5 mm), for finishing (optional)

Change needle size if necessary to obtain correct gauge.

NOTIONS
Stitch markers; waste yarn (optional)

GAUGE
17 sts and 24 rows = 4" (10 cm) in Slip Stitch Mesh, washed and blocked

STITCH PATTERNS

Slip Stitch Mesh
(even number of sts; 6-row repeat)

ROW 1 (RS): Purl.

ROW 2: Knit.

ROW 3: K2, *slip 1 wyib, k1; repeat from * to end.

ROW 4: *K1, slip 1 wyif; repeat from * to last 2 sts, k2.

ROW 5: K1, *yo, k2tog; repeat from * to last st, k1.

ROW 6: Purl.

Repeat Rows 1–6 for Slip Stitch Mesh.

SLIP STITCH MESH

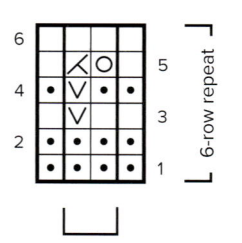

Tongue and Groove Stripes
(multiple of 6 sts + 2; 12-row repeat)

NOTE: Use Lake Ice as L and Shale as D.

ROW 1 (RS): Using D, k1, *k3, slip 1, k1, slip 1; repeat from * to last st, k1.

ROW 2 AND ALL WS ROWS: Using current color, knit the purl sts and slip the slipped sts as they face you.

ROW 3: Using L, k1, *slip 1, k1, slip 1, k3; repeat from * to last st, k1.

ROW 5: Using D, k1, *k1, slip 1, k3, slip 1; repeat from * to last st, k1.

ROW 7: Using L, k1, *k2, [slip 1, k1] twice; repeat from * to last st, k1.

ROW 9: Using D, k1, *[k1, slip 1] twice, k2; repeat from * last st, k1.

ROW 11: Using L, k1, *slip 1, k3, slip 1, k1; repeat from * to last st, k1.

ROW 12: Repeat Row 2.

Repeat Rows 1–12 for Tongue and Groove Stripes.

TONGUE AND GROOVE STRIPES

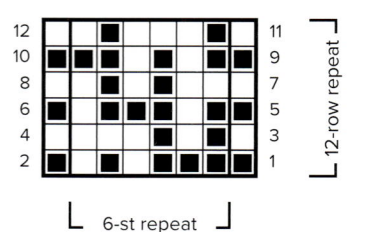

Chains

(multiple of 10 sts + 3; 12-row repeat)

NOTE: Use Lake Ice as L and Black Swan as D.

ROW 1 (RS): Using D, k1, *[k3, slip 1] twice, k2; repeat from * to last 2 sts, k2.

ROW 2 AND ALL WS ROWS: Using current color, knit the purl sts and slip the slipped sts as they face you.

ROW 3: Using L, k1, *k2, slip 1, k5, slip 1, k1; repeat from * to last 2 sts, k2.

ROW 5: Using D, k1, *slip 2, k7, slip 1; repeat from * last 2 sts, slip 1, k1; repeat from * to end.

ROW 7: Repeat Row 3.

ROW 9: Repeat Row 1.

ROW 11: Using L, k1, *k4, slip 3, k3; repeat from * to last 2 sts, k2.

ROW 12: Repeat Row 2.

Repeat Rows 1–12 for Chains.

CHAINS

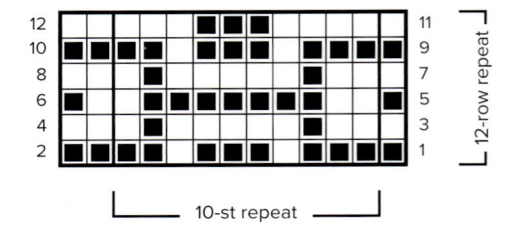

10-st repeat

12-row repeat

NOTES

This cowl begins with a Provisional CO; the two ends are grafted with Kitchener stitch or joined using 3-Needle BO. Or you may use your preferred CO, then sew the ends together.

The yarn colors used for D and L in the mosaic patterns change from one pattern to the next; make sure to refer to the stitch patterns for the correct colors to use.

COWL

Using Provisional CO (see Special Techniques, page 280) and waste yarn, CO 46 sts. Change to Lake Ice.

NEXT ROW (RS): K2 (edge sts, keep in Garter st), pm, work in Slip St Mesh to last 2 sts, pm, k2 (edge sts, keep in Garter st). Keep first and last 2 sts in Garter st throughout remainder of piece.

Work even until piece measures 20" (51 cm) from beginning, ending with Row 6 of pattern, and increasing 2 sts evenly between markers on last row—48 sts.

NEXT ROW (RS): K2, sm, work in Tongue and Groove Stripes to last 2 sts, sm, k2.

Work even until piece measures 40" (101.5 cm) from beginning, ending with a WS row in L, and decreasing 1 st between markers on last row—47 sts remain. Cut D.

NEXT ROW (RS): K2, sm, work in Chains to last 2 sts, sm, k2.

Work even until piece measures 60" (152.5 cm) from beginning, ending with a WS row in L, and decreasing 1 st between markers on last row—46 sts remain. Cut D.

FINISHING

Carefully unravel Provisional CO and place resulting 46 sts on spare needle. Using Lake Ice and Kitchener st or 3-Needle BO (see Special Techniques, page 280), graft or join ends together. Block as desired.

DESIGNING FROM SCRATCH

THESE SIX "FROM SCRATCH" formulas are easy, fun ways to dip your toe—or, shall we say, knitting needle—into the design world. Consider each formula a design-it-yourself framework into which you can add your own personal, creative flair. You can work any of them from the bottom up or from the top down, so the only decisions you need to make are which yarn, needle, and stitch pattern you want to use.

PROJECTS

SOCKS IN TWO DIRECTIONS
CAPS IN TWO DIRECTIONS
TRIANGULAR SHAWLS IN TWO
DIRECTIONS

SOCKS IN TWO DIRECTIONS

Socks are easy to knit on the go—once you've knitted a couple of pairs, the formula is easy enough to remember that a line-by-line pattern isn't even necessary. Just choose from one of the many beautiful sock yarns available, select a stitch pattern, and begin.

I offer two basic sock formulas, one worked from the top-down and the other worked from the toe up. Although I give cast-on numbers, if you need to center a motif or make accommodations for a stitch multiple, you can add or subtract stitches as needed.

The darker green pair of socks shown in the photo above is a basic top-down version with the Fern Grotto Lace Top-Down stitch pattern (page 170) centered on the instep. The lighter pair is worked toe-up with the bottom-up version of Fern Grotto Lace (page 168) centered on the instep. Both pairs of socks used two hanks of Spud & Chloe Fine. The lighter green is #7801 Glow Worm, and the darker green is #7804 Cricket.

Basic Top-Down Sock Pattern

SIZES
Children's Large/Women's Small (Women's Medium, Women's Large/Men's Small, Men's Medium, Men's Large)

FINISHED MEASUREMENTS
7 (7½, 8, 8½, 9)" [18 (19, 20.5, 21.5, 23) cm] Foot circumference

8½ (9½, 10, 10½, 11)" [21.5 (24, 25.5, 26.5, 28) cm] Foot length from back of Heel

8¾ (9½, 10¼, 11, 11½)" [22 (24, 26, 28, 29) cm] Leg length from Cuff to base of Heel

YARN
Fingering weight yarn, approximately 250 (300, 350, 400, 450) yards

NEEDLES
One set of five double-pointed needles (dpn) size US 1 (2.25 mm)

Note: This pattern is written for dpns, but you may use your preferred needle style for working in the rnd.

Change needle size if necessary to obtain correct gauge.

NOTIONS
Stitch markers

GAUGE
32 sts and 40 rows = 4" (10 cm) in Stockinette stitch (St st)

STITCH PATTERN

1x1 Rib
(even number of sts)
ALL RNDS: *K1, p1; repeat from * to end.

CUFF

CO 56 (60, 64, 68, 72) sts. Divide sts among 3 needles. Join for working in the rnd, being careful not to twist sts. Begin 1x1 Rib or rib of your choice; work even for 1" (2.5 cm).

LEG

Change to St st or desired st pattern; work even until Leg measures 6 (6½, 7, 7½, 8)" [15 (16.5, 18, 19, 20.5) cm] from the beginning.
NOTE: The last 28 (30, 32, 34, 36) sts are the Instep sts. If you want to work an Instep pattern, center it across these sts.

HEEL FLAP

Arrange stitches so that you have 28 (30, 32, 34, 36) sts on the first needle; you will work the Heel Flap on these sts only.
ROW 1 (RS): *Slip 1 wyib, k1; repeat from * to end.
ROW 2 (WS): Slip 1 wyif, purl to end.
Repeat Rows 1 and 2 until you have worked a total of 28 (30, 32, 34, 36) rows.

TURN HEEL

ROW 1 (RS): K16 (17, 18, 19, 20) sts, ssk, k1, turn.
ROW 2: Slip 1 wyif, p5, p2tog, p1, turn.
ROW 3: Slip 1 wyib, knit to 1 st before gap, ssk (the 2 sts on either side of gap), k1, turn.
ROW 4: Slip 1 wyif, purl to 1 st before gap, p2tog (the 2 sts on either side of gap), p1, turn.
Repeat Rows 3 and 4 until you have worked all Heel sts, omitting final k1 and p1 in last repeat of Rows 3 and 4 if necessary—16 (18, 18, 20, 20) sts remain.

GUSSET

NEXT ROW (RS): Knit across Heel sts, pick up and knit 14 (15, 16, 17, 18) sts along left side of Heel Flap, pm; work across 28 (30, 32, 34, 36) Instep sts to other side of Gusset, pm; pick up and knit 14 (15, 16, 17, 18) sts along right side of Heel Flap, k8 (9, 9, 10, 10) Heel sts—72 (78, 82, 88, 92) sts. Join for working in the rnd; pm for beginning of rnd.
NOTE: Rather than using markers, you may place Instep, Heel, and Gusset sts on separate needles if you prefer. If you place all the Heel sts on 1 needle, you will need to keep the beginning-of-round marker in place at the center of the Heel.
DECREASE RND: Knit to 3 sts before marker, k2tog, k1, sm, work across Instep sts to next marker, sm, k1, ssk, knit to end—2 sts decreased. Work even for 1 rnd. Repeat Decrease Rnd every other rnd 7 (8, 8, 9, 9) times to return to original st count—56 (60, 64, 68, 72) sts remain.

FOOT

Work even until piece measures 6¼ (7, 7½, 7¾, 8)" [16 (18, 19, 19.5, 20.5) cm], or to 2 (2¼, 2½, 2¾, 3)" [5.5 (6.5, 6.5, 7, 7.5) cm] less than desired length from back of Heel.

TOE

Rearrange sts if necessary so that Instep sts are on 2 needles and Sole sts are on another 1 or 2 needles. Work across Sole sts to beginning of Instep.
DECREASE RND: K1, k2tog, work to last 3 Instep sts, ssk, k1, sm, k1, k2tog, work to last 3 Sole sts, ssk, k1—4 sts decreased. Knit 1 rnd. Repeat Decrease Rnd every other rnd until the desired number of sts remains, usually between 10 and 12. Break yarn, leaving a long tail. Rearrange sts if necessary so that Instep sts are on 1 needle and Sole sts are on another. Using Kitchener st (see Special Techniques, page 280), graft Toe sts. Block as desired.

Basic Toe-Up Sock Pattern

SIZES

Children's Large/Women's Small (Women's Medium, Women's Large/Men's Small, Men's Medium, Men's Large)

FINISHED MEASUREMENTS

7 (7½, 8, 8½, 9)" [18 (19, 20.5, 21.5, 23) cm] Foot circumference

8½ (9½, 10, 10½, 11)" [21.5 (24, 25.5, 26.5, 28) cm] Foot length from back of Heel

8¾ (9½, 10¼, 11, 11½)" [22 (24, 26, 28, 29) cm] Leg length from Cuff to base of Heel

YARN

Fingering weight yarn, approximately 250 (300, 350, 400, 450) yards

NEEDLES

One set of five double-pointed needles (dpn) size US 1 (2.25 mm)

NOTE: This pattern is written for dpns, but you may use your preferred needle style for working in the rnd.

Change needle size if necessary to obtain correct gauge.

NOTIONS

Stitch markers, waste yarn

GAUGE

32 sts and 40 rows = 4" (10 cm) in Stockinette stitch (St st)

STITCH PATTERN

1x1 Rib

(even number of sts)

ALL RNDS: *K1, p1; repeat from * to end.

TOE

Using waste yarn and Provisional CO (see Special Techniques, page 280), CO 10 (12, 12, 12, 12, 12) sts. Change to working yarn. Work in St st for 4 rows, beginning with a purl row; do not cut yarn. Rotate the Toe so that the Provisional CO is on top. Carefully unravel the CO and place resulting 10 (12, 12, 12, 12, 12) sts onto 2 empty dpns; divide other live sts onto 2 dpns. Join for working in the rnd; pm for beginning of rnd.

SET-UP RND: *Needle 1:* K1, M1-r, k4 (5, 5, 5, 5); *Needle 2:* K4 (5, 5, 5, 5), M1-l k1; *Needles 3 and 4:* Repeat Needles 1 and 2—28 (32, 32, 32, 32) sts. Join for working in the rnd, being careful not to twist sts; pm for beginning of rnd.

INCREASE RND: *Needle 1:* K1, M1-r, knit to end; *Needle 2:* Knit to last st, M1-l, k1; *Needles 3 and 4:* Repeat Needles 1 and 2—4 sts increased. Knit 1 rnd. Repeat Increase Rnd every other rnd until there are 56 (60, 64, 68, 72) sts on the needles.

FOOT

Work in St st until piece measures 6½ (7½, 8, 8½, 9)" [16.5 (19, 20.5, 21.5, 23) cm], or to 2" (5 cm) less than desired Foot length from beginning. **NOTE:** The last 28 (30, 32, 34, 36) sts are the Instep sts. If you want to work an Instep pattern, center it across these sts.

HEEL

Arrange stitches so that you have 28 (30, 32, 34, 36) sts on the first needle; you will work the Heel Flap on these sts only. **NOTE:** Heel is shaped using short rows (see Special Techniques, page 280).

SHORT ROW 1 (RS): K27 (29, 31, 33, 35) sts, w&t.

SHORT ROW 2 (WS): P26 (28, 30, 32, 34) sts, w&t.

SHORT ROW 3: Knit to 1 st before wrapped st from previous RS row, w&t.

SHORT ROW 4: Purl to 1 st before wrapped st from previous WS row, w&t. Repeat Rows 3 and 4 until 12 (14, 14, 14, 14) sts remain between wraps in the middle of the Heel.

SHORT ROW 5: Knit to wrapped st, pick up wrap and knit it together with wrapped st, w&t.

SHORT ROW 6: Purl to wrapped st, pick up wrap and purl it together with wrapped st, w&t.

SHORT ROW 7: Knit to double-wrapped st, pick up both wraps and knit them together with wrapped st, w&t.

SHORT ROW 8: Purl to double-wrapped st, pick up both wraps and purl them together with wrapped st, w&t. Repeat Short Rows 7 and 8 until all wrapped sts have been worked. **NOTE:** On last repeat of Short Rows 7 and 8, you will work final w&t of each row on the first st on either side of Heel sts. Join for working in the rnd.

Knit 1 rnd across all sts, picking up remaining wraps and knitting them together with wrapped sts as you come to them, and ending at center of Heel; pm for beginning of rnd.

LEG

Work in St st or desired st pattern until piece measures 7¾ (8½, 9¼, 10, 10½)" [19.5 (21.5, 23.5, 25.5, 26.5) cm] from base of Heel. Change to 1x1 Rib or rib of your choice; work even for 1" (2.5 cm). BO all sts loosely in rib. Block as desired.

SOCKS AT A GLANCE

If you've knitted socks before and don't need a pattern, here are two charts that will help you determine the number of stitches you will need to work at key stages of basic sock-making, whether you're making top-down or toe-up socks. Note that these numbers are based on using a fingering weight yarn that works up at a gauge of 8 stitches to the inch.

Top Down

STITCHES TO CAST ON AT TOP OF LEG	56	60	64	68	72
STITCHES TO WORK FOR HEEL	28	30	32	34	36
ROWS TO WORK FOR HEEL	28	30	32	34	36
STITCHES TO WORK BEFORE TURN	16	17	18	19	20
STITCHES PICKED UP ALONG EACH GUSSET	14	15	16	17	18

Toe Up

STITCHES TO CAST ON AT TOE	10	12	12	12	12
NUMBER OF FOOT STITCHES TO INCREASE TO	56	60	64	68	72
NUMBER OF HEEL STITCHES	28	30	32	34	36
NUMBER OF STITCHES FOR FIRST SHORT ROW	27	29	31	33	35
NUMBER OF STITCHES FOR SECOND SHORT ROW	26	28	30	32	34
STITCHES REMAINING BETWEEN WRAPS BEFORE BEGINNING DOUBLE WRAP SHORT ROWS	12	14	14	14	14

CAPS IN TWO DIRECTIONS

There are benefits to knitting caps both from the bottom up or the top down. If you're trying out a new stitch pattern, sometimes it makes sense to start at the bottom so you have some time to practice before figuring out how you will divide up the stitches for the crown shaping. Or, if you are worried about running out of yarn, knitting from the top down makes a lot of sense because it allows you to try on the cap as you knit. If you do run out of yarn, you can always knit the brim in a contrasting color.

You can see that caps knit from the bottom up and the top down look exactly the same. Both the caps in the photo above feature Farrow Rib on the brim (page 66). The cap on the left (made with Blue Sky Alpacas Suri Merino, #411 Cloud) was knit top down, and the cap on the right (made with Blue Sky Alpacas Suri Merino, #413 Fog) was knit bottom up. Each cap required one hank of yarn to complete.

Basic Top-Down in-the-Round Cap Pattern

SIZES
Preemie–Men's (See table, Typical Head and Cap Measurements, page 271)

FINISHED MEASUREMENTS
See page 271

YARN
Approximately 100–200 yards (91.5–183 meters) for baby and child sizes; approximately 200–300 yards (183–274.5 meters) for adult sizes. NOTE: Exact yardage will depend upon hat size and gauge.

NEEDLES
One set of double-pointed needles (dpn) in size needed to obtain desired gauge

One 12–16" (30.5–40.5 cm) long circular needle (optional) in size needed to obtain desired gauge

NOTIONS
Stitch marker(s)

GETTING STARTED

Knit a gauge swatch in your stitch pattern and block it the same way you'll be blocking your cap, then fill in the blanks below.

STITCHES PER INCH (FROM YOUR SWATCH): _____ (A).

GOAL HEAD CIRCUMFERENCE FOR BRIM: _____ (B). (Negative ease is required for a close-fitting cap. Subtract an inch or two (2.5–5 cm) for best fit. For a slouchier version, use the actual head circumference. See table of Typical Head and Cap Measurements on page 271.)

STITCHES PER SECTION: (A x B) ÷ 8 = _____, rounded to a whole number (C).

CROWN

Using dpn and a CO of your choice, CO 8 sts. Note: You may wish to use a provisional CO and waste yarn to minimize the CO.

Join for working in the round, being careful not to twist sts; pm for beginning of rnd. You may also use the location of the CO tail to indicate the beginning of rnd for now. NOTE: If you use a finer gauge yarn and are concerned that you might twist your sts, you may work back and forth for a few rows, and then join to work in the rnd. At the end, you can use the yarn tail to join the edges of rows and cinch the crown.

RND 1: *K1-f/b; repeat from * to end—16 sts. Divide sts among 3 needles. NOTE: You may use any type of increase that you desire in place of k1-f/b, so that the following sts appear as you want them to.
RND 2: Knit.
RND 3: *K1, k1-f/b; repeat from * to end—24 sts.
RND 4: Knit, placing markers after every third st—8 markers, including beginning-of-rnd marker, which should be of a unique color.

SHAPE CROWN

NOTE: Change to circular needle if desired to accommodate number of sts on needle.
INCREASE RND: *K1-f/b, work to marker, sm; repeat from * to end—32 sts. Knit 1 rnd. Repeat the last 2 rnds until the stitch count per section equals C. Work even until the cap measures your desired depth to the beginning of the ribbing.
NEXT RND: Change to desired rib pattern. NOTE: You may have to increase or decrease a few sts to accommodate the multiples in your chosen rib or brim pattern. After ribbing is complete, BO all sts loosely in pattern.

FINISHING

Thread CO tail through CO sts or undo provisional CO, place sts onto 3 dpns, thread tail through live sts, and fasten off to WS. Block as desired.

Basic Bottom-Up in-the-Round Cap Pattern

SIZES
Preemie–Men's (See table, Typical Head and Cap Measurements, page 271)

FINISHED MEASUREMENTS
See page 271

YARN
Approximately 100–200 yards (91.5–183 meters) for baby and child sizes; approximately 200–300 yards (183–274.5 meters) for adult sizes. NOTE: Exact yardage will depend upon hat size and gauge.

NEEDLES
One set of double-pointed needles (dpn) in size needed to obtain desired gauge

One 12–16" (30.5–40.5 cm) long circular needle (optional) in size needed to obtain desired gauge

NOTIONS
Stitch marker(s)

GETTING STARTED

Knit a gauge swatch in your stitch pattern and block it the same way you'll be blocking your cap, then fill in the blanks below.

STITCHES PER INCH (FROM YOUR SWATCH): _____ (A).

GOAL HEAD CIRCUMFERENCE FOR BRIM: _____ (B). (Negative ease is required for a close-fitting cap. Subtract an inch or two (2.5–5 cm) for best fit. For a slouchier version, use the actual head circumference. See table of Typical Head and Cap Measurements on page 271.)

GOAL STITCHES: (A x B) = _____, rounded so that the multiple of sts matches your desired rib pattern (C).

BRIM

Using dpns or a short circular needle and a CO of your choice, CO C sts. Divide sts among 3 or 4 dpns if necessary. Join for working in the round, being careful not to twist sts; pm for beginning of rnd. You may also use the location of the CO tail to indicate the beginning of rnd for now. Note: If you use a finer gauge yarn and are concerned that you might twist your sts, you may work back and forth for a few rows, and then join to work in the rnd. At the end, you can use the yarn tail to join the edges of rows. Work your pattern to whatever depth you like, usually between 1 and 2 inches (2.5–5 cm). After that, knit your cap until it measures approximately:

PREEMIE:	4½" (11.5 cm)
BABY:	5" (12.5 cm)
TODDLER:	6" (15 cm)
KID	7" (18 cm)
SMALL ADULT:	8" (20.5 cm)
LARGE ADULT:	9" (23 cm)

(add about an inch [2.5 cm] for a slouchier version)

Adjust your st count so that it is divisible by 8 and evenly place 7 more markers to mark the 8 sections, plus a unique marker for the beginning of rnd if you haven't used one yet.

SHAPE CROWN

NOTE: Change to dpns if necessary to accommodate number of sts on needle.
NEXT RND: *K2tog, knit to next marker, sm; repeat from * to end. Knit 1 rnd. Repeat last 2 rnds until 8 or 16 sts remain.

FINISHING

Cut yarn, thread tail through remaining sts, pull tight, and fasten off to WS. Block as desired.

INCORPORATING STITCH PATTERNS

When planning a bottom-up cap, think about whether you want a ribbed brim, which will hug the head and won't roll, or a plain brim that is either worked in Stockinette stitch (which will roll) or in the same stitch pattern as the rest of the cap (which may roll, depending on the pattern you choose). Once you've made this selection, you'll want to decide on a goal circumference. To do this, check out your favorite stitch pattern and cast on the correct multiple of stitches that will yield you the correct size cap. For a top-down cap, your first design decision will be which stitch pattern you want to use for the body of the cap, and then last, the type of brim you want.

When it comes to incorporating stitch patterns, you can use any stitch pattern you like for the body of the hat. Once you select a stitch pattern, keep the crown shaping in mind, because at some point you will want to figure out a way to get your stitch pattern to flow into or out of the shaped portion. The more you practice a stitch pattern, the more likely that you will get a feel for how to manipulate the stitches so that they flow from one part of the hat to the other.

As an example, let's take a look at a top-down cabled cap idea with a 20" (50 cm) circumference and a gauge of 6 stitches per inch. Once you cast on the initial stitches, your goal will be to "grow" a crown of 8 sections with 15 stitches in each section (a total of 120 stitches). Knowing this, you can allow yourself a goal space of 15 stitches to hold a cable panel. One thing you could do is select the Little Pearls pattern on page 127, which is on a Reverse Stockinette stitch background. Next, cast on your initial stitches and purl all rounds, while increasing, until you have 6 stitches in each section. Place 8 markers, centering a panel of 4 stitches for your cable panel in each of the 8 sections, then begin your cables while shaping your crown and keeping all new stitches in Reverse Stockinette stitch. Once you've completed all the shaping, just continue working your cables in the center of each of the sections.

When working from the brim up toward the crown, the converse is true. As with the Woven Taffy Cap pattern in the cables chapter (opposite and on page 162), you'll notice that the Cable Fabric pattern appears on most of the cap. But as the crown is shaped, I altered the stitch pattern so that although the cables continued upward, they got thinner and thinner and no longer crossed. You can see that the crown is not cabled all over, but the transition from crossed cables to twists is more elegant looking than simply switching to Stockinette stitch. When working with other stitch patterns, again the key is to practice and get a feel for how you might want the body of the cap to flow into or out of the crown by using partial repeats of the pattern (or even "borrowing" an element like an eyelet or a crossed stitch) and echoing it in the crown so that the cap feels organic and makes sense to you.

TYPICAL HEAD AND CAP MEASUREMENTS

Circumference of Head

(Subtract up to 2" [5 cm] for a tighter fit; add 1" [2.5 cm] for a slouchier fit)

PREEMIE	BABY	TODDLER	CHILD	WOMAN	MAN
12" (30.5 cm)	15" (38 cm)	17" (43 cm)	18–19" (45.5-48.5 cm)	21" (53.5 cm)	22" (56 cm)

Approximate Cap Length

(including edge)

	PREEMIE	BABY	TODDLER	CHILD	WOMAN	MAN
Cap	5¼" (13.5 cm)	6" (15 cm)	7½" (19 cm)	9" (23 cm)	10¾" (27.5 cm)	12" (30.5 cm)
Slouch Cap	6¼" (16 cm)	8" (20.5 cm)	8½" (21.5 cm)	10" (25.5 cm)	11¾" (30 cm)	13" (33 cm)

TRIANGULAR SHAWLS IN TWO DIRECTIONS

There are a couple of different ways to make a basic double triangular shawl, the type of shawl with two inverted triangles separated by a center column of stitches. You can knit a shawl like this in either direction—it's totally up to you. If you like, you can make these shawls in Garter stitch as they are presented, or you can change it up and purl every wrong-side row, incorporate the shaping, and come up with a Stockinette stitch version. But if you're looking for something with a bit more interest, it's a cinch to add just about any stitch pattern—simply look through this collection of stitches and see what catches your eye.

When you design your shawl, you have lots of options: You can keep the first couple or several stitches along the edges in a nonrolling edge (like Garter stitch) and make your increases or decreases just inside them and use a stitch pattern on the interior portion. When you are working from the bottom up, you'll notice that as you increase, there may not initially be enough stitches to create a new full repeat in your chosen stitch pattern. Working from the top down, you will remove stitches from your stitch pattern. In either case, you will have an incomplete pattern repeat at either edge of the pattern as you go. Rather than getting knitter's graph paper and plotting everything out, you can work the stitches outside of the full pattern repeats in whatever the "background" stitch is in the pattern until you have a full pattern repeat at the increase or decrease edges.

If you prefer an allover pattern and really want to avoid having "white space," or a background of Reverse Stockinette, Stockinette, or Garter stitch (as with the shawl patterns here) you'll need to chart out the stitch pattern you've chosen. As stitches become available or are taken away, work a partial repeat of the multiple only and allow the stitch pattern to grow or shrink as you progress. If you are working in a lace pattern, make sure that you do not work any decreases in the stitch pattern without a corresponding increase, and vice versa. If you're working in a cable pattern and prefer not to just work Stockinette stitch as a cable is growing or decreasing, consider working fewer stitches in the cable cross until you have enough stitches to work a full repeat (for example, work C4B instead of C6B).

The photos on pages 274 and 276 show two customized double triangle shawls, one top down and the other bottom up. The darker version is top down and features Garter stitch (knit each row) for 68 rows, then bands of 14 rows of garter stitch separated by eyelet rows [work (k2tog, yo) across RS row, then knit following WS row]. The last section, at the bottom, has 4 vertical repeats of Miniature Leaves, which can be found on page 189 in the Lace chapter. This version measures 54" (137 cm) along the widest point and is approximately 27" (68.5 cm) deep. Three hanks of Blue Sky Alpacas Alpaca Silk were used in #137 Sapphire.

The lighter-colored version is bottom up. It begins with 3 rows of Garter stitch, then Welting Fantastic (page 115) is worked. Notice that the rows of Garter within the stitch pattern change from 5 to 3 and then to 1 row, with straight Welting for 13 rows. After that, 1 wrong-side row is knit before changing to straight Stockinette stitch for the remainder of the shawl. This larger version measures 66" (167.5 cm) across the top and is 30" (76 cm) deep. It took 5 hanks of Blue Sky Alpacas Alpaca Silk in #103 Plume.

Basic Bottom-Up Double Triangle Shawl Formula

FINISHED MEASUREMENTS
Refer to table below for typical measurements.

YARN
Refer to table below for yarn information.

NEEDLES
One 29" (74 cm) long or longer circular needle in size needed to obtain correct gauge. NOTE: Choose needle length based on desired width of piece.

NOTIONS
Stitch markers

GETTING STARTED

Make a gauge swatch and determine the number of stitches per inch in your desired stitch pattern.

Determine the desired bottom width of your shawl along the bottom edge; keep in mind that the bottom edge will form two sides of a triangle (see schematic), so your desired bottom width should be wider than the final width of the piece, which will be measured along the top edge. Multiply the desired width by the number of sts per inch (based on your gauge swatch) and round the resulting figure to an odd number, then cast on.

SHAPE SHAWL

ROW 1 (RS): K2, pm, knit to 1 st before center, pm, k1 (center spine st), pm, knit to last 2 sts, pm, k2.
ROW 2: Knit.
ROW 3: K2, sm, k2tog, work to 2 sts before marker, ssk, sm, k1, sm, k2tog, work to 2 sts before marker, ssk, sm, k2—4 sts decreased.
ROW 4: Knit.
Repeat Rows 3 and 4 until 3 or 5 sts remain. BO all sts.

FINISHING

Block as desired.

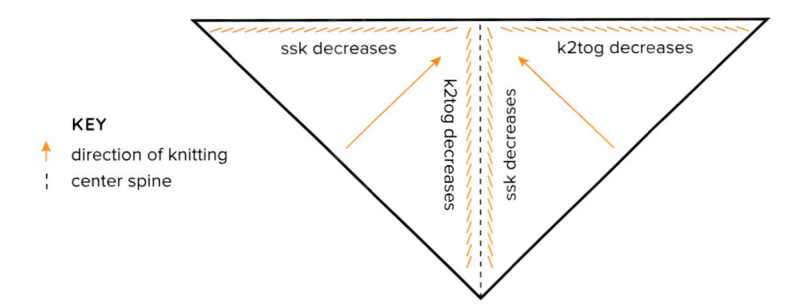

KEY
↑ direction of knitting
┊ center spine

MEASUREMENTS AND YARN REQUIREMENTS FOR TRIANGULAR SHAWLS

Yarn requirements will depend on a lot of factors, but to help you get started, take a look at this table for the approximate number of yards you might need. These numbers are based on a shawl that is twice as wide at its widest point as it is long at the center back, so any variation in the dimensions of the shawl will affect the amount needed. As with any on-the-fly, no-pattern project, check your retailer's return policy just in case you end up with more yarn than you need.

YARN WEIGHT	SHAWL LENGTH AT CENTER BACK 20–32 INCHES (51–81.5 CM)	34–42 INCHES (86.5–107 CM)
Lace	390–1,000 yards (355–915 meters)	1,130–1,720 yards (1,035–1,575 meters)
Fingering	320–820 yards (295–750 meters)	930–1,420 yards (850–1,300 meters)
Sport / DK	280–720 yards (255–660 meters)	810–1,240 yards (740–1,135 meters)
Worsted	250–640 yards (230–585 meters)	730–1,110 yards (670–1,015 meters)

Basic Top-Down Double Triangle Shawl Formula

FINISHED MEASUREMENTS
Refer to table on page 275 for typical measurements.

YARN
Refer to table on page 275 for yarn information.

NEEDLES
One 29" (74 cm) long or longer circular needle in size needed to obtain correct gauge. NOTE: Choose needle length based on desired width of piece.

NOTIONS
Stitch markers

GETTING STARTED

Make a gauge swatch and determine the number of stitches per inch in your desired stitch pattern.

GARTER TAB

Start with a Garter tab cast-on as follows:
CO 3 sts.
Knit 5 rows.

SHAWL SET-UP

SET-UP ROW (WS): Knit to end; do not turn. Rotate piece 90 degrees clockwise, pick up and knit 3 sts (1 in each purl bump along edge); rotate piece clockwise again, pick up and knit 3 sts along cast-on edge—9 sts.

SHAPE SHAWL

ROW 1 (RS): [K2, pm] twice, k1 (center spine st), [pm, k2] twice.
ROW 2: Knit.
ROW 3: K2, [sm, yo, knit to marker, yo, sm, k1] twice, k1—4 sts increased.
ROW 4: Knit.
Repeat Rows 3 and 4 until shawl is your desired width and length.
BO all sts.

FINISHING

Block as desired.

KEY

↑ direction of knitting
⋮ center spine

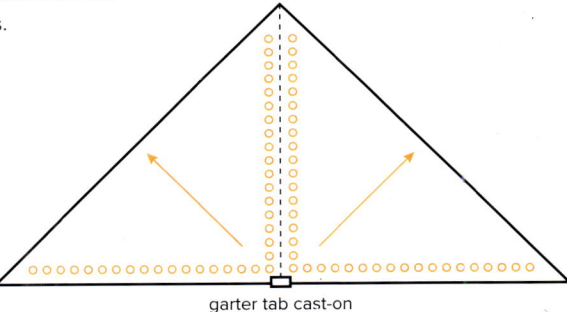

garter tab cast-on

A NOTE ABOUT NEEDLE SIZES

When you look at yarn labels, you'll probably notice that they often provide information about gauge and give a suggested needle size. Usually this information is intended for use in sweaters or socks or items that need to be knit into a reasonably solid fabric. If you want your shawl to have a similar drape to a sweater, then go ahead and use the yarn label information as a starting point. If you want a drapier shawl or one that is lacy, the rule of thumb is to use needles as many as 4 sizes larger than suggested on your yarn's label. In this situation, swatching is a perfect way to find a yarn and needle size combination that you like best.

1/2 LC: 1 over 2 Left Cross. Slip 1 stitch to cable needle, hold to front, k2, k1 from cable needle.

1/2 RC: 1 over 2 Right Cross. Slip 2 stitches to cable needle, hold to back, k1, k2 from cable needle.

2/1 LC: 2 over 1 Left Cross. Slip 2 stitches to cable needle, hold to front, k1, k2 from cable needle.

2/1 LC-P: 2 over 1 Left Cross, purled. Slip 2 stitches to cable needle, hold to front, p1, k2 from cable needle.

2/1 RC: 2 over 1 Right Cross. Slip 1 stitch to cable needle, hold to back, k2, k1 from cable needle.

2/1 RC-P: 2 over 1 Right Cross, purled. Slip 1 stitch to cable needle, hold to back, k2, p1 from cable needle.

2/2 LC-P: 2 over 2 Left Cross, purled. Slip 2 stitches to cable needle hold to front, p2, k2 from cable needle.

2/2 RC-P: 2 over 2 Right Cross, purled. Slip 2 stitches to cable needle, hold to back, k2, p2 from cable needle.

BO: Bind off.

C4B: Cable 4 Back. Slip 2 stitches to cable needle, hold to back, k2, k2 from cable needle.

C4B-P: Cable 4 Back, purled. Slip 2 stitches to cable needle, hold to back, p2, p2 from cable needle.

C4F: Cable 4 Front. Slip 2 stitches to cable needle, hold to front, k2, k2 from cable needle.

C4F-P: Cable 4 Front, purled. Slip 2 stitches to cable needle, hold to front, p2, p2 from cable needle.

C6B: Cable 6 Back. Slip 3 stitches to cable needle, hold to back, k3, k3 from cable needle.

C6F: Cable 6 Front. Slip 3 stitches to cable needle, hold to front, k3, k3 from cable needle.

C8B: Cable 8 Back. Slip 4 stitches to cable needle, hold to back, k4, k4 from cable needle.

C8F: Cable 8 Front. Slip 4 stitches to cable needle, hold to front, k4, k4 from cable needle.

C10B: Cable 10 Back. Slip 5 stitches to cable needle, hold to back, k5, k5 from cable needle.

C10F: Cable 10 Front. Slip 5 stitches to cable needle, hold to front, k5, k5 from cable needle.

CN: Cable needle

CO: Cast on.

D: Dark (used in Mosaic patterns)

DPN: Double-pointed needle(s)

K1B: Knit into stitch below next stitch on left-hand needle, dropping stitch from left-hand needle.

K1-F/B: Knit into front loop and back loop of same stitch—1 stitch increased.

K1-TBL: Knit 1 stitch through back loop.

K2TOG: Knit 2 stitches together—1 stitch decreased, right-slanting.

K3TOG: Knit 3 stitches together—2 stitches decreased, right-slanting.

K: Knit.

L: Light (used in Mosaic patterns)

LC: Left Cross. Insert needle from back to front between first and second stitches on left-hand needle and knit the second stitch through the front loop. Knit first stitch; slip both stitches from left-hand needle together.

M1-L: Make 1 left-slanting. With tip of left-hand needle inserted from front to back, lift strand between 2 needles onto left-hand needle; knit strand through back loop—1 stitch increased.

M1-R: Make 1 right-slanting. With tip of left-hand needle inserted from back to front, lift strand between 2 needles onto left-hand needle; knit strand through front loop—1 stitch increased.

P1-TBL: Purl 1 stitch through back loop.

P2TOG: Purl 2 stitches together—1 stitch decreased, right-slanting.

P3TOG: Purl 3 stitches together—2 stitches decreased, right-slanting.

P: Purl.

PM: Place marker.

PSSO: Pass slipped stitch over. Pass slipped stitch on right-hand needle over stitch(es) indicated in the instructions, as in binding off.

RC: Right Cross. On right-side rows, insert tip of right-hand needle into front of second stitch, bringing tip to front of work between second and first stitches, knit stitch, knit first stitch through front loop, slip both stitches from left-hand needle together. On wrong-side rows, purl into front of second stitch, then purl into front of first stitch, slip both stitches from left-hand needle together.

REV ST ST: Reverse Stockinette stitch. When working flat, purl on right-side rows, knit on wrong-side rows. When working in the round, purl all sts.

RND(S): Round(s)

RS: Right side

RT: Right Twist. K2tog, but do not drop stitches from left-hand needle; insert right-hand needle between 2 stitches just worked and knit first stitch again, slip both stitches from left-hand needle together.

S2KP2: Slip next 2 stitches together to right-hand needle as if to knit 2 together, k1, pass the 2 slipped stitches over—2 stitches decreased, centered.

SKP: Slip next stitch knitwise to right-hand needle, k1, pass slipped stitch over knit stitch—1 stitch decreased, left-slanting.

SK2P: Slip next stitch knitwise to the right-hand needle, k2tog, pass slipped stitch over stitch from k2tog—2 stitches decreased, left-slanting.

SM: Slip marker

SSK: Slip next 2 stitches to right-hand needle one at a time as if to knit; return them to left-hand needle one at a time in their new orientation; knit them together through back loops—1 stitch decreased, left-slanting.

SSP: Slip next 2 stitches to right-hand needle one at a time as if to knit; return them to left-hand needle one at a time in their new orientation; purl them together through back loops—1 stitch decreased, left-slanting.

ST(S): Stitch(es)

TBL: Through the back loop

TOG: Together

WS: Wrong side

W&T: Wrap and turn (see Special Techniques: Short Row Shaping, page 280).

WYIB: With yarn in back

WYIF: With yarn in front

YO: Yarnover

BACKWARD LOOP CO: Make a loop (using a slip knot) with the working yarn and place it on the right-hand needle (first st CO), *wind yarn around thumb clockwise, insert right-hand needle into the front of the loop on thumb, remove thumb and tighten st on needle; repeat from * for remaining sts to be CO, or for casting on at the end of a row in progress.

KITCHENER STITCH: Using a blunt tapestry needle, thread a length of yarn approximately 4 times the length of the section to be joined. Hold the pieces to be joined wrong sides together, with the needles holding the sts parallel, both ends pointing to the right. Working from right to left, insert tapestry needle into first st on front needle as if to purl, pull yarn through, leaving st on needle; insert tapestry needle into first st on back needle as if to knit, pull yarn through, leaving st on needle; *insert tapestry needle into first st on front needle as if to knit, pull yarn through, remove st from needle; insert tapestry needle into next st on front needle as if to purl, pull yarn through, leave st on needle; insert tapestry needle into first st on back needle as if to purl, pull yarn through, remove st from needle; insert tapestry needle into next st on back needle as if to knit, pull yarn through, leave st on needle. Repeat from *, working 3 or 4 sts at a time, then go back and adjust tension to match the pieces being joined. When 1 st remains on each needle, cut yarn and pass through last 2 sts to fasten off.

PROVISIONAL CO: Using waste yarn, CO the required number of sts; work in Stockinette st for 3-4 rows; change to main yarn and continue as directed. When ready to work the live sts, pull out the CO, placing the live sts on a spare needle.

SHORT ROW SHAPING: Work the number of sts specified in the instructions, wrap and turn (w&t) as follows:

To wrap a knit st, bring yarn to the front (purl position), slip the next st purlwise to the right-hand needle, bring yarn to the back of work, return the slipped st on the right-hand needle to the left-hand needle purlwise; turn, ready to work the next row, leaving the remaining sts unworked. To wrap a purl st, work as for wrapping a knit st, but bring yarn to the back (knit position) before slipping the st, and to the front after slipping the st.

When short rows are completed, or when working progressively longer short rows, work the wrap together with the wrapped st as you come to it as follows: If st is to be worked as a knit st, insert the right-hand needle into the wrap, from below, then into the wrapped st; k2tog; if st to be worked is a purl st, insert needle into the wrapped st, then down into the wrap; p2tog. (Wrap may be lifted onto the left-hand needle, then worked together with the wrapped st if this is easier.)

THREE-NEEDLE BO: Place the sts to be joined onto two same-size needles; hold the pieces to be joined with the right sides facing each other and the needles parallel, both pointing to the right. Holding both needles in your left hand, using working yarn and a third needle same size or one size larger, insert third needle into first st on front needle, then into first st on back needle; knit these two sts together; *knit next st from each needle together (two sts on right-hand needle); pass first st over second st to BO one st. Repeat from * until one st remains on third needle; cut yarn and fasten off.

☐ Knit on RS, purl on WS.

☐ In mosaic charts, work using color L.

■ In mosaic charts, work using color D.

• Purl on RS, knit on WS.

ℚ K1-tbl on RS, p1-tbl on WS.

↓ Knit st in row below.

○ Yo

∨ Slip 1 wyib on RS, slip 1 wyif on WS.

⩒ Slip 1 wyif on RS, slip 1 wyib on WS.

▨ No st

ẟ M1-l

⟍ K1-f/b on RS, p1-f/b on WS.

⟱ [K1, p1, k1] in next st.

╱ K2tog on RS, p2tog on WS.

⤬ P2tog on RS, k2tog on WS.

╲ Skp on RS.

╲ Ssk on RS, ssp on WS.

╱ K3tog on RS, p3tog on WS.

⤬ P3tog on RS, k3tog on WS.

╱ Sk2p

人 S2kp2

RC: Right Cross. On RS rows, insert tip of right-hand needle into front of second st, bringing tip to front of work between second and first sts, knit st, knit first st through front loop, slip both sts from left-hand needle together. On WS rows, purl into front of second st, then purl into front of first st, slip both sts from left-hand needle together.

LC: Left Cross. Insert needle from back to front between first and second sts on left-hand needle and knit the second st through the front loop. Knit first st; slip both sts from left-hand needle together.

1/2 RC: 1 over 2 Right Cross. Slip 2 sts to cable needle, hold to back, k1, k2 from cable needle.

1/2 LC: 1 over 2 Left Cross. Slip 1 st to cable needle, hold to front, k2, k1 from cable needle.

2/1 RC: 2/1 Right Cross. Slip 1 st to cable needle, hold to back, k2, k1 from cable needle.

2/1 LC: 2/1 Left Cross. Slip 2 sts to cable needle, hold to front, k1, k2 from cable needle.

2/1 RC-p: 2 over 1 Right Cross, purled. Slip 1 st to cable needle, hold to back, k2, p1 from cable needle.

2/1 LC-p: 2 over 1 Left Cross, purled. Slip 2 sts to cable needle hold in front, p1, k2 from cable needle.

C4B: Cable 4 Back. Slip 2 sts to cable needle, hold to back, k2, k2 from cable needle.

C4F: Cable 4 Front. Slip 2 sts to cable needle, hold to front, k2, k2 from cable needle.

C4F-p: Cable 4 Front, purled. Slip 2 sts to cable needle, hold to front, p2, k2 from cable needle.

C6B: Cable 6 Back. Slip 3 sts to cable needle, hold to back, k3, k3 from cable needle.

C6F: Cable 6 Front. Slip 3 sts to cable needle, hold to front, k3, k3 from cable needle.

C8B: Cable 8 Back. Slip 4 sts to cable needle, hold to back, k4, k4 from cable needle.

C8F: Cable 8 Front. Slip 4 sts to cable needle, hold to front, k4, k4 from cable needle.

C10 B: Cable 10 Back. Slip 5 sts to cable needle, hold to back, k5, k5 from cable needle.

C10 F: Cable 10 Front. Slip 5 sts to cable needle, hold to front, k5, k5 from cable needle.

STITCH MULTIPLE INDEX

INDEX

Acknowledgments

I am often asked how I made my way into the realm of designing garments and writing knitting books. The truth is, I never pursued knitting or designing—knitting and designing found me. Little did I know that a hobby that I wrote about on a blog years ago would lead me into a world rich with tradition, creativity, expression, and community. I really have been so lucky.

This book would not have been possible without the help of a distinguished and talented group of people.

Thanks to Melanie Falick, who offered thoughtful guidance, and to Cristina Garces, my editor, who was an absolute delight to work with. Thanks also to Sarah Gifford, whose keen sense of design brought this book together.

I can't imagine not having Sue McCain, my trusty technical editor sidekick, work with me on my books. It is because of Sue that I can sleep soundly at night instead of lying awake worrying that there might be an error somewhere. Thanks also to Robin Melanson for a second pair of technical eyes.

Blue Sky Alpacas generously provided all of the yarn for this book, and for that I am grateful. I have always loved their yarns and appreciated the wide array of colors they offer. I personally knit each of the swatches in this book, and using their yarns made the huge task more pleasurable.

Thanks also to my family for their unfailing support and encouragement.

Lastly, I want to dedicate this book to Helen Cowle. Helen was my grandmother who taught me to knit when I was eight years old. Last time I saw Helen, several years ago, she had just been diagnosed with Alzheimer's Disease. I remember that she didn't recognize me at first. But then, after a little while, I knelt down and placed my knitting in her hands. She squished the yarn, looked up at me, and wistfully said, "Oh, I wish I knew how to knit."

Friends, teach your children and grandchildren how to knit. Helen's gift will forever live within me, and hopefully with you and yours as well.

Be well and knit on!

Wendy.

About the Author

Wendy Bernard is a knitwear designer based in Southern California. She is the author of the Custom Knits series and *The Up, Down, All-Around Stitch Dictionary*. Her knitwear patterns have been published in the magazines *Interweave Knits* and *Knitscene,* and in several edited volumes. She is also an instructor for Creativebug.com and Craftsy.com.

Published in 2016 by Stewart, Tabori & Chang
An imprint of ABRAMS

Text copyright © 2016 by Wendy Bernard
Photographs copyright © 2016 by Thayer Allyson Gowdy

Library of Congress Control Number: 2015948559
ISBN: 978-1-61769-195-9

Editor: Cristina Garces
Designer: Sarah Gifford
Technical Editor: Sue McCain
Production Manager: True Sims

The text of this book was composed in Proxima Nova and Quicksand.

Printed and bound in China

10 9 8 7 6 5 4 3 2 1

Stewart, Tabori & Chang books are available at special discounts when
purchased in quantity for premiums and promotions as well as fundraising
or educational use. Special editions can also be created to specification.
For details, contact specialsales@abramsbooks.com or the address below.

THE ART OF BOOKS SINCE 1949

115 West 18th Street
New York, NY 10011
www.abramsbooks.com